T0331787

AI MEETS BI
Artificial Intelligence and Business Intelligence

AI MEETS BI
Artificial Intelligence and Business Intelligence

Lakshman Bulusu
Rosendo Abellera

CRC Press
Taylor & Francis Group
Boca Raton London New York

CRC Press is an imprint of the
Taylor & Francis Group, an **informa** business
AN AUERBACH BOOK

Press

or & Francis Group

Broken Sound Parkway NW, Suite 300

Raton, FL 33487-2742

21 by Taylor & Francis Group

Press is an imprint of Taylor & Francis Group, an Informa business

laim to original U.S. Government works

ed on acid-free paper

national Standard Book Number-13: 978-0-367-33260-0 (Hardback) 978-0-367-64381-2 (Paperback)

the Taylor & Francis Web site at
://www.taylorandfrancis.com

the CRC Press Web site at
://www.crcpress.com

Trademarks Covered in This Book

BIS3® is a registered trademark of Business Intelligence Software Service Solution.

Facebook™ is a trademark of Facebook, Inc.

IBM® and IBM Watson® are registered trademarks of International Business Machines Corporation.

Keras is neural network–based deep learning library under the open source umbrella. It is licensed by MIT.

Microsoft® is a registered trademark of Microsoft Corporation.

MNIST is a database of images of handwritten digits created from National Institute of Standards and Technology (NIST) data sets.

Oracle® is a registered trademark of Oracle Corporation

Python® is a registered trademark of the Python Software Foundation.

Qteria® is a BIS3® company.

SparkCognition™ is a trademark of SparkCognition.

Tableau® is a registered trademark of Tableau Software.

TensorFlow® is a registered trademark of Google, Inc.

Dedication

I dedicate this book to the memory of my parents, Professor B.S.K.R. Somayajulu and Smt. B. Sita, for their untiring efforts in nurturing me to become who I am today and their inspiring acumen and advice that have been a constant beacon throughout my career.

I also dedicate this book to my uncle, Professor B.L. Deekshatulu, and my aunt, the late Smt. B. Kameswari, for their blessings, which have enabled me to rise in life, both professionally and personally.

And, finally, I dedicate this book to all the readers of my previous books and their invaluable feedback, which has gone a long way in shaping this book.

— Lakshman Bulusu

Contents

Dedication   vii

Contents   ix

Preface by Lakshman Bulusu   xiii

Preface by Rosendo Abellera   xv

Acknowledgments   xvii

About the Author   xix

Chapter 1   Introduction   1

In This Chapter   1
1.1   Introduction   1
1.2   Traditional Ways of Enabling BI   3
1.3   Three Generations of BI   3
1.4   How Business Fits into BI—From Business Data to Business
      Decision Making   7
1.5   Summary   8

Chapter 2   AI and AI-Powered Analytics   9

In This Chapter   9
2.1   Introduction   9
2.2   AI and Its Rise in the Modern Enterprise   9
2.3   How AI Changes the Enterprise BI Landscape   10
2.4   The Analytics Sphere   10
2.5   BI-Enabled vs. AI-Powered Analytics   13
2.6   From Data to Intelligent Decision Making to Insightful Decisions   13
2.7   AI-Powered Techniques for BI   15
2.8   Summary   17

Chapter 3   Industry Uses Cases of Enterprise BI—A Business Perspective   19

In This Chapter   19
3.1   Introduction   19
3.2   Classifying Commodity Saleable Grade Based on Its Attributes   20
        3.2.1   Descriptive Analytics   20
3.3   Predicting Commodity Prices in Advance   33
        3.3.1   Predictive Analytics   33
3.4   Recommender Systems to Suggest Optimal Choices Based on Score   46
3.5   Automatic Image Recognition   46
3.6   Summary   48

Chapter 4   Industry Use Cases of Enterprise BI—The AI-Way of Implementation   49

In This Chapter   49
4.1   Introduction   49
4.2   Classifying Commodity Saleable Grade Based on Their Attributes   50
        4.2.1   The AI-Methodology—Descriptive Analytics—Using the Random Forest Machine Learning Algorithm and Comparing It with Decision Trees   50
        4.2.2   The BI-Enablement and Its Impact on the Enterprise   112
4.3   Predicting Commodity Prices in Advance   113
        4.3.1   The AI-Methodology—Predictive Analytics—Using Neural Networks   113
        4.3.2   The BI-Enablement and Its Impact on the Enterprise   121
4.4   Recommender Systems to Suggest Optimal Choices Based on Score   122
        4.4.1   The AI-Methodology—Prescriptive Analytics by Recommending Viable Sources Based on Score Prediction (using DNNs) and Predictive Analytics by Predicting "How the Product Fares in the Market" Based on the Recommended Choices   122
        4.4.2   The BI-Enablement and Its Impact on the Enterprise   182
4.5   Automatic Image Recognition   195
        4.5.1   The AI-Methodology—Prescriptive and Augmented Analytics—Using Deep Learning–Based Convolutional Neural Networks for Classification   195
4.6   Summary   207
4.7   References   208

Chapter 5   What's Next in AI Meets BI?   209

In This Chapter   209
5.1   Introduction   209
5.2   AI-Powered Cognitive Computing   209
5.3   Security and Governance in AI-Powered BI   211

5.4   The Trust Factor in AI-Powered BI   212
5.5   Summary   213

Index   **215**

Preface

This book focuses on the primary aspect of "AI meets BI" and details the intersection of AI, data science, machine learning, deep learning, and cognitive computing and how these technologies can assist and/or automate BI and decision making, resulting in more informed business insights. It stands out as the first publication to address the integration of artificial intelligence tools and technologies from the multitude of such tools and technologies available today to boost and enhance business intelligence. It covers various AI-powered analytics for BI-enabled decision making. Specifically, it discusses four industry use cases and their implementation, using AI-enabled machine learning and deep learning techniques along with their integration into enterprise BI platforms, by making use of the abovementioned technologies. It also discusses how all types of data, including Big Data, can be scaled to enterprise level and thereby enhance customer experience. Details are discussed from a business perspective and the AI-way of implementation.

The intended audience for this book includes business and data analysts who need to interpret the output of AI-powered BI systems from a business perspective; data scientists; data engineers; AI and BI practitioners, designers, programmers, and technical/project managers involved in AI/BI solution implementations; academia and research scientists involved in teaching/training of AI/BI models; and, last but not least, teachers and students of data science/AI/BI courses at the graduate level and/or in career-based learning courses. It is also intended for anyone involved in instructor-led or online training in AI and BI who will benefit from augmenting their courses with proven AI techniques for BI that will prepare the students for on-the-job solutions and certifications.

From data sources to deployment models (of AI), enterprise BI has most recently entered its third phase—one powered by AI. There are many aspects that address renewing focus on the capabilities of today's artificial intelligence. However, in light of how the corporate world touches our everyday lives, artificial intelligence–enhanced business intelligence would now seem to have the utmost importance in affecting how we work on a daily basis. It is for this reason that this book helps to pave the technological path of AI meets BI. In addition, this topic, never before offered, will provide important details about new ways and tools that will lead us into the future of business intelligence—a future enhanced with opportunities never before effectively available and only imagined for artificial intelligence.

Beginning with an outline of the traditional methods for implementing BI in the enterprise and how BI has evolved into using self-service analytics, data discovery, and, most recently, AI-powered BI, Chapter 1 lays out the three typical architectures of the first, second, and third generations of BI in the enterprise. It touches upon the "business" paradigm in the context of BI in the enterprise and how both BI and business analytics complement each other to provide a holistic BI solution—one that empowers all types of users, from business analysts to end users.

Chapter 2 outlines AI and AI-powered analytics in some depth, describing the various types of analytics using an analytics sphere and highlights how each of these can be implemented using AI-enabled algorithms and deep learning models. In particular, it touches upon AI and its rise in the modern enterprise. It provides a compare-and-contrast discussion of BI-enabled and AI-powered analytics and shows how businesses can leverage these techniques to tailor business processes to provide insight into how enterprises can gain a competitive edge. Chapter 2 also provides information on how AI techniques can be used to work upon the data, not vice versa, including the leveraging of data augmentation, data discovery, augmented analytics, and other such techniques. It demonstrates how the implementation of such AI-based techniques can be done right in the BI platform, and how to integrate the results into the same.

Chapters 3 and 4 form the crux of the book. They discuss, in great detail, the four industry use cases.

Chapter 3 focuses on the business perspective of these use cases. It describes how an enterprise can access, assess, and perform analytics on data by way of discovering data, defining key metrics that enable the same, defining governance rules, and activating metadata for AI/ML recommendations. It highlights how business users can explain key variables that serve as drivers for the business process in context, perform interactive correlations to determine variable importance, associate results with time, and, most important, how to predict outcomes based on data using AI-powered deep learning models—business analytics anytime and anywhere—and on all kinds of data and in real time. In addition, Chapter 3 highlights how enabling power users to create visuals based on these and other embedded metrics for deep-dive analysis in an interactive fashion is key for an enterprise to remain competitive. Four use cases that describe descriptive and predictive analytics in terms of predicting likelihood as well as forecasting and predicting measures for the future, along with prescriptive analytics, are outlined.

Chapter 4 takes a very in-depth approach in describing the implementation specifics of each of these four use cases by way of using various AI-enabled machine learning and deep learning algorithms and shows how the results enable actionable BI. The key component of predictive capabilities that was missing in the second generation of BI is brought to light, and it explains how it can be executed by way of AI-powered BI. Complete code for each of the implementations is provided, along with the output of the code supplemented by visuals that aid in BI-enabled decision making.

Chapter 5 touches upon what's next in AI meets BI. It begins with a brief discussion of the cognitive computing aspects of AI as well as augmented analytics and automated and autonomous BI. It then outlines how security and governance can be addressed in AI-powered BI. It ends with a note on the ethical aspects of BI and the trust factor involved in AI-powered decision making.

BI has evolved from its initial landscape of OLAP-based reporting and analysis to *ad hoc* querying, operational BI, and self-service analytics to AI-powered business analytics and big data discovery. And many of the industry's leading BI vendors, such as Tableau®, Microsoft®, Oracle®, IBM®, etc., have already started offering AI-powered capabilities to enable all kinds of users (technical and nontechnical) to take advantage of these new technologies and trends and derive intelligent insights that can lead to better, smarter, faster BI. This book comes at a time when this changing landscape for BI is in place, and the pragmatics of AI in the production and democratization/monetization of AI, as well as their implementation specifics from a BI perspective, are entering the mainstream of enterprises worldwide. It provides specifics regarding the most widely used AI-based technologies and their role in enterprise BI, thus positively reflecting the real-world scenarios that make AI-powered BI a reality.

— Lakshman Bulusu

Preface

Business Intelligence is dead. Long live Business Intelligence—with Artificial Intelligence, that is!

With the emergence of Artificial Intelligence (AI) in the business world, a new era of Business Intelligence (BI) has been ushered in to create real-world business solutions using analytics. These analytical capabilities, which were previously either not available or just difficult to use, have now become feasible and readily usable. For BI developers and practitioners, we now have new tools and technologies to complete and enhance the job that we set out to do—that is, provide our users (or customers) with the systems and solutions needed to provide effective decision making that stems from reliable and accurate information and intelligence, which, in turn, leads to valuable, actionable insights for business.

Oftentimes in the past, BI was stymied by bad or incomplete data, poorly architected solutions, or even just outright incapable systems or resources. The industry has come a long way in combating these obstacles, and now, with the advent of AI, BI has renewed hope for true effectiveness. This is a long-awaited phase for practitioners and developers, and moreover, for executives and leadership depending on knowledgeable and intelligent decision making for their respective organizations.

More than 20 years ago, after serving in military intelligence and with a passion for software development, I began my career in BI. I met Lakshman about 10 years ago. By that time, he was already an established, published author, and he introduced me to his world of book writing. I quickly embraced his expertise, and, together, we began this partnership of writing about a subject of our choice that we both so deeply enjoyed—that is, BI and analytics. Therefore, when it became evident that AI was becoming more prevalent and, more importantly, feasible to augment BI, we quickly jumped at the opportunity to write about this game changer. Together, we authored the first published book on Oracle BI and AI with machine learning.[*] It was received quite well. An audience began to form around it, and many even reached out for help in implementing the system and using it to provide a solution to their AI problems. In that book, we used a single case study to illustrate how AI could be effectively applied to BI.

With its success, Lakshman suggested and pushed for us to go beyond a single vendor and a single case study. Thus, this book begins that journey, as it presents numerous ways that AI can be applied to BI. Our hope is that it opens up a dialog about how we can best proceed and further augment and enhance BI to effectively fulfill its promise of successfully implementing advanced and predictive analytics in various applications for a multitude of industries—especially, with vital case studies that may affect many people.

---

[*] Abellera, R. and Bulusu, L. (2017). *Oracle Business Intelligence with Machine Learning,* 1st ed. New York (NY): Apress.

For instance, it was about 5 years ago that we, as a company, began to develop a software application with the goal of utilizing genomics for prescriptive treatments. This goal was only possible with the use of AI coupled with BI. It was rather an early attempt, as we used the first version (1.0, in fact) of Microsoft®'s machine learning tool. We struggled to implement it with this early tool and to convince investors of the capabilities, or even feasibility, of our vision for healthcare. This was back in the 2014, and in software development years, that seems like a lifetime ago. Many new developments and improvements in AI have materialized since then. Now it is 2020, and with a global pandemic, I can't help but think of the many ways that the new technologies in AI and machine learning could have possibly aided and been effectively used to accurately predict, prescribe, and prevent the unfortunate events that have transpired. If we had somehow been able to clearly foresee the future, we certainly would have focused on that goal. Perhaps that could be the ultimate use and application for AI, as it satisfies the demands of BI as it pertains specifically to healthcare in matters of life and death. For those case studies, providing a solution would definitely be a worthwhile cause. In that field, we've only really begun to scratch the surface.

The possibilities are truly endless. New capabilities are now at hand as AI meets BI. For our future, we can only hope.

— Rosendo Abellera

Acknowledgments

I thank my immediate family for their cooperation and patience during the time that I wrote this book.

I thank my brother Dr. B. Rama for his guidance on predictive analytics, which helped me to write related parts of this book.

I thank Mr. Linesh Dave and Mr. Praveen Sharma for judging my book proposal and giving the go-ahead to this book project.

And I thank Theron R. Shreve (Director) and Marje Pollack (copy editor and typesetter) at Derryfield Publishing Services, as well as the publisher, CRC Press/Taylor & Francis Group, for the support, feedback, reviews, and production work they provided to enable this book project to see the light of day.

— Lakshman Bulusu

About the Authors

Lakshman Bulusu is a veteran IT professional and data scientist, with 28 years of experience in the IT industry. He has worked at major industry verticals in the retail, banking, pharma/health care, insurance, media, telecom, and education fields. He currently consults for a major banking client in the New York/New Jersey metropolitan area. He has expertise in RDBMS technologies, including Oracle®, MS SQL Server, and Vertica and their related technologies. He is also well versed in the latest-and-greatest technologies such as artificial intelligence, data science, and business intelligence.

Lakshman also serves as Vice President of Research at Qteria.com. When not at his job, he lectures at various technical schools, user group conferences and summits, and data science meetings. He also devotes his free time to writing poetry in English and in his native language, Telugu.

He holds a Masters credential from Oracle Corporation and Master certifications from Brainbench, and he is an OCP-certified Professional. He is a Barnes & Noble Educator and holds a Certification of Appreciation from Barnes & Noble.

He has authored 10 books spanning topics such as Oracle, Oracle BI, Open Source DW/BI, and Oracle and machine learning, as well a host of papers in technical magazines and journals.

— Lakshman Bulusu

With a long and proven track record of success in the Business Intelligence (BI) industry throughout several decades, **Rosendo Abellera** is a subject matter expert and expert practitioner in business intelligence and analytics. As a career consultant, he has serviced numerous leading global commercial clients and major US government organizations. A strategist as well as a hands-on developer, he architected and implemented complete, holistic, and data-centric decision-making systems and solutions from the ground up— from complex data warehouses for Revenue Recognition to advanced dashboards for Financial Analytics.

Rosendo has held key management positions in establishing the Business Intelligence and Analytics practices of several global consulting organizations. Moreover, he founded and established BIS3®, a successful consulting firm started more than 10 years ago, specializing in what was then Oracle®'s new BI strategy with OBIEE and Essbase—both of which are subjects of his previously published books (jointly with Lakshman Bulusu). In an additional role for the company, he is the chief architect of Qteria®, an AI and machine learning platform.

Rosendo is a veteran of the US Air Force and the National Security Agency (NSA), where he served worldwide as a cryptologist and linguist for several languages. With these beginnings in the intelligence community, he provides unique insight and knowledge for utilizing data as a critical asset.

— Rosendo Abellera

Chapter 1

Introduction

In This Chapter

1.1 Introduction
1.2 Traditional Ways of Enabling BI
1.3 Three Generations of BI
1.4 How Business Fits into BI—From Business Data to Business Decision Making
1.5 Summary

1.1 Introduction

This chapter begins with an outline of the conventional methods for implementing BI in an enterprise and highlights how BI has evolved into using self-service analytics and, most recently, AI-powered BI. It touches upon the three generations of BI and how DW/BI solutions have changed the landscape of business decision making for the better. Finally, it ends with notes on how the commonly used term "business" aligns with and can be fit into a comprehensive BI solution that is not only state of the art but also one that continually and automatically evolves on metrics or key performance indicators (KPIs) that the BI solution outputs, which, in turn, can be refueled into the same architecture as input, leading to more insightful decisions. **The primary aspect of "pairing AI with BI" on a one-on-one basis** as well as its details, including the intersection of AI, data science, machine learning, deep learning, cognitive computing, and how this can lead to the automation of BI and decision-making processes resulting in more informed business decision making, is briefly covered in Section 1.3. There are many topics with renewed focus on the capabilities of today's artificial intelligence. On the surface, admittedly, it may not seem as interesting, perhaps, as artificial intelligence, which is igniting new interest, for example, in the areas of self-driving cars or robotics. However, in light of how the corporate world touches our everyday lives, artificial intelligence enhancing business intelligence would now seem to have the utmost importance in affecting how we work on a daily basis. It is for this reason that Chapters 2 through 5 of this book provide the coverage needed to define a technological path that is filled with new methods and tools that will bring us to business intelligence's future—a future never before effectively available and only imagined for artificial intelligence.

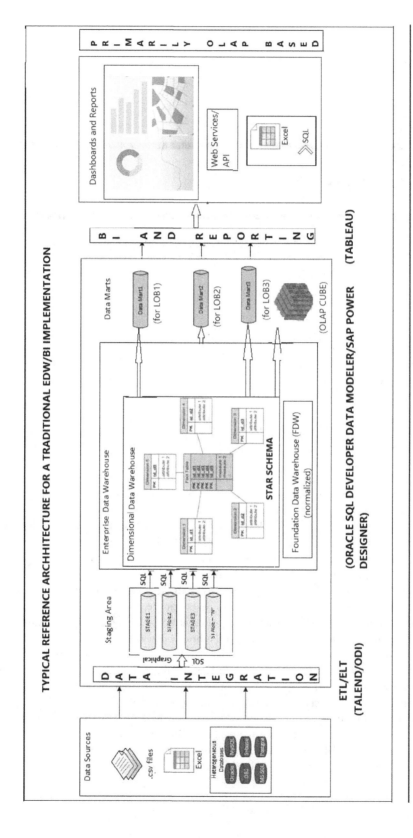

Figure 1.1 A typical architecture of a traditional (first-generation) EDW/BI implementation.

1.2 Traditional Ways of Enabling BI

Any BI-enabled ecosystem involves the integration of all of the tools and technologies—from data preparation (including data quality) to data integration (via ETL/ELT or data virtualization) to data warehousing (including data lakes that act as sources to data warehouse) to data presentation (via data marts, data warehouses, and/or BI dashboards) to data visualization, and from decision support to decision making—presented by today's plethora of artificial intelligence tools and technologies to boost and enhance business intelligence. In addition, data governance needs to be applied to each of these phases to meet regulatory requirements etc.

Data virtualization and data lakes entered the EDW/BI scenario as part of the so-called Data Integration 2.0 technologies.

Figure 1.1 shows a typical architecture of a comprehensive EDW/BI solution. As can be seen from this figure, there are three major components of the EDW/BI solution:

1. Data Integration—This consists of collecting data from multiple sources and in multiple formats, including mostly structured or relational data that can be massaged into a common format that can be then be integrated into the subsequent data warehousing component.
2. Data Warehousing—This consists of staging the data from the data integration component into a landing zone that is responsible for massaging the data. On the basis of the data sources and the type of data, a logical dimensional model is constructed that clearly lays out the dimensions and facts based on business processes. This results in a STAR schema wherein a fact is surrounded by multiple dimensions in a star format. This logical model forms the core of the EDW that stores data in a semantic model for inter-day and as-is and as-of reporting. Multiple Data Marts are created off of the EDW to cater to reporting on a departmental level of the enterprise. Each data mart is modeled as a STAR schema.
3. Business Intelligence (BI) and Reporting Component—This consists of the dashboarding and reporting of data (based on canned reports using a BI tool that is integrated with the EDW to enable business analysts and user interaction of the data. These users are given access to the data to use predefined KPIs.

Although the above architecture shows EDW/BI at an enterprise level, it had limitations, such as no intra-day reporting (Operational BI), no real capability to enable users to create their own KPIs via interactive dashboarding (self-service analytics), and *ad hoc* reporting. The next section outlines how the EDW/BI landscape evolved to result in second- and third-generation EDW/BI solutions.

1.3 Three Generations of BI

The first generation of BI was based on a primarily OLAP-based solution, which supported mostly relational data formats and used ETL/ELT for data integration. The EDW was designed based on the STAR-schema, which was also relational and could be extended to Multidimensional Online Analytical Processing (MOLAP). Figure 1.1 depicts a typical first-generation BI architecture. First-generation reporting and BI were limited to nightly reporting based on batch loads and support for real-time data integration but no ad hoc reporting. In addition, operational BI or, in other words, analysis of data as it was created was not feasible, and BI capabilities did not extend to enable users to create their own KPIs or self-service analytics.

These needs were addressed by *the second generation of BI architecture, which introduced analytics as part of BI* and, additionally, took advantage of Data Integration 2.0, which came with robust data integration technologies such as data virtualization and data integration pipelines and EDW enhancements such as data lakes (that housed raw data) and could be used as a source for EDW.

The three main capabilities of second-generation BI included *ad hoc* querying, operational BI, and self-service analytics. It could also leverage data virtualization, which enabled data integration at scale. Second-generation BI also took care of BI at scale by enabling the use of data lakes and data agility.

---

*With the ability to perform analytics on data, enterprises could find the whys of what occurred in the past using such data or sometimes predict the future using this information (**business analytics part**) in addition to getting to know what happened and how it happened in the past based on the data (**business intelligence part**). This meant that causation and correlation are part of the analyses and are both needed to perform the analyses. In addition, both are not the same. The second generation of BI supports business intelligence and business analytics, leading to a holistic view of business and the ability to make decisions that are more insightful. This could also pave the way for predicting the future using these analytics and intelligence such as how a particular decision could evolve if and when the data evolves. **In addition, a key component of the second generation of BI was to put business analytics in the hands of the business analyst or end user, thus leading to self-service analytics**. Accordingly, BI tools were enhanced to include these new trends as new ways to integrate into already-existing BI ecosystems. From a business analyses perspective, BI happens before Business Analytics, and while the former can discern what the criteria are that lead to business competition, the latter allows you to discern why such criteria lead to business competition of your enterprise. And both BI and BA fall under the larger umbrella of business analyses.*

By using analytics, an enterprise can design metrics that aid in decision making, which, in turn, enables competition—also called competitive intelligence. In comparison, BI uses metrics that measure the effectiveness of a business goal within your enterprise. Metrics are like atomic measures that track business processes.

Figure 1.2 depicts a typical second generation of BI architecture.

Third-generation BI is based on AI meets BI (artificial intelligence meets business intelligence), and it enables various AI-powered analytics for BI-enabled decision making. It is unique in the sense that it leverages the intersection of AI, data science, machine learning, deep learning, and cognitive computing and how these technologies can assist and/or automate BI and decision making. The major aspects of AI-powered BI are as follows:

- Real-time EDW and BI.
- Automated, augmented, and autonomous BI, including augmented analytics that uses a combination of human and machine intelligence and **the automation of content-and-context involved** for relevance and importance of BI-enabled insights and accuracy and transparency of the same across the enterprise level. Simply put, it enables automated and extended data analyses and analytics.
- Big Data Discovery using AI-powered search and its integration into the BI landscape that is efficient and facilitates informed decision making at the enterprise level and scale via transformed (big) data analytics.
- AI-powered EDW/BI has eased the ability to harness data in varied formats, such as structured, semi-structured, and unstructured and real-time data. It has also handled the rate at which such data was created, as well as the huge volume of the same, while simultaneously enabling validation of the data and maintaining the quality of such data.
- Agile analytics.
- Enterprise-level scalability and how customer experience can thereby be enhanced.

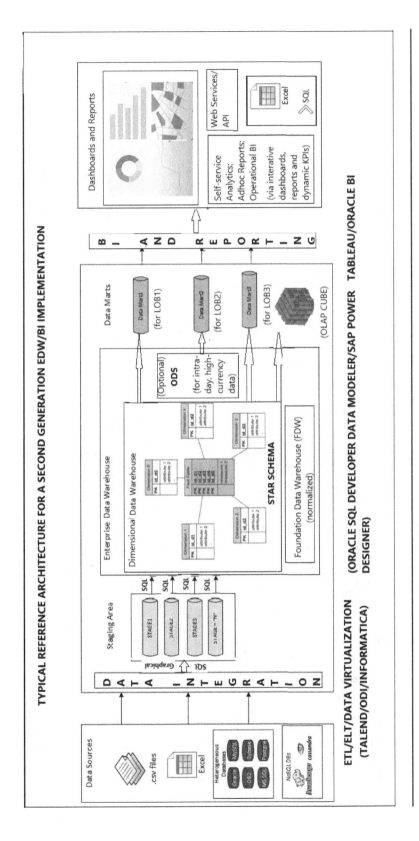

Figure 1.2 A typical second-generation EDW/BI architecture.

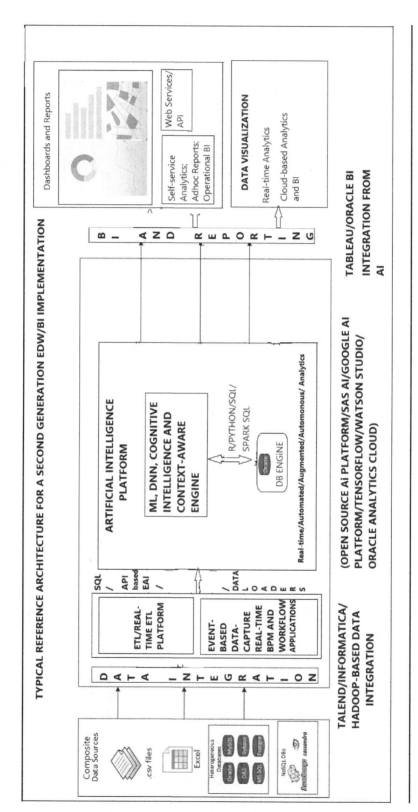

Figure 1.3 A typical third-generation AI meets BI architecture.

- A holistic EDW/BI solution that can be used by both technical and non-technical users at all levels of the enterprise.
- Intelligent automation of business and operational processes.
- Delivery of BI-as-a-service for mobility and on-the-go customer analytics.
- Data monetization at the enterprise level.
- Acceleration and enhancement of competitive BI. As an example, BI can have deep neural network solutions embedded within its implementation stack to realize competitive results. Use cases of such an implementation include image tagging and image-recognition solutions.

Using AI for BI leverages how to use an AI model in context from business by recommending a particular AI model/machine learning algorithm based on the use case inputs and outputs. It details the aspects that have not yet been deeply explored in the BI landscape, such as the relevance and importance of BI-enabled insights and accuracy and transparency of the same across the enterprise/corporate industry level.

Figure 1.3 depicts a typical third-generation BI architecture that is powered by AI.

Third-generation BI is of specific advantage to business analysts, data analysts, data scientists, and data engineers as well as end users. As stated in the beginning of this section, BI has evolved from its initial landscape of OLAP-based reporting and analysis (first generation of BI) to *ad hoc* querying, operational BI, and self-service analytics (second generation of BI) to AI-powered business analytics and big data discovery (third generation of BI). And many of the industry's leading BI vendors, such as Tableau®, Microsoft®, Oracle®, IBM®, etc., have already started offering AI-powered capabilities to enable all kinds of users (technical and non-technical) to take advantage of these new technologies and trends and to derive intelligent insights that can lead to better, smarter, faster BI.

1.4 How Business Fits into BI—From Business Data to Business Decision Making

Every enterprise has a business landscape that has certain objectives or goals to meet to remain competitive in the industry. To this end, it is composed of a number of business processes that define how the enterprise is organized to meet its goals. For example, a product manufacturing enterprise has the objectives of maximizing its sales, profit, and its supply chain, which help it stay ahead of the competition. And each of these objectives comprises one or more business processes that are, in turn, measured by metrics that track their status. In addition, there are KPIs that track and measure how well the enterprise is meeting a certain business objective. These KPIs measure the effectiveness of a business goal and constitute what is called the business intelligence component of the enterprise. BI needs data that is current as well as historical to determine the KPI measurements based on which analyses are done that, in turn, determine the "what happened" and "how it happened" aspects. In addition, these two aspects determine whether and how well the enterprise has met its goals. To this end, data visualization based on this data enables a business user and/or end user to perform "what" and "how" analyses that eventually aid in determining how well a particular business objective was met and provide an idea of what can be done to further improve the KPI that led to enterprise growth. As an example, visual charts that depict the trend analysis and dashboards that group charts based on combinations of data and drill-up/drill-down/drill-across capabilities can aid business users to discern the correlation between data effects. But BI alone cannot determine the why of data analysis that is very important to actually make decisions based on the reasoning. This is where business analytics enters the picture. As a second aspect of business analyses, business analytics helps in the decision-making process by aiding the prescriptive part (business action to be taken) of a solution as well as, sometimes, the predictive piece of the solution. Both the business decision made and the business action taken help in determining whether the decisions made and subsequent actions taken can help. Furthermore, enabling business users to create their own analytics based on the data presented goes a long way in insightful decision making that drives the enterprise to competitive success. Coming back to the product manufacturing enterprise example, business analytics can help in determining what decisions can be taken when a particular product evolves by way of forecasting sales growth in such a scenario. It is in this predictive analytics scenario that AI can make a difference by way of intelligent decision support.

Business and business users play a pivotal role by describing the enterprise goals and business processes, the KPIs, and the metrics necessary for BI as well as the decisions and the subsequent actions to be taken. Business can also define the type of data visualizations required for analysis as well as those that enhance the decision-making process.

1.5 Summary

This chapter discussed the traditional method of data warehousing and BI and then outlined the three generations of BI by way of a typical architecture based on each. Finally, it touched upon how "business" fits into the BI land analytics landscape. The next chapter describes AI and AI-powered analytics and their role in BI-enablement.

Chapter 2

AI and AI-Powered Analytics

In This Chapter

2.1 Introduction
2.2 AI and Its Rise in the Modern Enterprise
2.3 How AI Changes the Enterprise BI Landscape
2.4 The Analytics Sphere
2.5 BI-Enabled vs. AI-Powered Analytics
2.6 From Data to Intelligent Decision Making to Insightful Decisions
2.7 AI-Powered Techniques for BI
2.8 Summary

2.1 Introduction

Recent years have seen a remarkable rise in AI and AI adoption in the enterprise. From smart data discovery to data standardization to AI-powered models applied to the data, AI has empowered the user landscape from technical user and data scientist to business analyst, citizen scientist, power users, and end users, enabling them to create analytics from business context in real time and on data as it is created. This chapter looks into these details and how AI and AI-powered analytics have resulted in a BI solution that delivers intelligent insights from any and all kinds of data and, at the same time, is next-gen, scalable, contextually relevant, and one that is customizable and personalized—from on-premise to on-the-go.

2.2 AI and Its Rise in the Modern Enterprise

The rise of AI has benefitted the enterprise in the following ways:

- It has enabled unlock data science and its application in solving enterprise business problems.
- It has provided an area in which AI and cognitive computing can work together, resulting in an optimal autonomous, augmented, and adaptive intelligence platform.

- Through AI, cognitive computing can consist of the following technologies: natural language processing (NLP), machine learning with neural networks and deep neural networks, algorithms that learn and adapt with AI, deep learning, image recognition, reason and decision automation, and emotional intelligence.
- AI has become a convergence of three powerful technologies, namely, machine learning, natural language processing, and cognitive computing. This is where the future of AI is heading.
- Further, pragmatics can be defined by way of cognition and recommend the "optimal" choice, thereby boosting competition. This integrates "cognition" into the model and trains it using the cognitive computing–based recommender model for decision making in terms of outputting the "most optimal" choice to be used, as well as *comprehend" why the particular choice is optimal to be used (i.e., the next best action)*—from decision support to insightful decision making.
- Typical levels of data analytics include descriptive analytics, diagnostic analytics, predictive analytics, prescriptive analytics, and cognitive computing. The fifth type of data analytics—cognitive computing—answers questions such as, What is the next best action that can be taken? This involves the computing context with respect to the business use case.

2.3 How AI Changes the Enterprise BI Landscape

AI changes the enterprise landscape of business intelligence (BI) by way of adaptive intelligence whereby applications and analytics can be integrated together by applying and embedding AI/ML-based techniques. Starting from storing all data (preferably in a catalog), performing discovery on data, applying data quality and governance on such data, and using metadata for AI/ML-based recommendations to building a machine learning platform for all data, augmenting data by embedding ML (e.g., adding relevant context to data such as by adding ethnicity and demographics data based on ethnicity to a person's name), enterprises can gain a competitive edge in the specific industry.

Enabling data enrichment, visualized recommendations, predictive analytics, and personalized analytics from on-premise to on-the-go, BI solutions have gone a long way in accelerating data-driven insights, thus making AI meets BI a reality. And accelerating decisions with AI and ML using intelligent data discovery, interactive visualizations and dashboarding, smart data enrichment, customizable AI for creating predictive model-enabled charts, and determining outliers faster and without the need to code or requiring extra skills or tools are all the ways in which AI-powered analytics have and are changing the enterprise BI landscape. And all of this without losing flexibility, business continuity, scalability, performance, and collaboration and in an automated fashion.

Add to this natural language capabilities such as natural language querying (NLQ), natural language processing (NLP), and natural language generation (NLG), today we have BI solutions that have these features embedded within them, delivering analytics that tell a story based on data on the fly that is both relevant and performant.

Figure 2.1 shows a typical AI-powered BI system.

2.4 The Analytics Sphere

The so-called analytics sphere contains descriptive analytics at its core and progresses outward in enclosing spherical circles that encompass diagnostic analytics, predictive analytics, prescriptive analytics, and cognitive computing. A next-gen kind of analytics called augmented analytics that consists of machine intelligence and human intuition is part of cognitive computing and adaptive AI. And when adaptive AI is integrated with BI, a new world of BI opens up that can align vis-à-vis business processes to deliver intelligent insights. This helps an enterprise acquire competitive intelligence that, in turn,

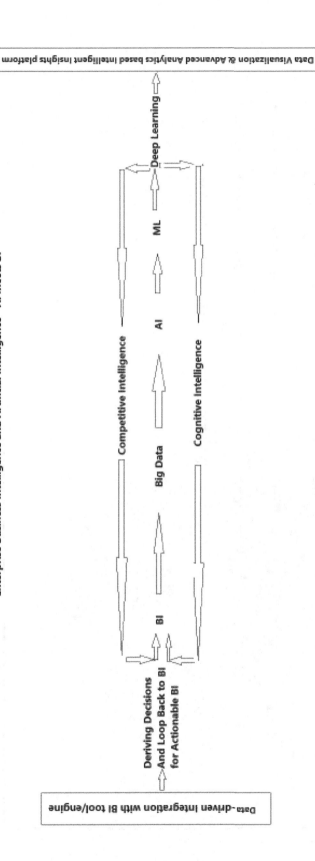

Figure 2.1 A typical AI-powered BI system.

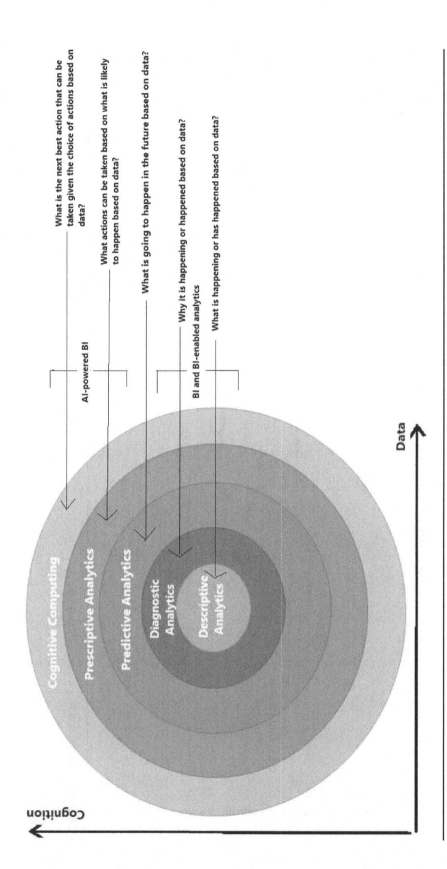

Figure 2.2 Typical analytics sphere.

What is the next best action that can be taken given the choice of actions based on data?

What actions can be taken based on what is likely to happen based on data?

What is going to happen in the future based on data?

Why it is happening or happened based on data?

What is happening or has happened based on data?

AI-powered BI

BI and BI-enabled analytics

Cognitive Computing

Prescriptive Analytics

Predictive Analytics

Diagnostic Analytics

Descriptive Analytics

Cognition

Data

enables its business stay at the cutting edge in the industry. Figure 2.2 depicts a typical analytics sphere, along with the key drivers of each type of analytics.

2.5 BI-Enabled vs. AI-Powered Analytics

Business intelligence has the ability to deliver results based on canned reports and visual analyses (first-generation BI), self-service analytics, and data discovery (second-generation BI). These techniques also enable performing trends and trend-based projections based on the data but lack the ability to make predictions, such as the likelihood of a certain event occurring—for example, what would happen to the sales if a product evolves with time, etc.—or more deep-dive analytics, such as why a particular segment of customers cancelled their subscriptions to a particular product. With the introduction of AI-powered analytics into BI, a new wave of BI—called third-generation of BI—emerged that could provide predictive analytics and much more.

So, what types of answers can a BI system provide and what types of answers can an AI-powered BI system provide that an enterprise can leverage to boost business competition? It is to be noted that BI-enabled analytics are still needed for any type of analysis for an enterprise, and AI-powered analytics provide extensibility to these analytics by way of integration with AI, leading to deeper, smarter, faster, and adaptive analytics and in an augmented, automated, and autonomous fashion.

Table 2.1 provides a compare-and-contrast view of BI-enabled versus AI-powered analytics.

2.6 From Data to Intelligent Decision Making to Insightful Decisions

When processed and fed into a BI tool, data can aid in decision making that can, in turn, help enterprises meet their goals. For example, projecting the growth of sales of a product based on past trends in the sales of the product can help a business make decisions such as to expand its operations base and/or enhance its product line. This kind of decision making is descriptive in nature in that it seems the decisions made are based on facts or events that have happened in the past. Taking the product sales example, it is the sales trend. And the projections here are a look into how the future looks in terms of product growth. Although projections are predictive. they cannot explain why the projections made can boost sales in the future, or why they cannot. Applying business analytics can answer questions pertaining to the why of events that happened in the past. Taking the product sales example in context, they can explain why a sales trend was good at a given point in time.

However, questions such as why a product line did not see growth in a particular region are tougher to answer, for the following reasons: First, the relevance to the answers obtained cannot be personalized or customized over time. Second, what actions to be taken next and why such actions need to be taken next to see an improvement in sales growth are not quite unambiguously answerable. This is where intelligent decision making comes into the picture.

BI-enabled analytics can help in customizing relevance as of a given time frame. It can answer the what and when of past events that occurred based on data, and the business analytics part can answer why the events happened based on past data, but not the what, when, and why next, and, more specifically, the why next based on predictions. This includes descriptive, diagnostic, comparative (to a certain extent), and predictive (to a lesser degree—primarily projections into the future based on past data and events).

Table 2.1 BI-Enabled versus AI-Powered Analytics

BI-Enabled Analytics	AI-Powered Analytics
Suggest data lineage–based descriptive factors and derive analytics based on it. Here, it does not suggest new data that can be augmented for better analyses (**only analysis**).	Suggest everything about the data just by looking at its source as well as suggest new data that can be used for deriving analytics. In addition, it can generate new data based on the existing data by way of data augmentation techniques (**analyses and synthesis**).
Responsive and visual in nature—data can be used to suggest metrics based on dashboards and other types of visual components. Additionally, the why of data is attainable based on responses obtained from the how of data-based events—decision support.	Proactive and dynamically visualizable based on the proactive results for deep-dive insights—decision making.
Non-conversational in nature—aids in the business decision process by way of interactive analytics and visualizations.	Both conversational and visual analytics—the former enables asking questions in natural language, and the latter integrates the results into instant visualizations created on the fly for further analytics, yet retaining the context.
Uses query-based analysis that works on certain types of data. This might present an obstacle when performing an in-depth exploration of data for business users.	Enables analysis on all types of datasets by bringing the algorithms to the data, thus helping in data exploration without any stratified limits for business users.
BI-enabled queries mostly use the row set returned by the query to perform analyses, derive analytics, and learn from it.	AI-powered exploration predominantly uses the inclusion as well as the exclusion set of queries—both to learn from and to derive new analytics. In addition, this type of learning enables studying the correlations involved and using them to determine variable importance (key business drivers' importance).
Analytical flexibility is a function of business drivers, key performance indicators (KPIs), and self-service analytics. As an example, BI-enabled analytics can determine Gross Margin and Gross Revenue, along with their respective trends over time. However, relating the two to define custom analytics that is most relevant to every type of user is not easily achievable with BI alone—even when visualizations are available.	In contrast, AI-powered analytics not only takes into account the context behind the two, but also the correlations across the same, over time, by way of suggesting new data and generating new data to aid in computing the context (augmented analytics) and comparative analysis. Additionally, it studies what is happening and what is not happening from learning from and exploring the inclusion and exclusion sets. Last, it learns from the changes each type of user makes to the best practice visualizations as well as from the changes in the selections in the visualization This provides ease and flexibility in defining custom analytics that are tailored to each type of user.
Advanced analytics and custom analytics integration that go beyond the capability of a particular BI-enabled engine can be a challenge.	Can easily integrate with other third-party engines that provide deep-dive analytics, predictive analytics, and other AI/ML models.
Embedded analytics confined to BI tool limits.	Extensive embedded analytics with enhancement features that address a wide range of business contexts, resulting in new insights and thereby enabling adaptive BI.
BI-enabled analytics can help in customizing relevance as of a given time frame. It can answer the *what and when* of past events that occurred based on data, and the business analytics part can answer *why* the events happened based on past data, but not the *what, when, and why next*, and more specifically the *why next* based on predictions. This includes descriptive, diagnostic, comparative (to a certain extent), and predictive (to a lesser degree—primarily projections into the future based on past data and events).	AI-powered analytics can be used to customize and improve relevance over time, thus providing insights for *what, why, and where to go next*. The *why* part of what and where to go next is the unique part AI can aid in determining. This includes narrative, visual, diagnostic, comparative, and predictive analytics.
Find a product by way of its features—declarative classification using KPIs and/or descriptive analytics.	Find a product by analyzing a photo-image classification using deep learning.

AI-powered analytics can be used to customize and improve relevance over time, thus providing insights for what, why, and where to go next. The why part of what and where to go next is the unique part AI can aid in determining. This includes narrative, visual, diagnostic, comparative, and predictive analytics.

Machine learning algorithms and predictive AI models can be embedded into BI platforms to compute contextual relevance using various techniques that, in turn, can aid in answering questions such as the above, which are more important in terms of business drivers as well as relevant to the context in question. The journey from data to insightful decisions by way of AI-powered analytics can typically comprise the following steps:

1. Discover issues and the key business drivers pertaining to them
2. Perform self-service data import from all relevant data sources
3. Enrich the data leveraging AI-based machine learning and advanced analytics pair (integrated into the BI platform)
4. Perform additional exploration of data with embedded AI and convert visualizations into narratives, as necessary, using NLG techniques
5. Discover data-driven insights powered by AI/ML and deep learning that best align with the key business drivers in context. Use augmented analytics in combination with AI/ML to arrive at smarter insights
6. Autogenerate visuals for the data-driven insights using AI/ML and save them as reusable components, for example, PDF or graphical formats
7. Create voice-based visuals using NLP and add narratives to visuals using NLG
8. Automate the above AI-powered analytics by way of deployable and schedulable workflows or otherwise as supported by AI/ML-embedded BI platforms
9. Mobile-enable the above for on-the-go AI-powered BI solutions
10. Enrich the solution to learn and explore further based on user feedback that can be fed into the solution and leveraged using AI/ML inherent in it

The above steps can be followed as a blueprint for a typical AI-powered BI solution that enables any and all kinds of data that tell a story that is in real time, visualizable, and insightful.

2.7 AI-Powered Techniques for BI

A plethora of AI-powered techniques exist that can be either embedded into BI platforms or integrated with third-party AI systems. Beginning with embedded analytics and guided analytics to more advanced analytics such as augmented analytics and those that are deep learning–based to conversational AI, today's BI platforms are modernized to address multiple business problems across the analytics spectrum. This section outlines certain AI-powered techniques that are relevant to the four industry use cases that are covered in depth in Chapters 3 and 4. Here's a list of the same:

1. Classification machine learning algorithm using random forests and decision trees—used to classify commodity saleable grade based on its attributes (descriptive analytics).
2. Deep learning–based techniques (using neural networks) for predicting commodity pricing in advance (predictive analytics).
3. Neural networks–based ML algorithms for recommender systems to suggest optimal choices based on score (prescriptive and predictive analytics). As an example, the pragmatics of using deep neural networks for making recommendations from a business standpoint can include

recommending viable product sources by predicting the "score" of each source—a prescriptive analytics solution **and** predicting how the product fares in the market based on the recommended source—a predictive analytics solution. And the output of recommendation can be visually integrated in BI dashboards for actionable insight (e.g., Tableau® Dashboard, Oracle® BI, Microsoft® BI, etc.).

4. Automatic image recognition (for classification of images).

Consider an example of a BI system that discovers and recommends wearables based on the personal choice of customers. There are two approaches it can take, namely,

1. Obtain the customer's details along with details of the attire and other wearables that the customer has purchased recently and compare them with similar metrics on a month-by-month basis over the last six months. Then, recommend similar or improved wearables in the same category by way of descriptive analytics. The results can be sent to the customer's mobile device with descriptions of recommendations and any associated pictures of the wearables.

2. Identify the customer using face recognition as well as the attire and other wearables by looking at the same picture of the customer as he or she enters a store and discern facial features, perform image recognition to identify the wearables of that person as seen in the image, and correlate the findings of the two. Then merge the results of the image recognition with sales data pertaining to the customer in an embeddable manner on the fly, perform deep-dive analytics and come up with recommendations, and send the results back to the same customer by using the recognized face images and wearable details (machine intelligence using embedded AI/ML—face recognition, image processing, smart discovery, product association, and personalized visual analytics. An important part of this deep learning–based analysis that comes first is the face recognition from the image of the customer that is captured in-store. This step itself involves at least four substeps, as listed below:

   i. Feature extraction—what features should be extracted from a face to form a feature set that can aid in identifying a particular face.

   ii. Feature selection—what features from the extracted set above should be used to best identify a "face." In others words, what are the best features to be used out of the set of extracted features.

   iii. Feature engineering—how to improvise the selected features in step (ii) to identify a different image to be classified as a "face."

   iv. Image classification—how to classify the detected "face" as belonging to a particular person.

The second approach (driven by AI) has the advantages of giving smarter data-driven results in real time, improved relevance, customized recommendations, and the ability to justify why those recommendations are actionable for a win-win situation.

Some business applications of AI-based deep learning models are as follows:

- IT-automation
- Sentiment analysis
- Social intelligence and social engineering
- Prescriptive analytics—recommending products based on their "user ratings"
- Natural language generation and querying
- Image recognition—as in Facebook™ image tagging
- Visual analytics
- Weather prediction
- Contextual speech-to-text processing
- Genetic applications

BI can have deep neural network (DNN) solutions embedded within its implementation stack to realize competitive results. For example, for image tagging and image recognition–based applications, the convolutional neural network (CNN) model can be leveraged to that extent.

2.8 Summary

This chapter focused on explaining how AI-powered analytics using machine learning models can be implemented in BI platforms to enable fast and insightful decision making, which is achievable for BI purposes based on the data-driven results obtained. It outlined the various aspects of how an AI meets BI solution can be implemented in the modern enterprise—a solution that delivers real-time insights for any type of user, starting from IT to power users to end users. The next chapter deals with four real-world use cases covering descriptive, diagnostic, predictive, and prescriptive analytics from a business perspective, in detail, including how each of them fits into the BI landscape, but is implemented using AI-powered analytics.

Chapter 3

Industry Uses Cases of Enterprise BI—A Business Perspective

In This Chapter

3.1 Introduction
3.2 Classifying Commodity Saleable Grade Based on Its Attributes
3.3 Predicting Commodity Prices in Advance
3.4 Recommender Systems to Suggest Optimal Choices Based on Score
3.5 Automatic Image Recognition
3.6 Summary

3.1 Introduction

Today, we are into the third generation of business intelligence (BI), one that is powered by artificial intelligence (AI). Starting from data preparation and data wrangling to making decisions to monetizing AI-driven models for business processes, AI-powered BI has revolutionized intelligent decision making. Business analysts, data analysts, industry experts, and end users now have the ability to use all kinds of enterprise data at their disposal to generate new data, deduce key business drivers and anomalies from the generated data, and tell stories visually that are otherwise hard to realize. Taking it further, AI powered BI can allow businesses to create custom models with built-in intelligence that are smart enough to detect the edge competitive drivers and introduce them into analyses and analytic dashboards. This directly factors into delivering a state-of-the-art customer experience, one that is driven by an AI meets BI solution. This chapter describes four industry cases from a business perspective and an AI-powered BI standpoint as well as how these analyses can help in enterprise BI (including intelligent decision making).

3.2 Classifying Commodity Saleable Grade Based on Its Attributes

This section describes the use case of classifying commodity salability as grade in terms of cost deduced from its quality and other attributes. The primary drivers directly influencing grade, the anomalies, and the key performance metrics (F1 value, along with precision and recall) are visually depicted. The key point to note here is that an AI-powered machine learning model is used to arrive at the prediction of grade on new data, and a matrix of false positives versus true positives is shown from which business users can make insightful decisions in determining the cost to sell the commodity based on its grade.

3.2.1 Descriptive Analytics

3.2.1.1 Purpose of the Use Case

- Goal
  To classify commodity (wine) salability grade on the basis of its quality and other attributes. This allows decisions to be made, from a qualitative aspect, in regard to the cost and sale of wine. In this particular use case, we use two values for grade, namely, 'SaleableCheap' and 'SaleableCostly'.

- Business perspective
  To visualize data distribution, key drivers that influence the grade, anomalies of grade, and the AI- and ML-based model classification performance that can be used to quantitatively and qualitatively determine the cost of the wine based on the grade predicted and, hence, determine the salability of the wine.

- Input Dataset
  Wine grade dataset of white wine in a .csv file having grade and 11 other variables pertaining to it as fields.

3.2.1.2 Brief Introduction to Machine Learning–Based Random Forests and Decision Trees

For any data, given a set of data elements or attributes that it consists of, and the AI-powered model applied to this data that can ultimately be used to classify or predict the business outcome, there are at least six aspects by which it can be analyzed. Here is a list of these and what each of them represents:

1. The values and type of values of the data element or attribute and how the data elements relate to each other. If the attribute is categorical, the values in the attribute that it can be classified into, as well as the distribution of the classes, are also important. In our example use case. this means determining the values of grade and their distribution across the dataset.
2. The primary drivers of a particular attribute in the dataset. In other words, what attributes in the dataset best explain that attribute and, hence, best influence the feature importance. In our example use case, the question is, What are the primary drivers of the variable grade and how best can it be relied upon to score in business decisions that require grade as a key player?
3. The overall percentage of accuracy for predicting values of the attribute, that is, grade in the example use case.
4. The groups in the data that can be considered as outliers.
5. The type of AI-powered model that is built or applied to the training data (which can be a subset of the dataset) and the built model that can perform on this training data.

6. The performance of the AI-powered model built in Step 5 when applied to real-world enterprise data and the corresponding BI integration and analysis, including automation of the analytics involved and the cognitive capabilities of such a model to provide the **best context** of the BI-based decisions.

As pointed out in the previous section, the salability of grade is classified as SaleableCheap or SaleableCostly. Figure 3.1 shows the distribution of grade into these classes.

The following is a snapshot of training data:

```
 fixed.acidity volatile.acidity citric.acid residual.sugar chlorides free.sulfur.dioxide
total.sulfur.dioxide density   pH sulphates alcohol          grade
1            7.2              0.31        0.35            7.2     0.046                  45
              178 0.99550 3.14      0.53     9.7  SaleableCheap
2            7.0              0.20        0.33            4.7     0.030                  25
               76 0.99202 2.88      0.54    10.5 SaleableCostly
3            6.6              0.26        0.28            9.4     0.028                  13
              121 0.99254 3.17      0.34    12.1 SaleableCostly
4            7.3              0.19        0.27           13.9     0.057                  45
              155 0.99807 2.94      0.41     8.8 SaleableCostly
5            7.2              0.23        0.38            6.1     0.067                  20
               90 0.99496 3.17      0.79     9.7  SaleableCheap
6            7.9              0.35        0.24           15.6     0.072                  44
              229 0.99785 3.03      0.59    10.5 SaleableCostly
```

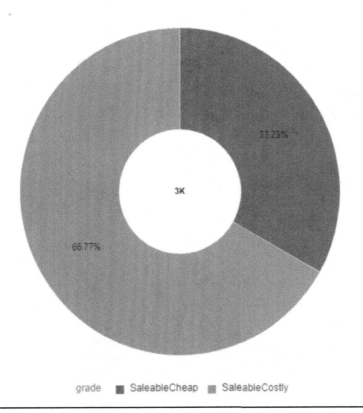

grade   ■ SaleableCheap ■ SaleableCostly

Figure 3.1 Distribution of the wine grade into two classes: SaleableCheap and SaleableCostly.

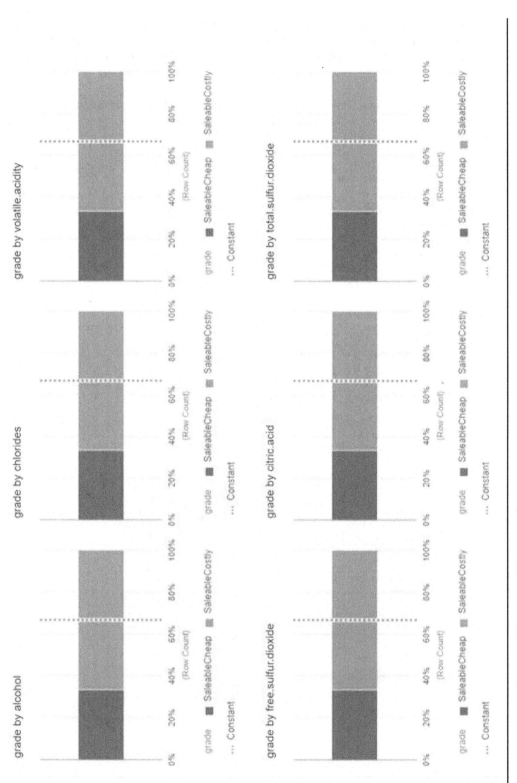

Figure 3.2 Primary drivers of the wine salability grade.

Other key criteria are the primary drivers of grade. Figure 3.2 demonstrates this in terms of what wine attributes influence the wine grade salability process.

Regarding the third aspect (as outlined above), the overall percentage for predicting outcomes of grade is 65% across 7 groups. These groups, along with the % accuracy and confidence, are depicted in Figures 3.3a and 3.3b.

Next, it is important to determine the anomalies of grade. These are demonstrated in Figure 3.4.

The AL/ML model used for the use case in question is random forest classification. After building the model on training data, the performance metrics obtained are as depicted in Figures 3.5 to 3.9.

During random forest AI-ML model creation, 30% of training data was indicated to be used for model validation. This means that out of 3,428 observations in the training dataset, 2,400 observations were used to build the model and 1,028 observations were used to validate the model built and, in the process, improve the model's accuracy. The validation process involved is termed k-fold validation, where k >= 2, and in the validation phase, the model will repeat the build and validate process so that the target variable(s) value(s) are optimal and the error rate is minimized. Figure 3.5 shows the confusion matrix (a cross table of counts of observations across actual and predicted classes). It also gives the % of accuracy of the model as well as the false positive rate. Another point to be noted in this figure is the number 1,028. This represents 30% of the training data that was used for validation, which, when calculated as 30% of 3,428 (the total number of observations), yields 1,028. And the predicted values come from the k-fold validation process that occurred during the model build process.

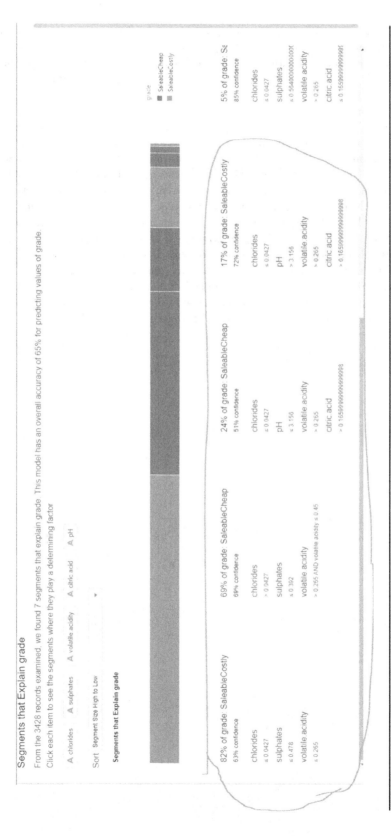

Figure 3.3a Overall % Accuracy for predicting outcomes of grade -1.

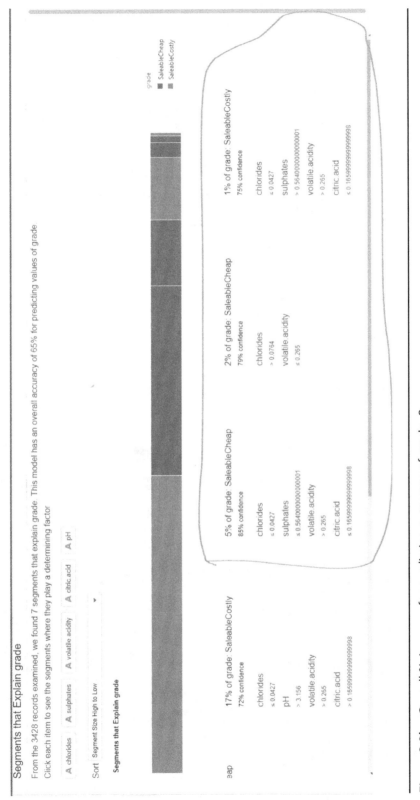

Segments that Explain grade

From the 3428 records examined, we found 7 segments that explain grade. This model has an overall accuracy of 65% for predicting values of grade

Click each item to see the segments where they play a determining factor

A chlorides   A sulphates   A volatile acidity   A citric acid   A pH

Sort   Segment Size High to Low   ▶

Segments that Explain grade

aap

17% of grade SaleableCostly
72% confidence

chlorides
≤ 0.0427

pH
> 3.156

volatile acidity
> 0.265

citric acid
> 0.1659999999999998

5% of grade SaleableCheap
85% confidence

chlorides
≤ 0.0427

sulphates
≤ 0.5640000000000001

volatile acidity
> 0.265

citric acid
≤ 0.1659999999999958

2% of grade SaleableCheap
79% confidence

chlorides
> 0.0764

volatile acidity
≤ 0.265

1% of grade SaleableCostly
75% confidence

chlorides
≤ 0.0427

sulphates
> 0.5640000000000001

volatile acidity
> 0.265

citric acid
≤ 0.1659999999999998

grade
■ SaleableCheap
■ SaleableCostly

Figure 3.3b   Overall % Accuracy for predicting outcomes of grade -2.

Anomalies of grade

55 combinations of 11 dimensions are being analyzed. Here are the top outliers for grade : SaleableCheap

When fixed acidity is 6, we expected {Row Count} for volatile acidity : 0.21 to be 2.00, however, it is 4.00, representing a difference of 2.00.

When fixed acidity is 5, we expected {Row Count} for volatile acidity : 0.61 to be 1.00, however, it is 1.00, representing a difference of 0.00.

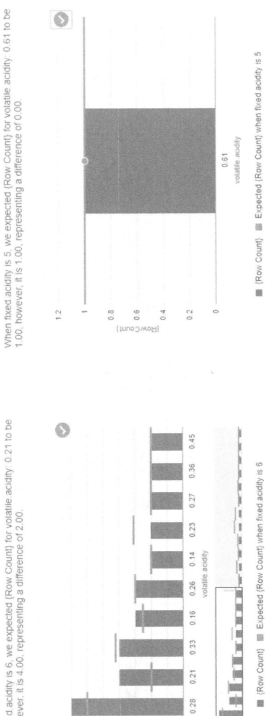

Figure 3.4 Anomalies of grade.

Figure 3.5 Cross table of actual and predicted value counts during validation of the AI-ML build process.

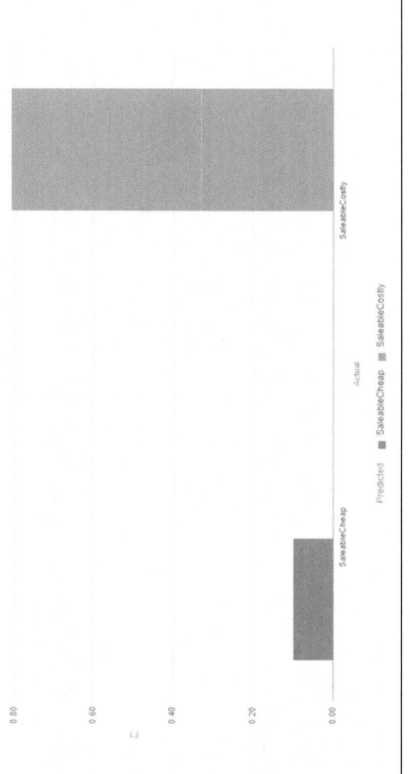

Figure 3.6 AI-ML Model Performance metric F1 by Actual, Predicted on training (validation) data.

The response variable in this use case is grade with values SaleableCheap and SaleableCostly. And both of these classes are to be considered in determining its prediction accuracy. From Figure 3.1 it can be seen that there is some class imbalance. As evident from Figures 3.5 and 3.6, in this case, our classifier has given **a high F1 score** to the class SaleableCostly (0.8) in terms of Predicted. Also, the misclassification rate for SaleableCostly is 0.7% (significantly low). However, the F1 score for SaleableCheap is around 0.1, with a misclassification rate of 94%. The F1 score is considered as the harmonic mean of recall and precision. Our classifier shows whether a particular wine has grade SaleableCheap or SaleableCostly. **This suggests that the grade SaleableCostly is favorable over SaleableCheap as it has a higher F1-score and lower misclassification rate. However, in our use case, it is important that both of the grades be evaluated, particularly because of class imbalance. We can do this by using two additional metrics: Precision and Recall.** To calculate precision and recall, we need to know four definitions, as stated below:

- True positive (TP): An outcome in which the model *correctly* predicts the positive class
- True negative (TN): An outcome in which the model *correctly* predicts the negative class
- False positive (FP): An outcome in which the model *incorrectly* predicts the positive class
- False negative (FN): An outcome in which the model *incorrectly* predicts the negative class

Translating this into the AI model that we built and scored, and taking into account the matrix in Figure 3.5, we can derive two tables (see Tables 3.1 and 3.2).

Table 3.1 Table for Class SaleableCheap Demonstrating the TP, FP, FN, and TN

True Positive Actual: SaleableCheap Predicted: SaleableCheap	False Positive Actual: SaleableCostly Predicted: SaleableCheap
False Negative Actual: SaleableCheap Predicted: SaleableCostly	True Negative Actual: SaleableCostly Predicted: SaleableCostly

Table 3.2 Table for Class SaleableCostly Demonstrating the TP, FP, FN, and TN

True Positive Actual: SaleableCostly Predicted: SaleableCostly	False Positive Actual: SaleableCheap Predicted: SaleableCostly
False Negative Actual: SaleableCostly Predicted: SaleableCheap	True Negative Actual: SaleableCheap Predicted: SaleableCheap

From a business perspective, the metrics Precision and Recall tend to answer the following questions:

- *For precision, what percentage of positive predictions were actually correct? In the use case discussed, this boils down to precisely identifying cheap grade from costly (and vice versa).*
- *For recall, what percentage of actual positives were correctly recognized? In the use case discussed, this boils down to identifying each class of grade from both classes.*

Taking into account both of the above statements, our model built must perform on both precision and recall.

Now, let us calculate the precision and recall for our model for each of the two classes. The following depicts how it can be done:

Precision (p) = TP/(TP+FP)
Recall (r) = TP/(TP+FN)

And from the above, we can calculate the F1-score as follows:

F1-score = 2/(1/r + 1/p)

Substituting the values into these formulas for each class from Figure 3.5 and Tables 3.1 and 3.2, we get the precision and recall as well as the F1-score for each of the two classes, as given below.

PrecisionSaleableCheap = TP/(TP+FP) = 18/(18+5) = 0.783
PrecisionSaleableCostly = TP/(TP+FP) = 684/(684+321) = 0.68
These two values match with that shown in Figure 3.7.

RecallSaleableCheap = TP/(TP+FN) = 18/(18+321) = 0.05
RecallSaleableCostly = TP/(TP+FN) = 684/(684+5) = 0.993
These two values match with that shown in Figure 3.8.

F1SaleableCheap = 2/(1/RecallSaleableCheap + 1/PrecisionSaleableCheap) = 0.094
F1SaleableCostly = 2/(1/RecallSaleableCostly + 1/RecallSaleableCostly) = 0.807
These two values match with that shown in Figure 3.6.

Precision relates to false positives (FPs) and having higher precision means less false positives. Having 0 or fewer FPs means that model prediction is good. In our use case, we had PrecisionSaleableCheap as 0.783 and PrecisionSaleableCostly as 0.68, which are significantly high compared to the measuring limit of 1.0.

Recall relates to false negatives (FNs) and having higher recall means less false negatives. Having 0 or fewer FNs means that model prediction is good. In our case, we had RecallSaleableCheap as 0.05 and RecallSaleableCostly as 0.993. The corresponding FNs for SaleableCheap and SaleableCostly were 321 and 5, respectively.

However, as the values for Precision increased, the corresponding values for Recall decreased, and vice versa for the two classes. This is expected behavior as, in most cases, there is a trade-off between Precision and Recall. ***Observing this, our model suggests that both classes—SaleableCheap and SaleableCostly—factor into business analyses and analytics.***

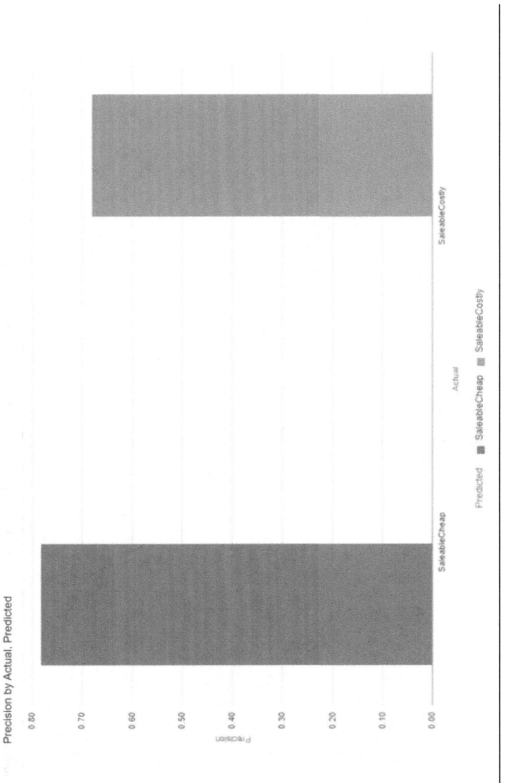

Figure 3.7 AI-ML Model Performance metric Precision by Actual, Predicted on training (validation) data.

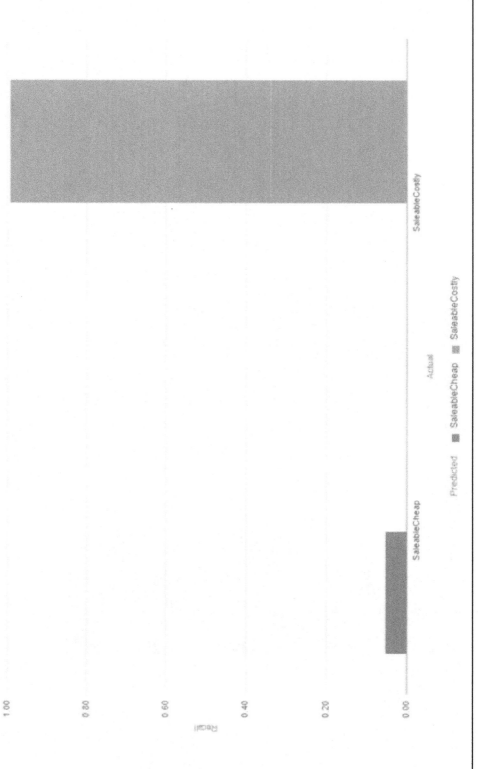

Figure 3.8 AI-ML Model Performance metric Recall by Actual, Predicted on training (validation) data.

**Confusion Matrix on test data for the AI-ML
Random Forest used to predict on test data**

Count by grade, Predictedgrade

grade	SaleableCheap Count	SaleableCostly Count
SaleableCheap	26	475
SaleableCostly	7	962

Figure 3.9   Confusion Matrix of AI-ML Model Performance on test (new) data.

When we calculate the precision and recall for the predictions versus actuals using the test data, the results are as follows:

PrecisionSaleableCheap = TP/(TP+FP) = 10/(10+2) = 0.83
RecallSaleableCheap = TP/(TP+FN) = 10/(10+491) = 0.019
PrecisionSaleableCostly = TP/(TP+FP) = 967/(967+491) = 0.663
RecallSaleableCostly = TP/(TP+FN) = 967/(967+2) = 0.998

And the corresponding F1 scores are as follows:

F1SaleableCheap = 0.037
F1SaleableCostly = 0.80

The above values exhibit behavior similar to that seen with validation data in terms of high precision with low recall and vice versa, as well as F1 scores, thereby suggesting that both classes count towards analysis and decision making when the model is applied to real-world data.

3.3 Predicting Commodity Prices in Advance

This section describes a case study in metallurgy by predicting precious metal prices based on available monthly data. The primary drivers directly influencing price, the anomalies, and key performance metrics (Accuracy, F1 value, along with precision and recall) are visually depicted. The key point to note here is that an AI-powered machine learning model is used to arrive at the prediction of price on new data, and a matrix of false positives versus true positives is shown from which business users can make insightful decisions in determining the cost to sell the precious metal.

3.3.1 Predictive Analytics

3.3.1.1 Purpose of the Use Case

- Goal
  To predict precious metal prices on the basis of the available monthly prices for years 1950 to 2019. This allows decisions to be made in regard to fixing the bullion rates in the market in

various currencies and different parts of the world. In this particular use case, we use two attributes—'Month' and 'Year'—with the day being the first day of each month.

- Business Perspective
Visualizing data distribution, key drivers that influence the price, anomalies of price, and the AI- and ML-based model classification performance that can be used to quantitatively and qualitatively predict the rate of metals.

- Input Dataset
Bullion rates at the beginning of each month, from 1950 to 2019, in a .csv file having Date and Price as fields.

3.3.1.2 Brief Introduction to the Use Case from an Analysis and Predictive Analytics Point of View

We analyze the input data as follows:

1. The values and type of values of the data element or attribute and how the data elements relate to each other. If the attribute is categorical, the values in the attribute that it can be classified into and the distribution of the classes are also important. In our example use case, our response variable is price that is continuous. In our use case, the visualization shows the graph of Price by Date on the prepared data, wherein Date represents a date value in the format MM/DD/YYYY and DD is always '01', representing the first day of each month.
2. The type of AI-powered model that is built or applied to the training data (which can be a subset of the dataset) and the built model performing on this training data. In our use case, we use three methods: Seasonal ARIMA, ARIMA, and ETS.
3. The same three AI-powered models used in Step 5 (above) when applied to real-world enterprise data and the corresponding BI integration and analysis, including automation of the analytics involved and the cognitive capabilities of such a model to provide the **best context** of the BI-based decisions.

Here is a snapshot of input data:

	Date	Price
1	1950-01	34.73
2	1950-02	34.73
3	1950-03	34.73
4	1950-04	34.73
5	1950-05	34.73
6	1950-06	34.73

Here is a subset of prepared training data:

	Date	Price
1	1950-01-01	34.73
2	1950-02-01	34.73
3	1950-03-01	34.73
4	1950-04-01	34.73
5	1950-05-01	34.73
6	1950-06-01	34.73

The following list briefly describes the three forecasting models used:

1. ARIMA represents the Auto-Regressive Integrated Moving Average, which is predominantly used when the overall past data is sufficient enough to project the future.
2. Seasonal ARIMA—This can be used when there are repeating patterns of changes in the data over specific time periods. This model can be considered a fit model for forecasting precious metal prices where there are repeating change patterns during some years (based on the price changes over months in those years).
3. Exponential Triple Smoothing (ETS)—This is a standard model that is used more frequently to model time series data.

For these three models, the number of periods represents the number of days to be considered a period. Figures 3.10 to 3.16 depict the Before and After Forecast visualizations applied to the training dataset using the above three types of forecasting models.

The graphs in Figures 3.10 to 3.19 reveal the following:

- *The metric being forecasted is the "Price" of the precious metal as of the beginning of each month of a specific year.*
- *The time series is the time period for which the forecast ML model is being built. In our use case, this ranges from January 1950 to January 2019.*
- *The dimension column(s) is the grain on which the forecast is based. In our use case, this is the first day of each month of a specific year.*
- *In the graphs that show the forecast, the outputs of the forecast ML are the predicted price, the (month, day, year) of the predicted price, the lower bound of the value of the interval, the upper bound of the prediction interval, and the value of the confidence prediction interval used for the ML forecast model.*

Figures 3.17 to 3.19 depict the visualizations on test data before forecast and after forecast using Seasonal ARIMA model.

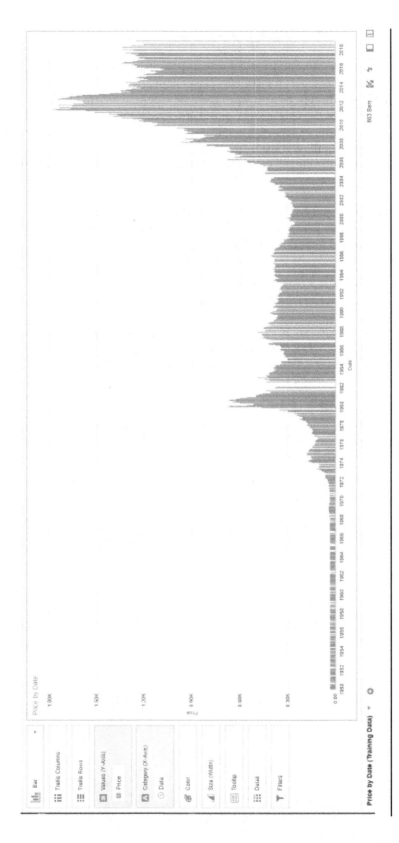

Figure 3.10 Price by Date training data—Before Forecast.

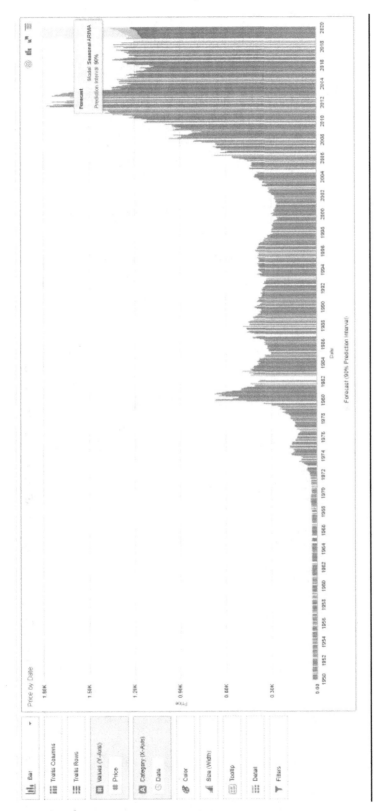

Figure 3.11 Forecast (Price by Date) using Seasonal ARIMA method (training data).

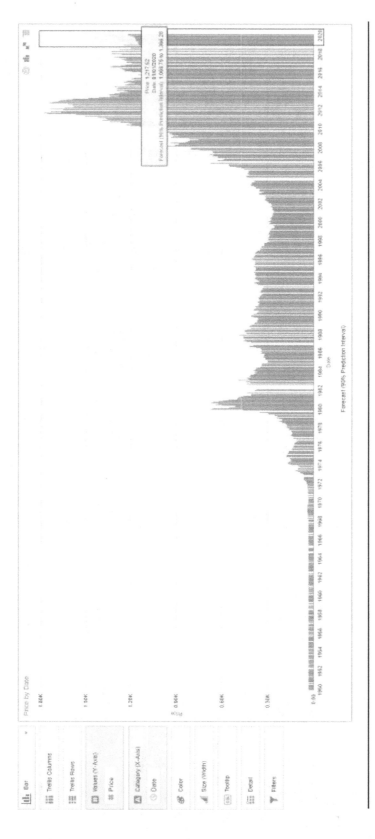

Figure 3.12 Forecast (Price by Date) using Seasonal ARIMA method (training data).

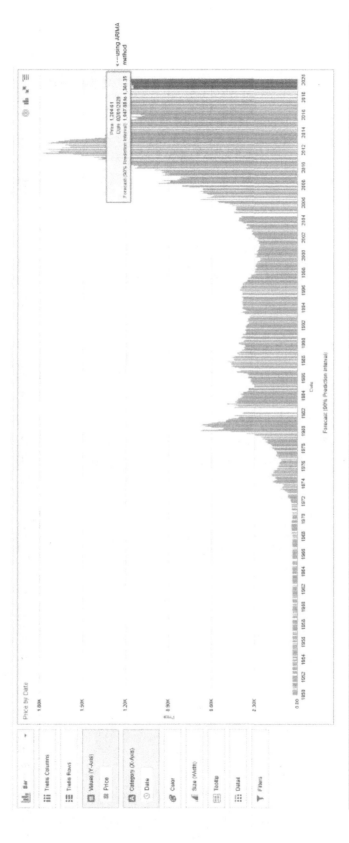

Figure 3.13 Forecast (Price by Date) using ARIMA method (training data) showing forecasted Price for February 2020 (new data point).

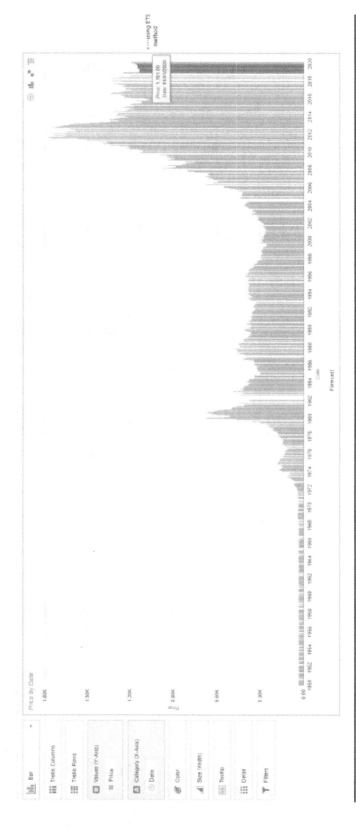

Figure 3.14 Forecast (Price by Date) using ETS method (training data) showing forecasted Price for January 2020 (new data point).

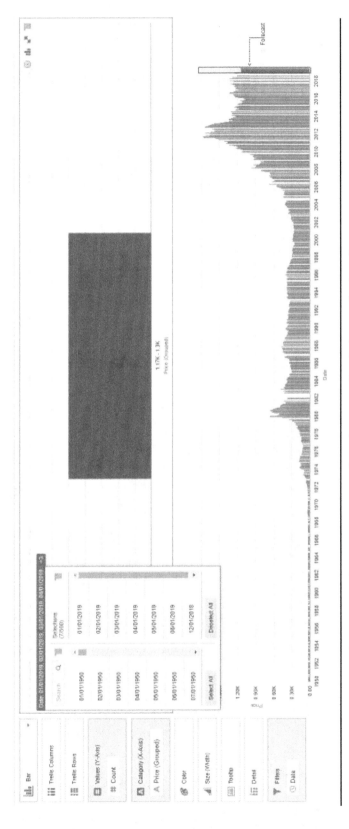

Figure 3.15 Forecast Price by Date visualization on training data showing a detailed view of values forecast.

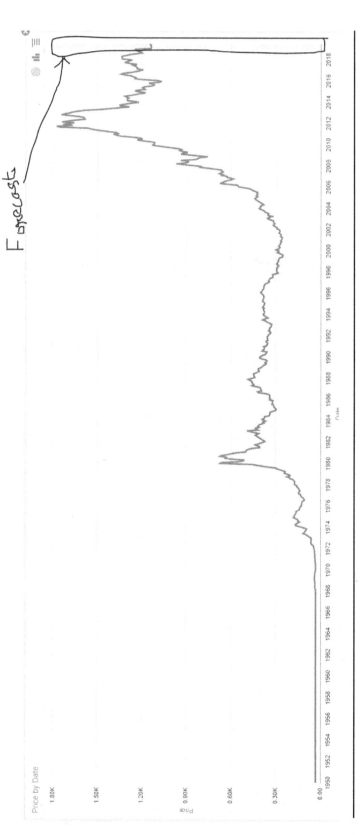

Figure 3.16 Forecast Price by Date visualization on training data using a continuous graph.

Figure 3.17 Price by Date test data—Before Forecast.

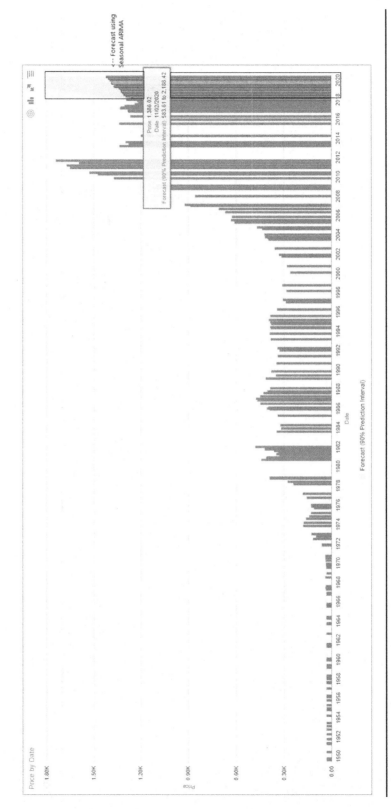

Figure 3.18 Forecast (Price by Date) using Seasonal ARIMA on test data.

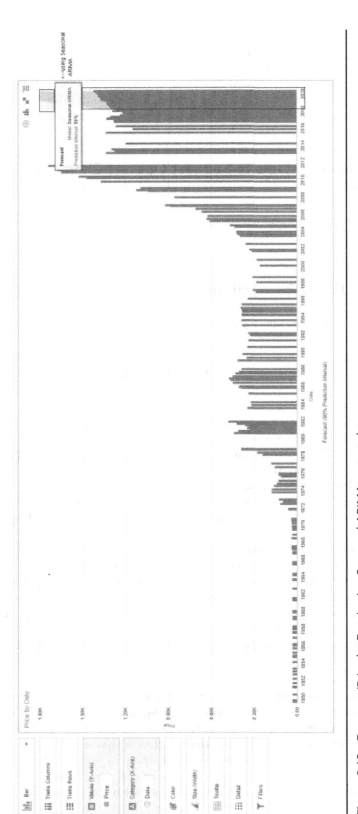

Figure 3.19 Forecast (Price by Date) using Seasonal ARIMA on test data.

As can be seen from the graphs with forecasted values, the time period of the forecast portion extends up to 2021, in some cases, and there is some overfitting in terms of predicted price. This is expected behavior for such a ML model that will generalize on enterprise real-world data. This forecasted data from the visualizations counts as augmented data for other enterprise data that, when combined with the latter, can be further analyzed through integration with BI dashboards to serve as augmented analytics, thereby yielding an AI meets BI solution—one that raises the bar on competitive insight.

3.4 Recommender Systems to Suggest Optimal Choices Based on Score

This use case is discussed from a business standpoint in a detailed manner based on implementation-oriented visualizations and a BI prespective in Chapter 4, Section 4.4.

3.5 Automatic Image Recognition

This use case is based on auto-recognizing the class of an input image as belonging to a predefined set of classes. This is used in many applications in the real world, such as image tagging by Facebook™, etc. It uses a deep learning–based convolutional neural network (CNN) that does the following tasks on an input image using what are termed layers of the neural network:

1. Input layer consisting of input image(s) as an nxn array of pixels.
2. Feature extraction layer that recognizes particular features in an input image. Examples are eyes, ear, nose, etc., in an image of a face.
3. Using an activation layer to trigger the nodes in the CNN for calculating the output at each node based on an activation function.
4. Max Pooling layer for dimensionality reduction.
5. Flatten layer for creating a 1D array of processed pixels from a multi-D array of pixels from an input image to ensure that these pixels are in the right shape to send to succeeding layer(s), called dense layer(s).
6. Dropout layer to reduce overfitting.
7. Dense layer to decide which nodes to activate and by how much based on the correlation between the 1D array in Flatten and Dense. It is called dense as each layer in dense is connected to each and every node in the next layer—in other words, it is fully connected.
8. Softmax layer to classify which class the input image belongs to. (Herein, a number of classes is assumed to be greater than 2.)
9. Output layer that returns the labels corresponding to nodes having the highest intensity turned on.

The CNN model first trains on training data and then classifies the images in the test data. This way, it recognizes the images in the test data by applying the AI-based model to it. The output of the classification (thereby recognition) is correctly determining the image label for any given image and checking the raster display of the same image in the test set.

The performance of a CNN is often measured by studying the loss and accuracy curves of the model. An example loss and accuracy curve for our use case in recognizing images from Fashion MNIST dataset is shown in Figure 3.20. The following observations can be made from this figure:

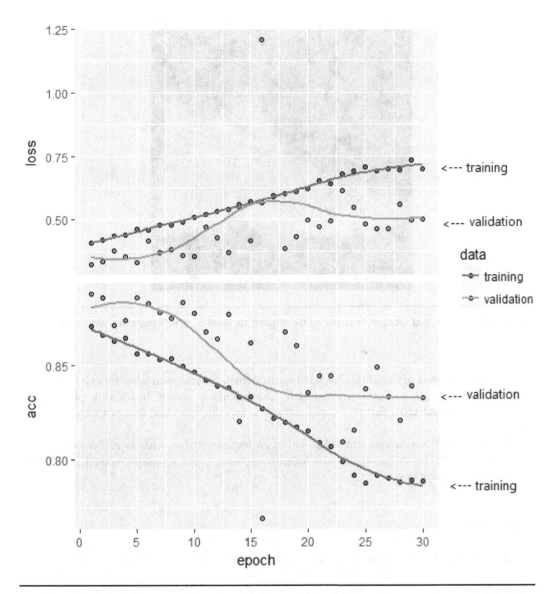

Figure 3.20 Loss and accuracy curves of the CNN model on training images and validation images.

1. As the number of batchwise epochs or training iterations increases, the loss increases and the accuracy decreases. The accuracy decreases by a small measure of ~0.05 and the loss increases by a measure of ~0.25.
2. However, based on the validation data, the accuracy is constant at 0.825 or 82.5%. And the loss on the validation data is constant at 0.5.

The classification accuracy of 82.5 correctly classifies an ankle shoe foot (in the test set) as belonging to label 9, as shown in Figure 3.21.

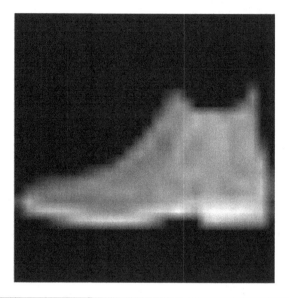

Figure 3.21   Predicted label in test set as belonging to label 9, which matches with that of the actual value of 9.

Checking the values of the labels (Predicted versus Actual) for any given label, for example, pred_ test[1] and test y-part[1], it is observed that each value belongs to class 9. In addition, plotting the raster image of original test x-part [1, ,], we see that it is an ankle foot shoe. (See raster image shown in Figure 3.21.)

BI can have DNN solutions embedded within its implementation stack to realize competitive results. For example, for image tagging and image recognition–based applications, the CNN model can be leveraged to that extent.

3.6 Summary

This chapter focused on discussing four use cases of AI- and ML-based solutions from a business perspective and an AI meets BI standpoint. The real-world use cases discussed are classifying Commodity Saleable Grade Based on Their Attributes (descriptive analytics solution), Predicting Commodity Prices in Advance (predictive analytics solution), Recommender Systems to Suggest Optimal Choices Based on Score (prescriptive and predictive analytics solution), and Automatic Image Recognition (prescriptive and augmented analytics solution). The description of each use case was presented with visualizations that depict and aid in analyses and deriving analytics useful for business analysts, data scientists, and end users. In certain cases, metrics that are performance-centric and help in decision making are also discussed. The following chapter details the implementation specifics of these use case solutions using AI- and ML-based models, ones based on classifications using random forests and decision trees, and deep learning–based neural networks. It shows how AI solutions can be implemented using machine learning models and R code along with how decision making can be achieved for BI purposes based on the results obtained.

Chapter 4

Industry Use Cases of Enterprise BI—The AI-Way of Implementation

In This Chapter

4.1 Introduction
4.2 Classifying Commodity Saleable Grade Based on Their Attributes
4.3 Predicting Commodity Prices in Advance
4.4 Recommender Systems to Suggest Optimal Choices Based on Score
4.5 Automatic Image Recognition
4.6 Summary
4.7 References

4.1 Introduction

Since AI and AI-based solutions, including those for business intelligence, have been in practice, there have been many real-world use cases demonstrating their implementation. AI practitioners and, more recently, data scientists have used AI-based machine learning and deep learning solutions to implement solutions that have achieved unimaginable results in the real world and enterprise BI. This chapter describes four such use cases, as outlined in Chapter 3, as well as their implementation and how it can help in enterprise BI (including intelligent decision making). This implementation uses R code and various machine learning algorithms and models to arrive at the desired solution and its role in the BI process, using multiple graphs and performance curves.

4.2 Classifying Commodity Saleable Grade Based on Their Attributes

This section describes the random forest algorithm and its relative classification performance with decision trees using an imbalanced dataset based on metrics such as the Area Under (ROC) Curve (AUC), Kappa measure, and F1 statistic, and why the accuracy metric is not as important as these other measures for imbalanced datasets.

4.2.1 The AI-Methodology—Descriptive Analytics—Using the Random Forest Machine Learning Algorithm and Comparing It with Decision Trees

4.2.1.1 Purpose of the Use Case

- Goal
  To classify commodity (wine) grade on the basis of its attributes. This allows decisions to be made, from a qualitative aspect, in regard to the sale of wine.

- Technology
  AI and ML using random forests and decision trees and comparing their relative classification performance.

- Implementation
  Using *rf* and *rpart* of *train()* machine learning libraries in R.

- Input Dataset
  Wine quality dataset of white wine in a .csv file having quality and 11 other variables pertaining to it as fields.

4.2.1.2 Brief Introduction to Machine Learning–Based Random Forests and Decision Trees

Random forests are a combination of single decision trees based a random sample of training data. This is also called an ensemble of decision trees. The sampled subset used for each decision tree is different and is chosen at random. The total number of trees can be specified at model build time. The trees are then aggregated to arrive at a classification decision based on the most important features factored into the model. Random forests exhibit greater accuracy when compared to decision trees. Table 4.1 summarizes the basic concepts of random forests and decision trees. In order to avoid overfitting, the right set of features needs to be chosen to build the classification model using a random forest. The number of features used to generate each tree is important as well. These features are selected at random defaulted to sqrt(total number of features) (but can be specified via the parameter mtry). This many features are used for splitting at each node. A very good introduction to decision trees and random forests for classification and regression can be found at "Decision Trees and Random Forests for Classification and Regression pt.1" (https://towardsdatascience.com/decision-trees-and-random-forests-for-classification-and-regression-pt-1-dbb65a458df)[1] and "Decision Trees and Random Forests for Classification and Regression pt. 2" (https://towardsdatascience.com/decision-trees-and-random-forests-for-classification-and-regression-pt-2-2b1fcd03e342).[2] In addition, it is important to pre-process data, especially when the dataset in use is unbalanced with reference to the classes involved in a classification model. A good introduction to this can be found at "Dealing with Unbalanced Data in Machine Learning" (https://shiring.github.io/machine_learning/2017/04/02/unbalanced).[3]

Table 4.1 Random Forests versus Decision Trees

Random Forests	Decision Trees
Ensemble of decision trees.	Single decision tree.
Can be used for both classification and regression.	Can be used for both classification and regression.
Easy to interpret.	Easy to interpret.
Do not require feature scaling and categorical feature encoding, such as one-hot encoding, when compared to neural nets.	Do not require feature scaling and categorical feature encoding, such as one-hot encoding, when compared to neural nets.
Demonstrate what features contribute to the variable selection and their relative importance based on depthwise location in the tree (using the variable importance plot).	Demonstrate what features contribute to the variable selection and their relative importance based on depthwise location in the tree.
RF tree is unpruned and learns on a random sample of training data for each decision tree.	A single decision tree is pruned on training data.
Exhibit feature bagging by splitting at each tree node using a random set of feature variables to achieve the optimal slit, thereby improving the accuracy. This enables increased accuracy in variable selection properties compared to decision trees. This can result in separable classes for classification, as the decision intervals will vary.	Splits at each node using a single feature variable at each split. This mostly uses the first variable to split, and, thus, the decision boundary often depends on the order of the features in the training set.
Less prone to overfitting, as the decision interval is often symmetric with respect to the classes when the trees are ensembled.	Overfitting can occur occasionally as the order of the features in a single tree factors into the classification or regression task at hand.
For the above reasons, decision accuracy is improved when compared with decision trees, especially when the dataset is large and the number of features is also large.	Still appreciably accurate and good for classification and regression tasks, especially when the dataset is small.

To build an optimal model and to determine the performance of a random forest, the following measures can be used:

1. **Use a combination of a number of trees and feature selections based on the most important features so as to minimize the Out-of-Bag (OOB) estimate of error rate,** as shown by printing the model after building. This can be done by first determining the optimal value of the number of trees (as given by the output of the *trainControl()* function on the training set to perform cross-validation to determine the optimal values of model parameters) and using it as a value to the *trControl()* parameter to the *train()* function along with the *method ="rf"* parameter to build the random forest. The *trainControl()* gives the value for *mtry* used in this cross-validation and can be used in taking the model building further using the *randomForest()* classifier (in R).

2. Use the **confusion matrix** to determine the performance of the RF model by looking at the number of misclassifications.

3. Use the **AUC metric** to determine the performance of the RF model by looking at the plotted ROC curve and the **Kappa value** *as opposed to the accuracy metric value.* The Kappa measure gives a more pragmatic value in the case of unbalanced datasets.

These are reflected in the pragmatics of the model implementation detailed in the next subsection.

4.2.1.3 Implementation Pragmatics

Random Forest Implementation

Listing 4.1 Build and Test a Random Forest Model for Classification

```
setwd("<directory-name>")
library(caret)
library(e1071)
# The file winequality-white.csv is in the working directory
winedata1 <- read.csv("winequality-white.csv", header=TRUE, sep=';')
head(winedata1)
class(winedata1$quality)
anyNA(winedata1)
# Mapping Wine Quality to Saleable Grade
# <=3 NotAccept
# 4 LessThanAvg
# 5 Avg
# 6 MoreThanAvg
# 7 Good
# 8 Great
# >=9 Excellent
winedata1$grade <- ifelse(winedata1$quality <= 3, 'NotAccept',
                 ifelse(winedata1$quality == 4, 'LessThanAvg',
                 ifelse(winedata1$quality == 5, 'Average',
                 ifelse(winedata1$quality == 6, 'MoreThanAvg',
                 ifelse(winedata1$quality == 7, 'Good',
                 ifelse(winedata1$quality == 8, 'Great',
                 ifelse(winedata1$quality >= 9, 'Excellent',
                 '')))))))
winedata1$grade <- as.factor(winedata1$grade)
set.seed(12345)
sample_size <- 0.70 * nrow(winedata1)
sampledata1 <-sample(seq_len(nrow(winedata1)), sample_size)
training_data1 <- winedata1[sampledata1, ]
test_data1 <- winedata1[-sampledata1, ]
nrow(training_data1) # 3428
nrow(test_data1) # 1470
training_data1 <- training_data1[,-12]
summary(training_data1$grade)
summary(test_data1$grade)
summary(winedata1$grade)
head(training_data1)
trctrl <- trainControl(method = "repeatedcv", number = 10, repeats = 10,
savePredictions = TRUE, verboseIter = FALSE)
set.seed(12345)
```

```r
model_rf <- train(grade ~ ., data = training_data1, method = "rf", preProcess =
c("scale", "center"), trControl = trctrl)
print(model_rf)
model_rf$finalModel$confusion
# Feature importance
imp2 <- model_rf$finalModel$importance
dim(imp2)
class(imp2)
imp2
imp2[order(imp2, decreasing = TRUE), ]
# estimate variable importance
importance2 <- varImp(model_rf, scale = TRUE)
plot(importance2)
# plot(imp2[order(imp2, decreasing = TRUE), ])
# predicting on test data
head(test_data1)
test_data_new1 <- test_data1[,-12]
head(test_data_new1)
test_data_new1 <- test_data_new1[,-12]
head(test_data_new1)
head(training_data1)
model_rf_pred <- predict(model_rf, test_data_new1)
cm_model_rf <- confusionMatrix(model_rf_pred, test_data1$grade)
cm_model_rf
# Measure model performance with ROCR and AUC
library(ROCR)
# Calculate the probability of new observations belonging to each class
# grade_pred_ROC_AUC will be a matrix with dimensions (data_set_size x number_of_classes)
grade_pred_ROC_AUC <- predict(model_rf,test_data_new1,type="prob")
# Use colors for roc curves for the classes (one for each grade measure):
colors <- c("green","orange","purple","yellow","blue","black","red")
# Specify the different classes
ROC_AUC_classes <- levels(test_data1$grade)
# For each class
for (i in 1:7)
{
 # Define observations belonging to each class i.e., class[i]
 Actualgrade_values <- ifelse(test_data1$grade==ROC_AUC_classes[i],1,0)
 # Assess the performance of classifier for class[i]
 pred <- prediction(grade_pred_ROC_AUC[,i],Actualgrade_values)
 perf <- performance(pred, "tpr", "fpr")
    pdf(paste("Random_Forest_ROC_Curve_for_",ROC_AUC_classes[i],".pdf"))
    plot(perf,main=paste("Random Forest ROC Curve for ",
    ROC_AUC_classes[i]),col=colors[i])
    dev.off()
 # Calculate the AUC and print it to screen
```

```
 auc.perf <- performance(pred, measure = "auc")
 print(paste("Random_Forest_AUC for ",ROC_AUC_classes[i],":",auc.perf@y.values))
}
results_rf <- data.frame(Actual = test_data1$grade, Predicted = predict(model_rf,
test_data_new1, type = "prob"))
head(results_rf)
results_rf$predicted_grade <- ifelse(results_rf$Predicted.Average > 0.5, "Average",
           ifelse(results_rf$Predicted.Excellent > 0.5, "Excellent",
             ifelse(results_rf$Predicted.Good > 0.5, "Good",
               ifelse(results_rf$Predicted.Great > 0.5, "Great",
                 ifelse(results_rf$Predicted.LessThanAvg > 0.5, "LessThanAvg",
                   ifelse(results_rf$Predicted.MoreThanAvg > 0.5, "MoreThanAvg",
                     ifelse(results_rf$Predicted.NotAccept > 0.5, "NotAccept",
                       ''))))))) 
results_rf$predicted_grade <- factor(results_rf$predicted_grade,
levels=levels(results_rf$Actual))
cm_original <-  confusionMatrix(results_rf$predicted_grade, test_data1$grade)
cm_original
pairs(table(model_rf_pred, test_data1$grade), main="Wine Quality Classification")
```

Listing 4.2 Random Forest Output (of code in Listing 4.1)

```
> setwd("<directory-name>")
> library(caret)
Loading required package: lattice
Loading required package: ggplot2

Attaching package: 'ggplot2'

The following object is masked from 'package:randomForest':

    margin


Warning messages:
1: package 'caret' was built under R version 3.4.4
2: package 'ggplot2' was built under R version 3.4.4
3: As of rlang 0.4.0, dplyr must be at least version 0.8.0.
x dplyr 0.7.8 is too old for rlang 0.4.2.
i Please update dplyr to the latest version.
i Updating packages on Windows requires precautions:
  <https://github.com/jennybc/what-they-forgot/issues/62>
> library(e1071)
Warning message:
package 'e1071' was built under R version 3.4.4
> # The file winequality-white.csv is in the working directory
> winedata1 <- read.csv("winequality-white.csv", header=TRUE, sep=';')
> head(winedata1)
```

```
     fixed.acidity volatile.acidity citric.acid residual.sugar chlorides free.sulfur.dioxide
1              7.0             0.27        0.36           20.7     0.045                  45
2              6.3             0.30        0.34            1.6     0.049                  14
3              8.1             0.28        0.40            6.9     0.050                  30
4              7.2             0.23        0.32            8.5     0.058                  47
5              7.2             0.23        0.32            8.5     0.058                  47
6              8.1             0.28        0.40            6.9     0.050                  30
  total.sulfur.dioxide density   pH sulphates alcohol quality
1                  170  1.0010 3.00      0.45     8.8       6
2                  132  0.9940 3.30      0.49     9.5       6
3                   97  0.9951 3.26      0.44    10.1       6
4                  186  0.9956 3.19      0.40     9.9       6
5                  186  0.9956 3.19      0.40     9.9       6
6                   97  0.9951 3.26      0.44    10.1       6
> class(winedata1$quality)
[1] "integer"
> anyNA(winedata1)
[1] FALSE
> # Mapping Wine Quality to Saleable Grade
> # <=3 NotAccept
> # 4 LessThanAvg
> # 5 Avg
> # 6 MoreThanAvg
> # 7 Good
> # 8 Great
> # >=9 Excellent
> winedata1$grade <- ifelse(winedata1$quality <= 3, 'NotAccept',
+                    ifelse(winedata1$quality == 4, 'LessThanAvg',
+                    ifelse(winedata1$quality == 5, 'Average',
+                    ifelse(winedata1$quality == 6, 'MoreThanAvg',
+                    ifelse(winedata1$quality == 7, 'Good',
+                    ifelse(winedata1$quality == 8, 'Great',
+                    ifelse(winedata1$quality >= 9, 'Excellent',
+                     '')))))))
> winedata1$grade <- as.factor(winedata1$grade)
> set.seed(12345)
> sample_size <- 0.70 * nrow(winedata1)
> sampledata1 <-sample(seq_len(nrow(winedata1)), sample_size)
> training_data1 <- winedata1[sampledata1, ]
> test_data1 <- winedata1[-sampledata1, ]
> nrow(training_data1) # 3428
[1] 3428
> nrow(test_data1) # 1470
[1] 1470
> training_data1 <- training_data1[,-12]
> summary(training_data1$grade)
```

```
      Average    Excellent       Good      Great LessThanAvg MoreThanAvg   NotAccept
         1014            4        618        126         110        1541          15
> summary(test_data1$grade)
      Average    Excellent       Good      Great LessThanAvg MoreThanAvg   NotAccept
          443            1        262         49          53         657           5
> summary(winedata1$grade)
      Average    Excellent       Good      Great LessThanAvg MoreThanAvg   NotAccept
         1457            5        880        175         163        2198          20
> head(training_data1)
     fixed.acidity volatile.acidity citric.acid residual.sugar chlorides
3531           7.2             0.31        0.35            7.2     0.046
4289           7.0             0.20        0.33            4.7     0.030
3726           6.6             0.26        0.28            9.4     0.028
4338           7.3             0.19        0.27           13.9     0.057
2235           7.2             0.23        0.38            6.1     0.067
815            7.9             0.35        0.24           15.6     0.072
     free.sulfur.dioxide total.sulfur.dioxide density   pH sulphates alcohol      grade
3531                  45                  178 0.99550 3.14      0.53     9.7    Average
4289                  25                   76 0.99202 2.88      0.54    10.5 MoreThanAvg
3726                  13                  121 0.99254 3.17      0.34    12.1 MoreThanAvg
4338                  45                  155 0.99807 2.94      0.41     8.8      Great
2235                  20                   90 0.99496 3.17      0.79     9.7    Average
815                   44                  229 0.99785 3.03      0.59    10.5 MoreThanAvg
> trctrl <- trainControl(method = "repeatedcv", number = 10, repeats = 10,
savePredictions = TRUE, verboseIter = FALSE)
> set.seed(12345)
> model_rf <- train(grade ~ ., data = training_data1, method = "rf", preProcess =
c("scale", "center"), trControl = trctrl)
> print(model_rf)
Random Forest

3428 samples
  11 predictor
   7 classes: 'Average', 'Excellent', 'Good', 'Great', 'LessThanAvg', 'MoreThanAvg',
'NotAccept'

Pre-processing: scaled (11), centered (11)
Resampling: Cross-Validated (10 fold, repeated 10 times)
Summary of sample sizes: 3084, 3085, 3086, 3088, 3082, 3086, ...
Resampling results across tuning parameters:

  mtry  Accuracy   Kappa
   2    0.6617835  0.4694894
   6    0.6580509  0.4671895
  11    0.6545221  0.4625398

Accuracy was used to select the optimal model using the largest value.
The final value used for the model was mtry = 2.
> model_rf$finalModel$confusion
```

```
            Average Excellent Good Great LessThanAvg MoreThanAvg NotAccept class.error
Average         661         0    9     0           6         338         0   0.3481262
Excellent         0         0    2     0           0           2         0   1.0000000
Good             10         0  330     2           0         276         0   0.4660194
Great             0         0   32    47           0          47         0   0.6269841
LessThanAvg      53         0    1     0          26          30         0   0.7636364
MoreThanAvg     214         0   91     0           0        1236         0   0.1979234
NotAccept         7         0    0     0           0           8         0   1.0000000
> # Feature importance
> imp2 <- model_rf$finalModel$importance
> dim(imp2)
[1] 11  1
> class(imp2)
[1] "matrix"
> imp2
                    MeanDecreaseGini
fixed.acidity              176.0452
volatile.acidity           230.2272
citric.acid                192.6936
residual.sugar             203.8580
chlorides                  206.5411
free.sulfur.dioxide        214.6507
total.sulfur.dioxide       211.3666
density                    239.4751
pH                         198.1514
sulphates                  185.8240
alcohol                    254.5991
> imp2[order(imp2, decreasing = TRUE), ]
          alcohol              density      volatile.acidity  free.sulfur.dioxide
         254.5991             239.4751              230.2272             214.6507
total.sulfur.dioxide         chlorides        residual.sugar                   pH
         211.3666             206.5411              203.8580             198.1514
      citric.acid            sulphates         fixed.acidity
         192.6936             185.8240              176.0452
> # estimate variable importance
> importance2 <- varImp(model_rf, scale = TRUE)
> plot(importance2)
> # plot(imp2[order(imp2, decreasing = TRUE), ])
> # predicting on test data
> head(test_data1)
   fixed.acidity volatile.acidity citric.acid residual.sugar chlorides free.sulfur.dioxide
5            7.2             0.23        0.32            8.5     0.058                  47
7            6.2             0.32        0.16            7.0     0.045                  30
8            7.0             0.27        0.36           20.7     0.045                  45
9            6.3             0.30        0.34            1.6     0.049                  14
12           8.6             0.23        0.40            4.2     0.035                  17
14           6.6             0.16        0.40            1.5     0.044                  48
```

```
      total.sulfur.dioxide density   pH sulphates alcohol quality     grade
5                      186  0.9956 3.19      0.40     9.9       6 MoreThanAvg
7                      136  0.9949 3.18      0.47     9.6       6 MoreThanAvg
8                      170  1.0010 3.00      0.45     8.8       6 MoreThanAvg
9                      132  0.9940 3.30      0.49     9.5       6 MoreThanAvg
12                     109  0.9947 3.14      0.53     9.7       5     Average
14                     143  0.9912 3.54      0.52    12.4       7        Good
> test_data_new1 <- test_data1[,-12]
> head(test_data_new1)
   fixed.acidity volatile.acidity citric.acid residual.sugar chlorides free.sulfur.dioxide
5            7.2             0.23        0.32            8.5     0.058                  47
7            6.2             0.32        0.16            7.0     0.045                  30
8            7.0             0.27        0.36           20.7     0.045                  45
9            6.3             0.30        0.34            1.6     0.049                  14
12           8.6             0.23        0.40            4.2     0.035                  17
14           6.6             0.16        0.40            1.5     0.044                  48
      total.sulfur.dioxide density   pH sulphates alcohol     grade
5                      186  0.9956 3.19      0.40     9.9 MoreThanAvg
7                      136  0.9949 3.18      0.47     9.6 MoreThanAvg
8                      170  1.0010 3.00      0.45     8.8 MoreThanAvg
9                      132  0.9940 3.30      0.49     9.5 MoreThanAvg
12                     109  0.9947 3.14      0.53     9.7     Average
14                     143  0.9912 3.54      0.52    12.4        Good
> test_data_new1 <- test_data_new1[,-12]
> head(test_data_new1)
   fixed.acidity volatile.acidity citric.acid residual.sugar chlorides free.sulfur.dioxide
5            7.2             0.23        0.32            8.5     0.058                  47
7            6.2             0.32        0.16            7.0     0.045                  30
8            7.0             0.27        0.36           20.7     0.045                  45
9            6.3             0.30        0.34            1.6     0.049                  14
12           8.6             0.23        0.40            4.2     0.035                  17
14           6.6             0.16        0.40            1.5     0.044                  48
      total.sulfur.dioxide density   pH sulphates alcohol
5                      186  0.9956 3.19      0.40     9.9
7                      136  0.9949 3.18      0.47     9.6
8                      170  1.0010 3.00      0.45     8.8
9                      132  0.9940 3.30      0.49     9.5
12                     109  0.9947 3.14      0.53     9.7
14                     143  0.9912 3.54      0.52    12.4
> head(training_data1)
      fixed.acidity volatile.acidity citric.acid residual.sugar chlorides
3531            7.2             0.31        0.35            7.2     0.046
4289            7.0             0.20        0.33            4.7     0.030
3726            6.6             0.26        0.28            9.4     0.028
4338            7.3             0.19        0.27           13.9     0.057
2235            7.2             0.23        0.38            6.1     0.067
815             7.9             0.35        0.24           15.6     0.072
```

	free.sulfur.dioxide	total.sulfur.dioxide	density	pH	sulphates	alcohol	grade
3531	45	178	0.99550	3.14	0.53	9.7	Average
4289	25	76	0.99202	2.88	0.54	10.5	MoreThanAvg
3726	13	121	0.99254	3.17	0.34	12.1	MoreThanAvg
4338	45	155	0.99807	2.94	0.41	8.8	Great
2235	20	90	0.99496	3.17	0.79	9.7	Average
815	44	229	0.99785	3.03	0.59	10.5	MoreThanAvg

```
> model_rf_pred <- predict(model_rf, test_data_new1)
> cm_model_rf <- confusionMatrix(model_rf_pred, test_data1$grade)
> cm_model_rf
Confusion Matrix and Statistics
```

```
                  Reference
Prediction    Average Excellent Good Great LessThanAvg MoreThanAvg NotAccept
  Average         302         0    6     0          33          79         1
  Excellent         0         0    0     0           0           0         0
  Good              3         0  143    13           1          42         0
  Great             0         0    1    17           0           1         0
  LessThanAvg       1         0    0     0           1           0         0
  MoreThanAvg     137         1  112    19          18         535         4
  NotAccept         0         0    0     0           0           0         0
```

```
Overall Statistics

              Accuracy : 0.6789     # This is less reliable as dataset is imbalanced
                95% CI : (0.6544, 0.7027)
   No Information Rate : 0.4469
   P-Value [Acc > NIR] : < 2.2e-16

                 Kappa : 0.4964 # This is a more reliable performance metric
 Mcnemar's Test P-Value : NA

Statistics by Class:
```

	Class: Average	Class: Excellent	Class: Good	Class: Great
Sensitivity	0.6817	0.0000000	0.54580	0.34694
Specificity	0.8841	1.0000000	0.95116	0.99859
Pos Pred Value	0.7173	NaN	0.70792	0.89474
Neg Pred Value	0.8656	0.9993197	0.90615	0.97795
Prevalence	0.3014	0.0006803	0.17823	0.03333
Detection Rate	0.2054	0.0000000	0.09728	0.01156
Detection Prevalence	0.2864	0.0000000	0.13741	0.01293
Balanced Accuracy	0.7829	0.5000000	0.74848	0.67277

	Class: LessThanAvg	Class: MoreThanAvg	Class: NotAccept
Sensitivity	0.0188679	0.8143	0.000000
Specificity	0.9992943	0.6421	1.000000
Pos Pred Value	0.5000000	0.6477	NaN
Neg Pred Value	0.9645777	0.8106	0.996599
Prevalence	0.0360544	0.4469	0.003401

```
Detection Rate                0.0006803        0.3639      0.000000
Detection Prevalence          0.0013605        0.5619      0.000000
Balanced Accuracy             0.5090811        0.7282      0.500000
> results_rf <- data.frame(Actual = test_data1$grade, Predicted = predict(model_rf,
test_data_new1, type = "prob"))
> head(results_rf)
        Actual Predicted.Average Predicted.Excellent Predicted.Good Predicted.Great
5   MoreThanAvg             0.142               0.000          0.024           0.004
7   MoreThanAvg             0.782               0.000          0.012           0.002
8   MoreThanAvg             0.232               0.000          0.038           0.006
9   MoreThanAvg             0.252               0.000          0.012           0.002
12      Average             0.188               0.000          0.066           0.006
14         Good             0.134               0.002          0.304           0.214
    Predicted.LessThanAvg Predicted.MoreThanAvg Predicted.NotAccept
5                   0.004                 0.826               0.000
7                   0.012                 0.190               0.002
8                   0.002                 0.722               0.000
9                   0.032                 0.702               0.000
12                  0.048                 0.662               0.030
14                  0.000                 0.344               0.002
> results_rf$predicted_grade <- ifelse(results_rf$Predicted.Average > 0.5, "Average",
+           ifelse(results_rf$Predicted.Excellent > 0.5, "Excellent",
+             ifelse(results_rf$Predicted.Good > 0.5, "Good",
+               ifelse(results_rf$Predicted.Great > 0.5, "Great",
+                 ifelse(results_rf$Predicted.LessThanAvg > 0.5, "LessThanAvg",
+                   ifelse(results_rf$Predicted.MoreThanAvg > 0.5, "MoreThanAvg",
+                     ifelse(results_rf$Predicted.NotAccept > 0.5, "NotAccept",
+                       ''))))))))
> results_rf$predicted_grade <- factor(results_rf$predicted_grade,
levels=levels(results_rf$Actual))
> cm_original <-  confusionMatrix(results_rf$predicted_grade, test_data1$grade)
> cm_original
Confusion Matrix and Statistics

            Reference
Prediction    Average Excellent Good Great LessThanAvg MoreThanAvg NotAccept
  Average         261         0    2     0          23          52         0
  Excellent         0         0    0     0           0           0         0
  Good              1         0  115     5           0          18         0
  Great             0         0    0    16           0           1         0
  LessThanAvg       0         0    0     0           1           0         0
  MoreThanAvg      88         0   63     7           7         405         2
  NotAccept         0         0    0     0           0           0         0

Overall Statistics

                Accuracy : 0.7479
                  95% CI : (0.7207, 0.7737)
```

```
No Information Rate : 0.4461
P-Value [Acc > NIR] : < 2.2e-16

              Kappa : 0.6027
Mcnemar's Test P-Value : NA
```

Statistics by Class:

	Class: Average	Class: Excellent	Class: Good	Class: Great
Sensitivity	0.7457	NA	0.6389	0.57143
Specificity	0.8926	1	0.9729	0.99904
Pos Pred Value	0.7722	NA	0.8273	0.94118
Neg Pred Value	0.8779	NA	0.9300	0.98857
Prevalence	0.3280	0	0.1687	0.02624
Detection Rate	0.2446	0	0.1078	0.01500
Detection Prevalence	0.3168	0	0.1303	0.01593
Balanced Accuracy	0.8192	NA	0.8059	0.78523

	Class: LessThanAvg	Class: MoreThanAvg	Class: NotAccept
Sensitivity	0.0322581	0.8508	0.000000
Specificity	1.0000000	0.7174	1.000000
Pos Pred Value	1.0000000	0.7080	NaN
Neg Pred Value	0.9718574	0.8566	0.998126
Prevalence	0.0290534	0.4461	0.001874
Detection Rate	0.0009372	0.3796	0.000000
Detection Prevalence	0.0009372	0.5361	0.000000
Balanced Accuracy	0.5161290	0.7841	0.500000

```
> pairs(table(model_rf_pred, test_data1$grade), main="Wine Quality Classification")
>
```

The variable importance plot, the pairs plot, and the ROC plots for the wine grades of the random forest implementation of the wine saleable grade classification are shown in Figures 4.1–4.9.

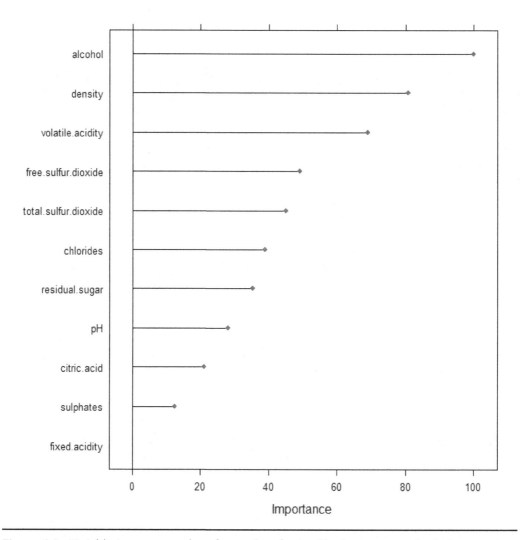

Figure 4.1   Variable importance plot of a random forest. The importance plot indicates a particular feature's contribution to the model's classification. It indicates a feature's impact on the model's accuracy, thereby enabling it to eliminate (or keep) features with least (or greatest) impact (also called feature selection). Doing this decreases the incorrect bias that otherwise would have creeped in with the least impact features.

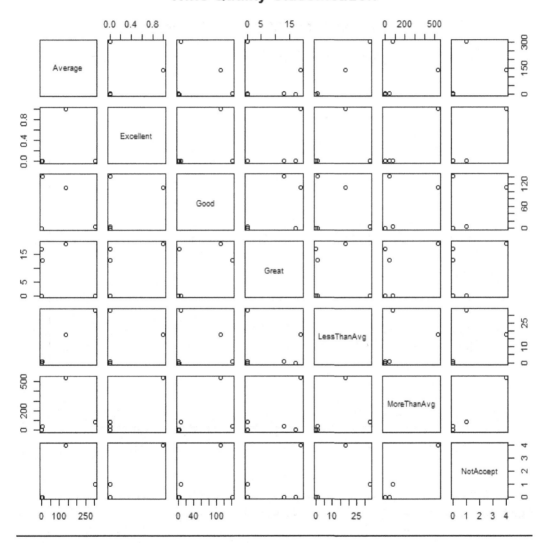

Figure 4.2 Pairs plot of Wine Grade Classification using Random Forest.

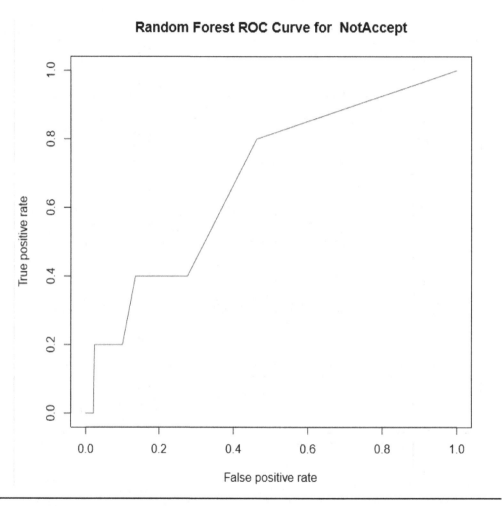

Figure 4.3 Random Forest ROC Curve for NotAccept.

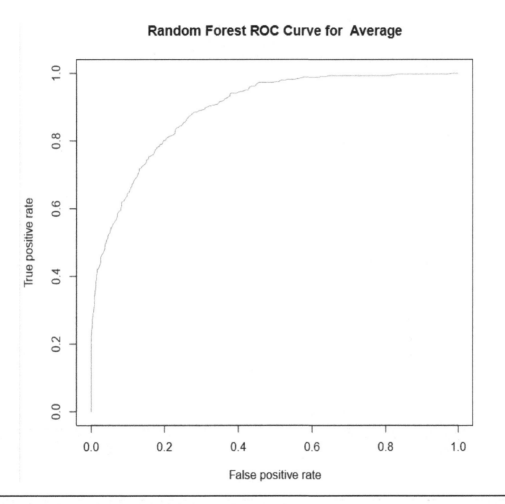

Figure 4.4   Random Forest ROC Curve for Average.

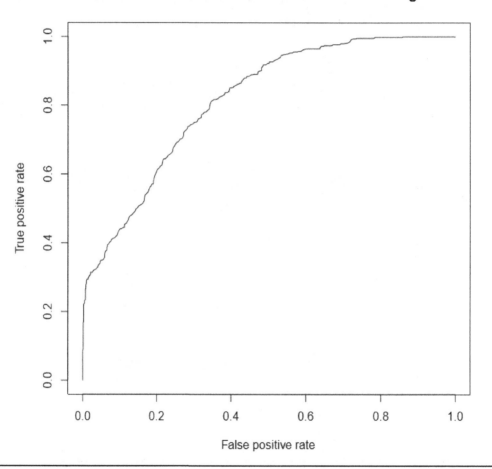

Figure 4.5 Random Forest ROC Curve for MoreThanAvg.

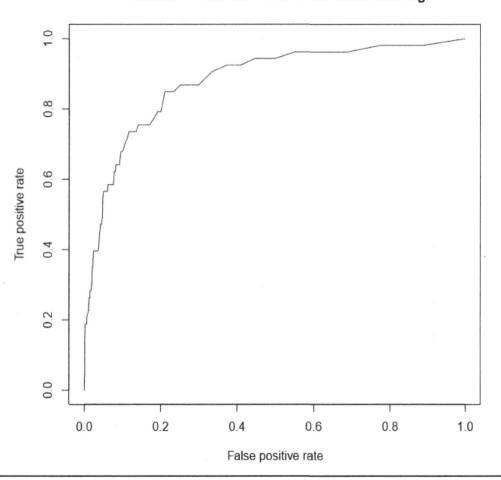

Figure 4.6 Random Forest ROC Curve for LessThanAvg.

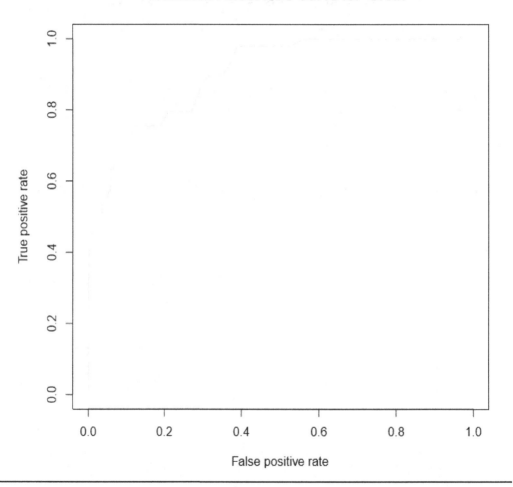

Figure 4.7   Random Forest ROC Curve for Great.

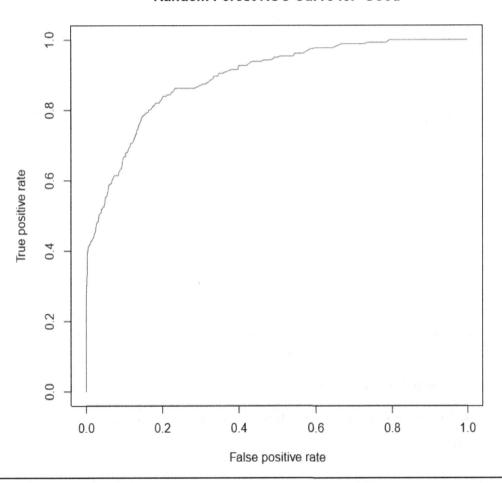

Figure 4.8   Random Forest ROC Curve for Good.

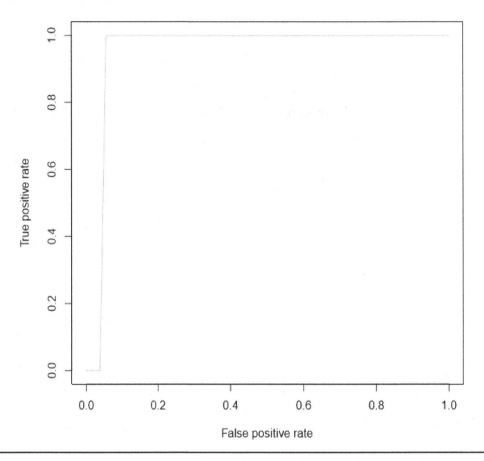

Figure 4.9   Random Forest ROC Curve for Excellent.

Comparison with Decision Trees

Listing 4.3 Build and Test a Decision Tree Model for Classification

```
setwd("<directory-name>")
library(caret)
library(e1071)
library(rpart.plot)
# The file winequality-white.csv is in the working directory
winedata1 <- read.csv("winequality-white.csv", header=TRUE, sep=';')
head(winedata1)
class(winedata1$quality)
anyNA(winedata1)
# Mapping Wine Quality to Saleable Grade
# <=3 NotAccept
# 4 LessThanAvg
# 5 Avg
```

```r
# 6 MoreThanAvg
# 7 Good
# 8 Great
# >=9 Excellent
winedata1$grade <- ifelse(winedata1$quality <= 3, 'NotAccept',
                   ifelse(winedata1$quality == 4, 'LessThanAvg',
                   ifelse(winedata1$quality == 5, 'Average',
                   ifelse(winedata1$quality == 6, 'MoreThanAvg',
                   ifelse(winedata1$quality == 7, 'Good',
                   ifelse(winedata1$quality == 8, 'Great',
                   ifelse(winedata1$quality >= 9, 'Excellent',
                     '')))))))

winedata1$grade <- as.factor(winedata1$grade)
set.seed(12345)
sample_size <- 0.70 * nrow(winedata1)
sampledata1 <-sample(seq_len(nrow(winedata1)), sample_size)
training_data1 <- winedata1[sampledata1, ]
test_data1 <- winedata1[-sampledata1, ]
nrow(training_data1) # 3428
nrow(test_data1) # 1470
training_data1 <- training_data1[,-12]
summary(training_data1$grade)
summary(test_data1$grade)
summary(winedata1$grade)
head(training_data1)

trctrl <- trainControl(method = "repeatedcv", number = 10, repeats = 10,
savePredictions = TRUE, verboseIter = FALSE)
set.seed(12345)
#model_rf <- train(grade ~ ., data = training_data1, method = "rf", preProcess =
c("scale", "center"), trControl = trctrl)
wine.dTree <- train(grade ~., data = training_data1, method = "rpart",
                parms = list(split = "information"),
                trControl=trctrl,
                tuneLength = 10)
# As an alternative to above call, the below statement using the rpart() can be run
# wine.dTree <- rpart(formula, data = training_data, method="class")
#summary(fit)
wine.dTree
prp(wine.dTree$finalModel) # Print Primary decision tree structure
head(test_data1)
test_data_new1 <- test_data1[,-12]
head(test_data_new1)
test_data_new1 <- test_data_new1[,-12]
head(test_data_new1)
head(training_data1)
```

```
test_pred <- predict(wine.dTree, newdata = test_data_new1)
cm <- confusionMatrix(test_pred, test_data1$grade )   #check accuracy
cm
#Training the Decision Tree Classifier with gini as criterion
set.seed(12345)
wine.dTree_gini <- train(grade ~., data = training_data1, method = "rpart",
                  parms = list(split = "gini"),
                  trControl=trctrl, tuneLength = 10)
wine.dTree_gini
prp(wine.dTree_gini$finalModel)
test_pred_gini <- predict(wine.dTree_gini, newdata = test_data_new1)
cm_gini <- confusionMatrix(test_pred_gini, test_data1$grade)   #check accuracy
cm_gini
table(test_pred, test_data1$grade)
table(test_pred_gini, test_data1$grade)


# Measure model performance with AUC
library(ROCR)
# Calculate the probability of new observations belonging tó each class
# Source_pred_ROC_AUC will be a matrix with dimensions (data_set_size x
number_of_classes)
grade_pred_ROC_AUC_dtree <- predict(wine.dTree,test_data_new1,type="prob")
# Use colors for roc curves for the three classes (one for each Source):
colors <- c("green","orange","purple","yellow","blue","black","red")
# Specify the different classes
ROC_AUC_classes <- levels(test_data1$grade)
# For each class
for (i in 1:7)
{
 # Define observations belonging to each class i.e., class[i]
 Actualgrade_values <- ifelse(test_data1$grade==ROC_AUC_classes[i],1,0)
 # Assess the performance of classifier for class[i]
 pred <- prediction(grade_pred_ROC_AUC_dtree[,i],Actualgrade_values)
 perf <- performance(pred, "tpr", "fpr")
    pdf(paste("Decision_Tree_v7_ROC_Curve_for_",ROC_AUC_classes[i],".pdf"))
    plot(perf,main=paste("Decision Tree ROC Curve for ",
    ROC_AUC_classes[i]),col=colors[i])
   dev.off()
 # Calculate the AUC and print it to screen
 auc.perf <- performance(pred, measure = "auc")
 print(paste("Decision Tree AUC for ",ROC_AUC_classes[i],":",auc.perf@y.values))
}


results_dTree_gini <- data.frame(Actual = test_data1$grade, Predicted = predict(wine.
dTree_gini, test_data_new1, type = "prob"))
head(results_dTree_gini)
```

```
results_dTree_gini$predicted_grade <- ifelse(results_dTree_gini$Predicted.Average >
0.5, "Average",
       ifelse(results_dTree_gini$Predicted.Excellent > 0.5, "Excellent",
         ifelse(results_dTree_gini$Predicted.Good > 0.5, "Good",
           ifelse(results_dTree_gini$Predicted.Great > 0.5, "Great",
             ifelse(results_dTree_gini$Predicted.LessThanAvg > 0.5, "LessThanAvg",
               ifelse(results_dTree_gini$Predicted.MoreThanAvg > 0.5, "MoreThanAvg",
                 ifelse(results_dTree_gini$Predicted.NotAccept > 0.5, "NotAccept",
                   ''))))))))
results_dTree_gini$predicted_grade <- factor(results_dTree_gini$predicted_grade,
levels=levels(results_dTree_gini$Actual))
cm_original_dtree_gini <-  confusionMatrix(results_dTree_gini$predicted_grade,
test_data1$grade)
cm_original_dtree_gini

pairs(table(test_pred_gini, test_data1$grade), main="Wine Quality Classification
using Decision Tree")
```

Listing 4.4 Decision Tree Output (of code in Listing 4.3)

```
# Output of above code
> # decision trees v7 regular
> setwd("<directory-name>")
> library(caret)
Loading required package: lattice
Loading required package: ggplot2
Warning messages:
1: package 'caret' was built under R version 3.4.4
2: package 'ggplot2' was built under R version 3.4.4
3: As of rlang 0.4.0, dplyr must be at least version 0.8.0.
x dplyr 0.7.8 is too old for rlang 0.4.2.
i Please update dplyr to the latest version.
i Updating packages on Windows requires precautions:
  <https://github.com/jennybc/what-they-forgot/issues/62>
> library(e1071)
Warning message:
package 'e1071' was built under R version 3.4.4
> library(rpart.plot)
Loading required package: rpart
> # The file winequality-white.csv is in the working directory
> winedata1 <- read.csv("winequality-white.csv", header=TRUE, sep=';')
> head(winedata1)
  fixed.acidity volatile.acidity citric.acid residual.sugar chlorides
1           7.0             0.27        0.36           20.7     0.045
2           6.3             0.30        0.34            1.6     0.049
3           8.1             0.28        0.40            6.9     0.050
4           7.2             0.23        0.32            8.5     0.058
5           7.2             0.23        0.32            8.5     0.058
6           8.1             0.28        0.40            6.9     0.050
```

```
   free.sulfur.dioxide total.sulfur.dioxide density   pH sulphates alcohol
1                   45                  170 1.0010 3.00      0.45     8.8
2                   14                  132 0.9940 3.30      0.49     9.5
3                   30                   97 0.9951 3.26      0.44    10.1
4                   47                  186 0.9956 3.19      0.40     9.9
5                   47                  186 0.9956 3.19      0.40     9.9
6                   30                   97 0.9951 3.26      0.44    10.1
   quality
1        6
2        6
3        6
4        6
5        6
6        6
> class(winedata1$quality)
[1] "integer"
> anyNA(winedata1)
[1] FALSE
> # Mapping Wine Quality to Saleable Grade
> # <=3 NotAccept
> # 4 LessThanAvg
> # 5 Avg
> # 6 MoreThanAvg
> # 7 Good
> # 8 Great
> # >=9 Excellent
> winedata1$grade <- ifelse(winedata1$quality <= 3, 'NotAccept',
+                    ifelse(winedata1$quality == 4, 'LessThanAvg',
+                    ifelse(winedata1$quality == 5, 'Average',
+                    ifelse(winedata1$quality == 6, 'MoreThanAvg',
+                    ifelse(winedata1$quality == 7, 'Good',
+                    ifelse(winedata1$quality == 8, 'Great',
+                    ifelse(winedata1$quality >= 9, 'Excellent',
+                    '')))))))
>
>
> winedata1$grade <- as.factor(winedata1$grade)
> set.seed(12345)
> sample_size <- 0.70 * nrow(winedata1)
> sampledata1 <-sample(seq_len(nrow(winedata1)), sample_size)
> training_data1 <- winedata1[sampledata1, ]
> test_data1 <- winedata1[-sampledata1, ]
> nrow(training_data1) # 3428
[1] 3428
> nrow(test_data1) # 1470
[1] 1470
```

```
> training_data1 <- training_data1[,-12]
> summary(training_data1$grade)
   Average   Excellent       Good     Great LessThanAvg MoreThanAvg
      1014           4        618       126         110        1541
 NotAccept
        15
> summary(test_data1$grade)
   Average   Excellent       Good     Great LessThanAvg MoreThanAvg
       443           1        262        49          53         657
 NotAccept
         5
> summary(winedata1$grade)
   Average   Excellent       Good     Great LessThanAvg MoreThanAvg
      1457           5        880       175         163        2198
 NotAccept
        20
> head(training_data1)
     fixed.acidity volatile.acidity citric.acid residual.sugar chlorides
3531           7.2             0.31        0.35            7.2     0.046
4289           7.0             0.20        0.33            4.7     0.030
3726           6.6             0.26        0.28            9.4     0.028
4338           7.3             0.19        0.27           13.9     0.057  ·
2235           7.2             0.23        0.38            6.1     0.067
815            7.9             0.35        0.24           15.6     0.072
     free.sulfur.dioxide total.sulfur.dioxide density   pH sulphates alcohol
3531                  45                  178 0.99550 3.14      0.53     9.7
4289                  25                   76 0.99202 2.88      0.54    10.5
3726                  13                  121 0.99254 3.17      0.34    12.1
4338                  45                  155 0.99807 2.94      0.41     8.8
2235                  20                   90 0.99496 3.17      0.79     9.7
815                   44                  229 0.99785 3.03      0.59    10.5
           grade
3531     Average
4289 MoreThanAvg
3726 MoreThanAvg
4338       Great
2235     Average
815  MoreThanAvg
>
> trctrl <- trainControl(method = "repeatedcv", number = 10, repeats = 10,
savePredictions = TRUE, verboseIter = FALSE)
> set.seed(12345)
> #model_rf <- train(grade ~ ., data = training_data1, method = "rf", preProcess =
c("scale", "center"), trControl = trctrl)
> wine.dTree <- train(grade ~., data = training_data1, method = "rpart",
+                  parms = list(split = "information"),
```

```
+                        trControl=trctrl,
+                        tuneLength = 10)
> # As an alternative to above call, the below statement using the rpart() can be run
> # wine.dTree <- rpart(formula, data = training_data, method="class")
> #summary(fit)
> wine.dTree
CART

3428 samples
  11 predictor
   7 classes: 'Average', 'Excellent', 'Good', 'Great', 'LessThanAvg', 'MoreThanAvg',
   'NotAccept'

No pre-processing
Resampling: Cross-Validated (10 fold, repeated 10 times)
Summary of sample sizes: 3084, 3085, 3086, 3088, 3082, 3086, ...
Resampling results across tuning parameters:

  cp            Accuracy    Kappa
  0.002543720   0.5345185   0.2621422
  0.002649709   0.5337576   0.2601781
  0.003179650   0.5285617   0.2464255
  0.003577107   0.5245704   0.2364919
  0.003709592   0.5242192   0.2349841
  0.005299417   0.5159950   0.1961872
  0.006006006   0.5173653   0.1901325
  0.007065889   0.5189706   0.1873288
  0.013778484   0.5139181   0.1815030
  0.059618442   0.4864673   0.1175249

Accuracy was used to select the optimal model using the largest value.
The final value used for the model was cp = 0.00254372.
> prp(wine.dTree$finalModel) # Print Primary decision tree structure
> head(test_data1)
   fixed.acidity volatile.acidity citric.acid residual.sugar chlorides
5            7.2             0.23        0.32            8.5     0.058
7            6.2             0.32        0.16            7.0     0.045
8            7.0             0.27        0.36           20.7     0.045
9            6.3             0.30        0.34            1.6     0.049
12           8.6             0.23        0.40            4.2     0.035
14           6.6             0.16        0.40            1.5     0.044
   free.sulfur.dioxide total.sulfur.dioxide density   pH sulphates alcohol
5                   47                  186  0.9956 3.19      0.40     9.9
7                   30                  136  0.9949 3.18      0.47     9.6
8                   45                  170  1.0010 3.00      0.45     8.8
9                   14                  132  0.9940 3.30      0.49     9.5
12                  17                  109  0.9947 3.14      0.53     9.7
14                  48                  143  0.9912 3.54      0.52    12.4
```

```
   quality        grade
5         6 MoreThanAvg
7         6 MoreThanAvg
8         6 MoreThanAvg
9         6 MoreThanAvg
12        5      Average
14        7         Good
> test_data_new1 <- test_data1[,-12]
> head(test_data_new1)
   fixed.acidity volatile.acidity citric.acid residual.sugar chlorides
5            7.2             0.23        0.32            8.5     0.058
7            6.2             0.32        0.16            7.0     0.045
8            7.0             0.27        0.36           20.7     0.045
9            6.3             0.30        0.34            1.6     0.049
12           8.6             0.23        0.40            4.2     0.035
14           6.6             0.16        0.40            1.5     0.044
   free.sulfur.dioxide total.sulfur.dioxide density   pH sulphates alcohol
5                   47                  186 0.9956 3.19      0.40     9.9
7                   30                  136 0.9949 3.18      0.47     9.6
8                   45                  170 1.0010 3.00      0.45     8.8
9                   14                  132 0.9940 3.30      0.49     9.5
12                  17                  109 0.9947 3.14      0.53     9.7
14                  48                  143 0.9912 3.54      0.52    12.4
          grade
5  MoreThanAvg
7  MoreThanAvg
8  MoreThanAvg
9  MoreThanAvg
12     Average
14        Good
> test_data_new1 <- test_data_new1[,-12]
> head(test_data_new1)
   fixed.acidity volatile.acidity citric.acid residual.sugar chlorides
5            7.2             0.23        0.32            8.5     0.058
7            6.2             0.32        0.16            7.0     0.045
8            7.0             0.27        0.36           20.7     0.045
9            6.3             0.30        0.34            1.6     0.049
12           8.6             0.23        0.40            4.2     0.035
14           6.6             0.16        0.40            1.5     0.044
   free.sulfur.dioxide total.sulfur.dioxide density   pH sulphates alcohol
5                   47                  186 0.9956 3.19      0.40     9.9
7                   30                  136 0.9949 3.18      0.47     9.6
8                   45                  170 1.0010 3.00      0.45     8.8
9                   14                  132 0.9940 3.30      0.49     9.5
12                  17                  109 0.9947 3.14      0.53     9.7
14                  48                  143 0.9912 3.54      0.52    12.4
```

```
> test_pred <- predict(wine.dTree, newdata = test_data_new1)
> cm <- confusionMatrix(test_pred, test_data1$grade )   #check accuracy
> cm
Confusion Matrix and Statistics

            Reference
Prediction   Average Excellent Good Great LessThanAvg MoreThanAvg NotAccept
  Average       206        0   10     0          31         103         1
  Excellent       0        0    0     0           0           0         0
  Good            3        1   68    17           0          52         0
  Great           1        0    2     3           0           1         0
  LessThanAvg     5        0    0     1           1           2         0
  MoreThanAvg   228        0  182    28          21         499         4
  NotAccept       0        0    0     0           0           0         0

Overall Statistics

               Accuracy : 0.5286
                 95% CI : (0.5027, 0.5544)
    No Information Rate : 0.4469
    P-Value [Acc > NIR] : 2.089e-10

                  Kappa : 0.2373
 Mcnemar's Test P-Value : NA

Statistics by Class:

                     Class: Average Class: Excellent Class: Good Class: Great
Sensitivity                  0.4650        0.0000000     0.25954     0.061224
Specificity                  0.8588        1.0000000     0.93957     0.997185
Pos Pred Value               0.5869              NaN     0.48227     0.428571
Neg Pred Value               0.7882        0.9993197     0.85403     0.968558
Prevalence                   0.3014        0.0006803     0.17823     0.033333
Detection Rate               0.1401        0.0000000     0.04626     0.002041
Detection Prevalence         0.2388        0.0000000     0.09592     0.004762
Balanced Accuracy            0.6619        0.5000000     0.59956     0.529205
                     Class: LessThanAvg Class: MoreThanAvg Class: NotAccept
Sensitivity                   0.0188679             0.7595         0.000000
Specificity                   0.9943543             0.4305         1.000000
Pos Pred Value                0.1111111             0.5187              NaN
Neg Pred Value                0.9644079             0.6890         0.996599
Prevalence                    0.0360544             0.4469         0.003401
Detection Rate                0.0006803             0.3395         0.000000
Detection Prevalence          0.0061224             0.6544         0.000000
Balanced Accuracy             0.5066111             0.5950         0.500000
> #Training the Decision Tree Classifier with gini as criterion
> set.seed(12345)
```

```
> wine.dTree_gini <- train(grade ~., data = training_data1, method = "rpart",
+                     parms = list(split = "gini"),
+                     trControl=trctrl, tuneLength = 10)
> wine.dTree_gini
CART

3428 samples
  11 predictor
   7 classes: 'Average', 'Excellent', 'Good', 'Great', 'LessThanAvg', 'MoreThanAvg',
   'NotAccept'

No pre-processing
Resampling: Cross-Validated (10 fold, repeated 10 times)
Summary of sample sizes: 3084, 3085, 3086, 3088, 3082, 3086, ...
Resampling results across tuning parameters:

  cp          Accuracy   Kappa
  0.002543720 0.5343409  0.2675094
  0.002649709 0.5338720  0.2656402
  0.003179650 0.5324351  0.2588795
  0.003577107 0.5295228  0.2522079
  0.003709592 0.5295229  0.2521572
  0.005299417 0.5193445  0.2253181
  0.006006006 0.5147324  0.2068900
  0.007065889 0.5131566  0.1882744
  0.013778484 0.5072367  0.1686660
  0.059618442 0.4852160  0.1150732

Accuracy was used to select the optimal model using the largest value.
The final value used for the model was cp = 0.00254372.
> prp(wine.dTree_gini$finalModel)
> test_pred_gini <- predict(wine.dTree_gini, newdata = test_data_new1)
> cm_gini <- confusionMatrix(test_pred_gini, test_data1$grade)   #check accuracy
> cm_gini
Confusion Matrix and Statistics

              Reference
Prediction    Average Excellent Good Great LessThanAvg MoreThanAvg NotAccept
  Average         246         0   14     1          30         138         1
  Excellent         0         0    0     0           0           0         0
  Good              7         0   93    20           1          81         0
  Great             0         0    0     1           0           0         0
  LessThanAvg       8         0    0     0           2           3         0
  MoreThanAvg     182         1  155    27          20         435         4
  NotAccept         0         0    0     0           0           0         0

Overall Statistics
```

```
            Accuracy : 0.5286
              95% CI : (0.5027, 0.5544)
 No Information Rate : 0.4469
 P-Value [Acc > NIR] : 2.089e-10

                Kappa : 0.2593
 Mcnemar's Test P-Value : NA
```

Statistics by Class:

	Class: Average	Class: Excellent	Class: Good	Class: Great
Sensitivity	0.5553	0.0000000	0.35496	0.0204082
Specificity	0.8208	1.0000000	0.90977	1.0000000
Pos Pred Value	0.5721	NaN	0.46040	1.0000000
Neg Pred Value	0.8106	0.9993197	0.86672	0.9673247
Prevalence	0.3014	0.0006803	0.17823	0.0333333
Detection Rate	0.1673	0.0000000	0.06327	0.0006803
Detection Prevalence	0.2925	0.0000000	0.13741	0.0006803
Balanced Accuracy	0.6881	0.5000000	0.63237	0.5102041

	Class: LessThanAvg	Class: MoreThanAvg	Class: NotAccept
Sensitivity	0.037736	0.6621	0.000000
Specificity	0.992237	0.5215	1.000000
Pos Pred Value	0.153846	0.5279	NaN
Neg Pred Value	0.964997	0.6563	0.996599
Prevalence	0.036054	0.4469	0.003401
Detection Rate	0.001361	0.2959	0.000000
Detection Prevalence	0.008844	0.5605	0.000000
Balanced Accuracy	0.514986	0.5918	0.500000

```
> table(test_pred, test_data1$grade)
```

test_pred	Average	Excellent	Good	Great	LessThanAvg	MoreThanAvg	NotAccept
Average	206	0	10	0	31	103	1
Excellent	0	0	0	0	0	0	0
Good	3	1	68	17	0	52	0
Great	1	0	2	3	0	1	0
LessThanAvg	5	0	0	1	1	2	0
MoreThanAvg	228	0	182	28	21	499	4
NotAccept	0	0	0	0	0	0	0

```
> table(test_pred_gini, test_data1$grade)
```

test_pred_gini	Average	Excellent	Good	Great	LessThanAvg	MoreThanAvg	NotAccept
Average	246	0	14	1	30	138	1
Excellent	0	0	0	0	0	0	0
Good	7	0	93	20	1	81	0
Great	0	0	0	1	0	0	0
LessThanAvg	8	0	0	0	2	3	0
MoreThanAvg	182	1	155	27	20	435	4
NotAccept	0	0	0	0	0	0	0

```
>
> # Measure model performance with AUC
> library(ROCR)
Loading required package: gplots

Attaching package: 'gplots'

The following object is masked from 'package:stats':

    lowess

Warning messages:
1: package 'ROCR' was built under R version 3.4.4
2: package 'gplots' was built under R version 3.4.4
> # Calculate the probability of new observations belonging to each class
> # Source_pred_ROC_AUC will be a matrix with dimensions (data_set_size x
number_of_classes)
> grade_pred_ROC_AUC_dtree <- predict(wine.dTree,test_data_new1,type="prob")
> # Use colors for roc curves for the three classes (one for each Source):
> colors <- c("green","orange","purple","yellow","blue","black","red")
> # Specify the different classes
> ROC_AUC_classes <- levels(test_data1$grade)
> # For each class
> for (i in 1:7)
+ {
+   # Define observations belonging to each class i.e., class[i]
+   Actualgrade_values <- ifelse(test_data1$grade==ROC_AUC_classes[i],1,0)
+   # Assess the performance of classifier for class[i]
+   pred <- prediction(grade_pred_ROC_AUC_dtree[,i],Actualgrade_values)
+   perf <- performance(pred, "tpr", "fpr")
+       pdf(paste("Decision_Tree_v7_ROC_Curve_for_",ROC_AUC_classes[i],".pdf"))
+       plot(perf,main=paste("Decision Tree ROC Curve for ",
        ROC_AUC_classes[i]),col=colors[i])
+     dev.off()
+   # Calculate the AUC and print it to screen
+   auc.perf <- performance(pred, measure = "auc")
+   print(paste("Decision Tree AUC for ",ROC_AUC_classes[i],":",auc.perf@y.values))
+ }
[1] "Decision Tree AUC for  Average : 0.770696828958966"
[1] "Decision Tree AUC for  Excellent : 0.466643975493533"
[1] "Decision Tree AUC for  Good : 0.754293893129771"
[1] "Decision Tree AUC for  Great : 0.763747863677491"
[1] "Decision Tree AUC for  LessThanAvg : 0.72961079080172"
[1] "Decision Tree AUC for  MoreThanAvg : 0.598024678876926"
[1] "Decision Tree AUC for  NotAccept : 0.437133105802048"
> results_dTree_gini <- data.frame(Actual = test_data1$grade, Predicted = predict(wine.
dTree_gini, test_data_new1, type = "prob"))
> head(results_dTree_gini)
```

```
        Actual Predicted.Average Predicted.Excellent Predicted.Good
5   MoreThanAvg          0.2214386                  0   0.142454161
7   MoreThanAvg          0.6749049                  0   0.007604563
8   MoreThanAvg          0.2666667                  0   0.133333333
9   MoreThanAvg          0.6749049                  0   0.007604563
12      Average          0.2214386                  0   0.142454161
14         Good          0.1805825                  0   0.213592233
    Predicted.Great Predicted.LessThanAvg Predicted.MoreThanAvg
5        0.01410437            0.01410437             0.6064880
7        0.00000000            0.05513308             0.2566540
8        0.00000000            0.00000000             0.6000000
9        0.00000000            0.05513308             0.2566540
12       0.01410437            0.01410437             0.6064880
14       0.05825243            0.01747573             0.5242718
    Predicted.NotAccept
5           0.001410437
7           0.005703422
8           0.000000000
9           0.005703422
12          0.001410437
14          0.005825243
> results_dTree_gini$predicted_grade <- ifelse(results_dTree_gini$Predicted.Average
> 0.5, "Average",
+     ifelse(results_dTree_gini$Predicted.Excellent > 0.5, "Excellent",
+       ifelse(results_dTree_gini$Predicted.Good > 0.5, "Good",
+         ifelse(results_dTree_gini$Predicted.Great > 0.5, "Great",
+           ifelse(results_dTree_gini$Predicted.LessThanAvg > 0.5, "LessThanAvg",
+             ifelse(results_dTree_gini$Predicted.MoreThanAvg > 0.5, "MoreThanAvg",
+               ifelse(results_dTree_gini$Predicted.NotAccept > 0.5, "NotAccept",
+                 ''))))))) 
> results_dTree_gini$predicted_grade <- factor(results_dTree_gini$predicted_grade,
levels=levels(results_dTree_gini$Actual))
> cm_original_dtree_gini <-   confusionMatrix(results_dTree_gini$predicted_grade,
test_data1$grade)
> cm_original_dtree_gini
Confusion Matrix and Statistics
```

```
          Reference
Prediction    Average Excellent Good Great LessThanAvg MoreThanAvg NotAccept
  Average         245         0   14     1          30         135         1
  Excellent         0         0    0     0           0           0         0
  Good              7         0   93    20           1          81         0
  Great             0         0    0     1           0           0         0
  LessThanAvg       8         0    0     0           2           3         0
  MoreThanAvg     182         1  155    27          20         435         4
  NotAccept         0         0    0     0           0           0         0
```

```
Overall Statistics
```

```
        Accuracy : 0.5293
          95% CI : (0.5034, 0.5551)
No Information Rate : 0.4461
P-Value [Acc > NIR] : 1.003e-10

           Kappa : 0.2607
Mcnemar's Test P-Value : NA
```

Statistics by Class:

	Class: Average	Class: Excellent	Class: Good	Class: Great
Sensitivity	0.5543	0.0000000	0.35496	0.0204082
Specificity	0.8232	1.0000000	0.90947	1.0000000
Pos Pred Value	0.5751	NaN	0.46040	1.0000000
Neg Pred Value	0.8106	0.9993179	0.86630	0.9672355
Prevalence	0.3015	0.0006821	0.17872	0.0334243
Detection Rate	0.1671	0.0000000	0.06344	0.0006821
Detection Prevalence	0.2906	0.0000000	0.13779	0.0006821
Balanced Accuracy	0.6888	0.5000000	0.63222	0.5102041

	Class: LessThanAvg	Class: MoreThanAvg	Class: NotAccept
Sensitivity	0.037736	0.6651	0.000000
Specificity	0.992215	0.5209	1.000000
Pos Pred Value	0.153846	0.5279	NaN
Neg Pred Value	0.964900	0.6589	0.996589
Prevalence	0.036153	0.4461	0.003411
Detection Rate	0.001364	0.2967	0.000000
Detection Prevalence	0.008868	0.5621	0.000000
Balanced Accuracy	0.514975	0.5930	0.500000

```
> pairs(table(test_pred_gini, test_data1$grade), main="Wine Quality Classification
using Decision Tree")
>
```

The primary structure of the decision tree used for the wine quality classification with "information gain" and "*gini*" as criteria is shown in Figures 4.10 and 4.11, respectively. The ROC curves for the Decision Tree model for each of the seven classes are shown in Figures 4.12 to 4.18, respectively.

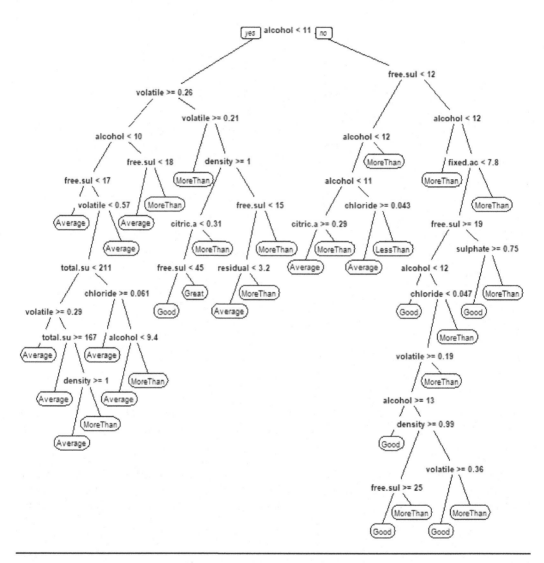

Figure 4.10   Primary structure of a Decision Tree (with Information as criterion).

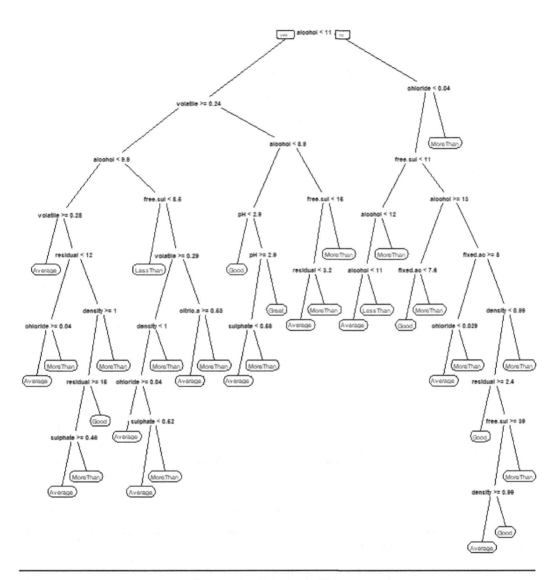

Figure 4.11   Primary structure of a Decision Tree (with Gini as criterion).

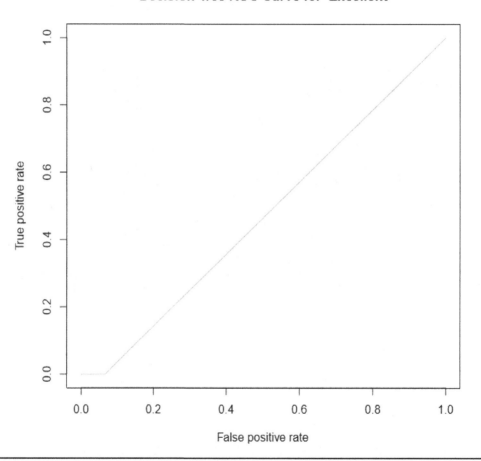

Figure 4.12   Decision Tree ROC Curve for Excellent.

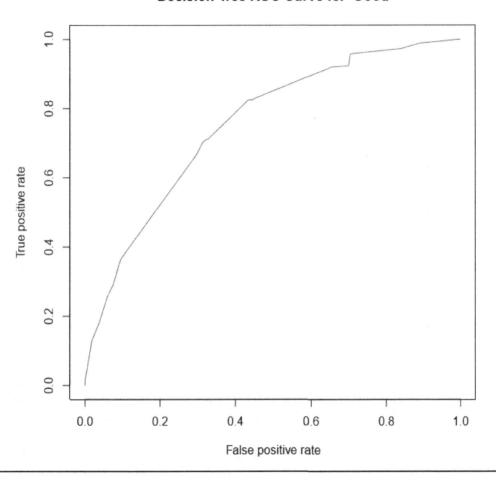

Figure 4.13 Decision Tree ROC Curve for Good.

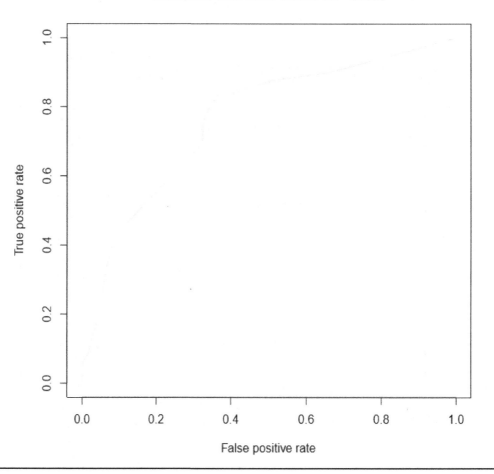

Figure 4.14 Decision Tree ROC Curve for Great.

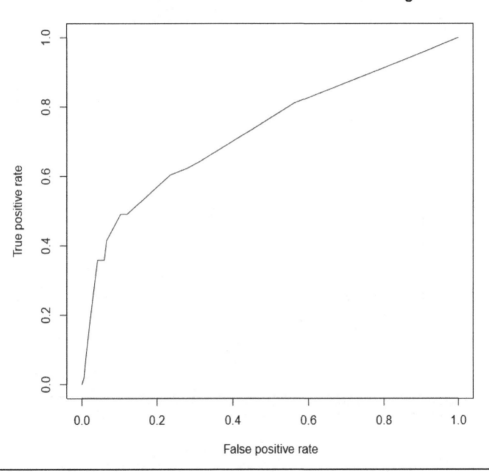

Figure 4.15   Decision Tree ROC Curve for LessThanAvg.

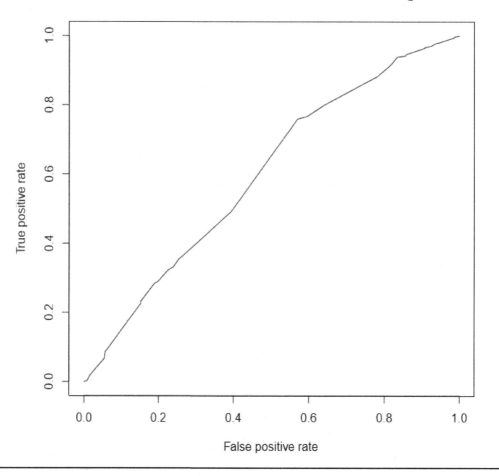

Figure 4.16   Decision Tree ROC Curve for MoreThanAvg.

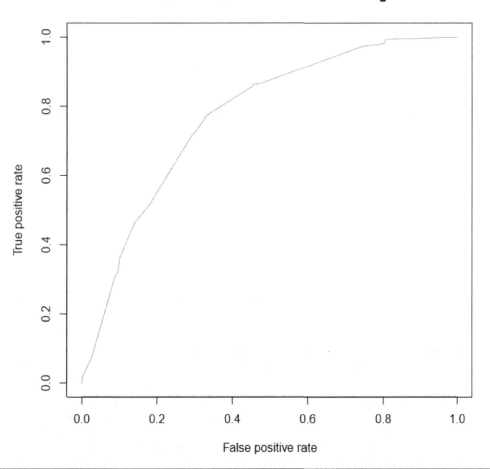

Figure 4.17 Decision Tree ROC Curve for Average.

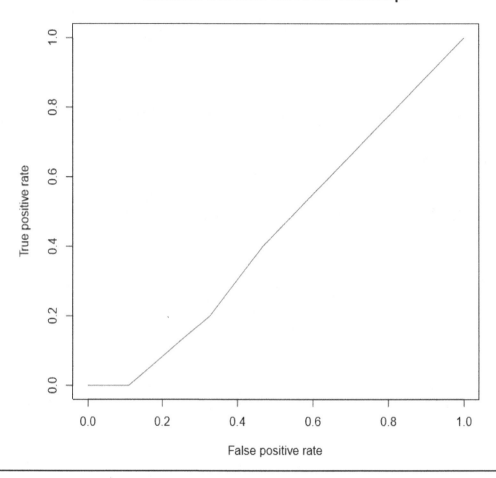

Decision Tree ROC Curve for NotAccept

Figure 4.18   Decision Tree ROC Curve for NotAccept

From the varImp plot of the random forest and the primary structure plot of the decision tree (with both information and Gini criteria), we see that "alcohol" was the most importance feature. However, the "Kappa" value (as opposed to the "accuracy" metric) varied from 49.64% to 60% in the case of the random forest model, whereas it varied from slightly more than 25% to 26% in the case of the decision tree model. In addition, overfitting is less, as observed from the ROC curves for the classes present in the test data versus the decision tree model. This shows that the random forest model performed better than the decision trees in this scenario. However, the imbalance in the dataset classes and building the model without any pre-processing of data factors into the process of feature and model selection as well as the overfitting involved. The performance of the random forest algorithm can be further improved by using a variety of resampling methods to balance out the distribution of data in each class, such as "up" sampling the less distributed classes in which random duplication of samples from the class with fewer instances or the generation of additional data to even out the distribution of data in each class is done, "down" sampling the more distributed classes in which a random selection of samples from more distributed class to even out data in each class is done, using a mix of "up" and "down" sampling called SMOTE, etc. These techniques are applied at the cross-validation stage before building the model to improve its performance.

Using "Up" Sampling on the Random Forest Model to Improve Performance[3]

As described in the inset above, in this subsection we show how "up" sampling in the cross-validation step improves the performance of the random forest model. Listings 4.5 and 4.6 provide the code for this, followed by the output of the code execution.

Listing 4.5 Using "Up" Sampling with the Random Forest Model

```
setwd("<directory-name>")
library(caret)
library(e1071)
library(DMwR)
# The file winequality-white.csv is in the working directory
winedata2 <- read.csv("winequality-white.csv", header=TRUE, sep=';')
head(winedata2)
winedata2$grade <- ifelse(winedata2$quality <= 3, 'NotAccept',
                   ifelse(winedata2$quality == 4, 'LessThanAvg',
                   ifelse(winedata2$quality == 5, 'Average',
                   ifelse(winedata2$quality == 6, 'MoreThanAvg',
                   ifelse(winedata2$quality == 7, 'Good',
                   ifelse(winedata2$quality == 8, 'Great',
                   ifelse(winedata2$quality >= 9, 'Excellent',
                    'CannotGrade')))))))
class(winedata2$grade)
winedata2$grade <- as.factor(winedata2$grade)
head(winedata2$grade)
anyNA(winedata2)
set.seed(12345)
sample_size2 <- 0.70 * nrow(winedata2)
sampledata2 <-sample(seq_len(nrow(winedata2)), sample_size2)
training_data2 <- winedata2[sampledata2, ]
test_data2 <- winedata2[-sampledata2, ]
nrow(training_data2) #
nrow(test_data2) #
head(training_data2$grade)
training_data2$grade <- as.factor(training_data2$grade)
summary(training_data2$grade) # to get distribution of each grade
training_data2 <- training_data2[,-12]
head(training_data2)
levels(training_data2$grade)
training_data2$grade <- factor(as.character(training_data2$grade))
levels(training_data2$grade)
# Using "up" to perform over-sampling for imbalanced training_data
# (Creating a balanced sataset for original TRAINING_SET for imbalanced classes)
trctrl5 <- trainControl(method = "repeatedcv", number = 10, repeats = 10,
savePredictions = TRUE, sampling = "up")
# Use same seed as used for splitting data to get better control
```

```
# model randomness i.e., for reusable results
set.seed(12345)
rf_up5 <- train(grade ~ ., data = training_data2, method = "rf",  preProcess =
c("scale", "center"), trControl = trctrl5)
print(rf_up5)
rf_up5$finalModel$confusion
# Feature importance
imp5 <- rf_up5$finalModel$importance
dim(imp5)
class(imp5)
imp5
imp5[order(imp5, decreasing = TRUE), ]
# estimate variable importance
importance <- varImp(rf_up5, scale = TRUE)
plot(importance)
# predicting on test data
head(test_data2)
test_data_new2 <- test_data2[,-12]
test_data_new2 <- test_data_new2[,-12]
head(test_data_new2)
head(training_data2)
rf_up5_pred <- predict(rf_up5, test_data_new2)
cm_up5 <- confusionMatrix(rf_up5_pred, test_data2$grade)
cm_up5

results_rf_over <- data.frame(Actual = test_data2$grade, Predicted = predict(rf_
up5, test_data_new2, type = "prob"))
head(results_rf_over)
results_rf_over$predicted_grade <- ifelse(results_rf_over$Predicted.Average > 0.5,
"Average",
        ifelse(results_rf_over$Predicted.Excellent > 0.5, "Excellent",
          ifelse(results_rf_over$Predicted.Good > 0.5, "Good",
            ifelse(results_rf_over$Predicted.Great > 0.5, "Great",
              ifelse(results_rf_over$Predicted.LessThanAvg > 0.5, "LessThanAvg",
                ifelse(results_rf_over$Predicted.MoreThanAvg > 0.5, "MoreThanAvg",
                  ifelse(results_rf_over$Predicted.NotAccept > 0.5, "NotAccept",
                    '')))))))

results_rf_over$predicted_grade <- factor(results_rf_over$predicted_grade,
levels=levels(results_rf_over$Actual))

cm_over <- confusionMatrix(results_rf_over$predicted_grade, test_data2$grade)
cm_over

# Measure model performance with ROCR and AUC
library(ROCR)
# Calculate the probability of new observations belonging to each class
```

```
# grade_pred_up_ROC_AUC will be a matrix with dimensions (data_set_size x
number_of_classes)
grade_pred_up_ROC_AUC <- predict(rf_up5,test_data_new2,type="prob")
# Use colors for roc curves for the classes (one for each grade measure):
colors <- c("green","orange","purple","yellow","blue","black","red")
# Specify the different classes
ROC_AUC_classes <- levels(test_data2$grade)
# For each class
for (i in 1:7)
{
 # Define observations belonging to each class i.e., class[i]
 Actualgrade_values <- ifelse(test_data2$grade==ROC_AUC_classes[i],1,0)
 # Assess the performance of classifier for class[i]
 pred <- prediction(grade_pred_up_ROC_AUC[,i],Actualgrade_values)
 perf <- performance(pred, "tpr", "fpr")
    pdf(paste("Random_Forest_up_ROC_Curve_for_",ROC_AUC_classes[i],".pdf"))
    plot(perf,main=paste("Random Forest up ROC Curve for ",
    ROC_AUC_classes[i]),col=colors[i])
   dev.off()
 # Calculate the AUC and print it to screen
 auc.perf <- performance(pred, measure = "auc")
 print(paste("Random_Forest_up_AUC for ",ROC_AUC_classes[i],":",auc.perf@y.values))
}
pairs(table(rf_up5_pred, test_data2$grade), main="Wine Quality Classification")
models2 <- list(original = model_rf, over = rf_up5)
resampling <- resamples(models2)
bwplot(resampling)
```

Listing 4.6 Output of Code in Listing 4.5

```
> setwd("<directory-name>")
> library(caret)
> library(e1071)
> library(DMwR)
> # The file winequality-white.csv is in the working directory
> winedata2 <- read.csv("winequality-white.csv", header=TRUE, sep=';')
> head(winedata2)
  fixed.acidity volatile.acidity citric.acid residual.sugar chlorides free.sulfur.dioxide
1          7.0            0.27        0.36          20.7      0.045                  45
2          6.3            0.30        0.34           1.6      0.049                  14
3          8.1            0.28        0.40           6.9      0.050                  30
4          7.2            0.23        0.32           8.5      0.058                  47
5          7.2            0.23        0.32           8.5      0.058                  47
6          8.1            0.28        0.40           6.9      0.050                  30
```

```
  total.sulfur.dioxide density   pH sulphates alcohol quality
1                  170 1.0010 3.00     0.45     8.8      6
2                  132 0.9940 3.30     0.49     9.5      6
3                   97 0.9951 3.26     0.44    10.1      6
4                  186 0.9956 3.19     0.40     9.9      6
5                  186 0.9956 3.19     0.40     9.9      6
6                   97 0.9951 3.26     0.44    10.1      6
> winedata2$grade <- ifelse(winedata2$quality <= 3, 'NotAccept',
+                    ifelse(winedata2$quality == 4, 'LessThanAvg',
+                    ifelse(winedata2$quality == 5, 'Average',
+                    ifelse(winedata2$quality == 6, 'MoreThanAvg',
+                    ifelse(winedata2$quality == 7, 'Good',
+                    ifelse(winedata2$quality == 8, 'Great',
+                    ifelse(winedata2$quality >= 9, 'Excellent',
+                    'CannotGrade')))))))
> class(winedata2$grade)
[1] "character"
> winedata2$grade <- as.factor(winedata2$grade)
> head(winedata2$grade)
[1] MoreThanAvg MoreThanAvg MoreThanAvg MoreThanAvg MoreThanAvg MoreThanAvg
Levels: Average Excellent Good Great LessThanAvg MoreThanAvg NotAccept
> anyNA(winedata2)
[1] FALSE
> set.seed(12345)
> sample_size2 <- 0.70 * nrow(winedata2)
> sampledata2 <-sample(seq_len(nrow(winedata2)), sample_size2)
> training_data2 <- winedata2[sampledata2, ]
> test_data2 <- winedata2[-sampledata2, ]
> nrow(training_data2) #
[1] 3428
> nrow(test_data2) #
[1] 1470
> head(training_data2$grade)
[1] Average     MoreThanAvg MoreThanAvg Great       Average     MoreThanAvg
Levels: Average Excellent Good Great LessThanAvg MoreThanAvg NotAccept
> training_data2$grade <- as.factor(training_data2$grade)
> summary(training_data2$grade) # to get distribution of each grade
   Average   Excellent        Good       Great LessThanAvg MoreThanAvg   NotAccept
      1014           4         618         126         110        1541          15
> training_data2 <- training_data2[,-12]
> head(training_data2)
     fixed.acidity volatile.acidity citric.acid residual.sugar chlorides
3531           7.2             0.31        0.35            7.2     0.046
4289           7.0             0.20        0.33            4.7     0.030
3726           6.6             0.26        0.28            9.4     0.028
4338           7.3             0.19        0.27           13.9     0.057
2235           7.2             0.23        0.38            6.1     0.067
815            7.9             0.35        0.24           15.6     0.072
```

```
     free.sulfur.dioxide total.sulfur.dioxide density   pH sulphates alcohol    grade
3531                  45                  178 0.99550 3.14      0.53     9.7   Average
4289                  25                   76 0.99202 2.88      0.54    10.5 MoreThanAvg
3726                  13                  121 0.99254 3.17      0.34    12.1 MoreThanAvg
4338                  45                  155 0.99807 2.94      0.41     8.8     Great
2235                  20                   90 0.99496 3.17      0.79     9.7   Average
815                   44                  229 0.99785 3.03      0.59    10.5 MoreThanAvg
> # Using "up" to perform over-sampling for imbalanced training_data
> # (Creating a balanced sataset for original TRAINING_SET for imbalanced classes)
> trctrl5 <- trainControl(method = "repeatedcv", number = 10, repeats = 10,
savePredictions = TRUE, sampling = "up")
> set.seed(12345)
> rf_up5 <- train(grade ~ ., data = training_data2, method = "rf",  preProcess =
c("scale", "center"), trControl = trctrl5)
> print(rf_up5)
Random Forest

3428 samples
  11 predictor
   7 classes: 'Average', 'Excellent', 'Good', 'Great', 'LessThanAvg', 'MoreThanAvg',
   'NotAccept'

Pre-processing: scaled (11), centered (11)
Resampling: Cross-Validated (10 fold, repeated 10 times)
Summary of sample sizes: 3084, 3085, 3086, 3088, 3082, 3086, ...
Addtional sampling using up-sampling prior to pre-processing

Resampling results across tuning parameters:

  mtry  Accuracy   Kappa
   2    0.6604751  0.4813420
   6    0.6487449  0.4692309
  11    0.6290210  0.4455761

Accuracy was used to select the optimal model using the largest value.
The final value used for the model was mtry = 2.
> rf_up5$finalModel$confusion
            Average Excellent Good Great LessThanAvg MoreThanAvg NotAccept class.error
Average        1354         0   15     0          11         161         0  0.12134977
Excellent         0      1541    0     0           0           0         0  0.00000000
Good              3         0 1482     4           0          52         0  0.03828683
Great             0         0    0  1541           0           0         0  0.00000000
LessThanAvg       0         0    0     0        1541           0         0  0.00000000
MoreThanAvg     253         0  151     2           4        1131         0  0.26606100
NotAccept         0         0    0     0           0           0      1541  0.00000000
> # Feature importance
> imp5 <- rf_up5$finalModel$importance
> imp5
                MeanDecreaseGini
```

```
fixed.acidity              872.4905
volatile.acidity           800.6993
citric.acid                733.8792
residual.sugar             731.9511
chlorides                  911.0409
free.sulfur.dioxide        995.7841
total.sulfur.dioxide       814.4053
density                    979.8786
pH                         830.4776
sulphates                  591.4882
alcohol                    980.1300
> imp5[order(imp5, decreasing = TRUE), ]
 free.sulfur.dioxide            alcohol              density             chlorides
         995.7841              980.1300             979.8786              911.0409
       fixed.acidity                 pH total.sulfur.dioxide       volatile.acidity
         872.4905              830.4776             814.4053              800.6993
         citric.acid     residual.sugar            sulphates
         733.8792              731.9511             591.4882
> # estimate variable importance
> importance <- varImp(rf_up5, scale = TRUE)
> plot(importance)
> head(test_data2)
   fixed.acidity volatile.acidity citric.acid residual.sugar chlorides free.sulfur.dioxide
5            7.2             0.23        0.32            8.5     0.058                  47
7            6.2             0.32        0.16            7.0     0.045                  30
8            7.0             0.27        0.36           20.7     0.045                  45
9            6.3             0.30        0.34            1.6     0.049                  14
12           8.6             0.23        0.40            4.2     0.035                  17
14           6.6             0.16        0.40            1.5     0.044                  48
   total.sulfur.dioxide density   pH sulphates alcohol quality       grade
5                   186  0.9956 3.19      0.40     9.9       6 MoreThanAvg
7                   136  0.9949 3.18      0.47     9.6       6 MoreThanAvg
8                   170  1.0010 3.00      0.45     8.8       6 MoreThanAvg
9                   132  0.9940 3.30      0.49     9.5       6 MoreThanAvg
12                  109  0.9947 3.14      0.53     9.7       5     Average
14                  143  0.9912 3.54      0.52    12.4       7        Good
> test_data_new2 <- test_data2[,-12]
> test_data_new2 <- test_data_new2[,-12]
> head(test_data_new2)
   fixed.acidity volatile.acidity citric.acid residual.sugar chlorides free.sulfur.dioxide
5            7.2             0.23        0.32            8.5     0.058                  47
7            6.2             0.32        0.16            7.0     0.045                  30
8            7.0             0.27        0.36           20.7     0.045                  45
9            6.3             0.30        0.34            1.6     0.049                  14
12           8.6             0.23        0.40            4.2     0.035                  17
14           6.6             0.16        0.40            1.5     0.044                  48
```

```
     total.sulfur.dioxide density   pH sulphates alcohol
5                     186 0.9956 3.19     0.40     9.9
7                     136 0.9949 3.18     0.47     9.6
8                     170 1.0010 3.00     0.45     8.8
9                     132 0.9940 3.30     0.49     9.5
12                    109 0.9947 3.14     0.53     9.7
14                    143 0.9912 3.54     0.52    12.4
> head(training_data2)
       fixed.acidity volatile.acidity citric.acid residual.sugar chlorides
3531             7.2             0.31        0.35            7.2     0.046
4289             7.0             0.20        0.33            4.7     0.030
3726             6.6             0.26        0.28            9.4     0.028
4338             7.3             0.19        0.27           13.9     0.057
2235             7.2             0.23        0.38            6.1     0.067
815              7.9             0.35        0.24           15.6     0.072
     free.sulfur.dioxide total.sulfur.dioxide density   pH sulphates alcohol      grade
3531                  45                  178 0.99550 3.14     0.53     9.7    Average
4289                  25                   76 0.99202 2.88     0.54    10.5 MoreThanAvg
3726                  13                  121 0.99254 3.17     0.34    12.1 MoreThanAvg
4338                  45                  155 0.99807 2.94     0.41     8.8      Great
2235                  20                   90 0.99496 3.17     0.79     9.7    Average
815                   44                  229 0.99785 3.03     0.59    10.5 MoreThanAvg
> rf_up5_pred <- predict(rf_up5, test_data_new2)
> cm_up5 <- confusionMatrix(rf_up5_pred, test_data2$grade)
> cm_up5
Confusion Matrix and Statistics

          Reference
Prediction   Average Excellent Good Great LessThanAvg MoreThanAvg NotAccept
  Average        314         0    8     0          34          84         0
  Excellent        0         0    0     0           0           0         0
  Good             5         0  164    15           1          65         0
  Great            0         0    1    19           0           1         0
  LessThanAvg      3         0    0     1           3           2         0
  MoreThanAvg    121         1   89    14          13         505         5
  NotAccept        0         0    0     0           2           0         0

Overall Statistics

               Accuracy : 0.6837
                 95% CI : (0.6592, 0.7074)
    No Information Rate : 0.4469
    P-Value [Acc > NIR] : < 2.2e-16

                  Kappa : 0.5144
 Mcnemar's Test P-Value : NA
```

Statistics by Class:

	Class: Average	Class: Excellent	Class: Good	Class: Great
Sensitivity	0.7088	0.0000000	0.6260	0.38776
Specificity	0.8773	1.0000000	0.9288	0.99859
Pos Pred Value	0.7136	NaN	0.6560	0.90476
Neg Pred Value	0.8748	0.9993197	0.9197	0.97930
Prevalence	0.3014	0.0006803	0.1782	0.03333
Detection Rate	0.2136	0.0000000	0.1116	0.01293
Detection Prevalence	0.2993	0.0000000	0.1701	0.01429
Balanced Accuracy	0.7931	0.5000000	0.7774	0.69317

	Class: LessThanAvg	Class: MoreThanAvg	Class: NotAccept
Sensitivity	0.056604	0.7686	0.000000
Specificity	0.995766	0.7011	0.998635
Pos Pred Value	0.333333	0.6751	0.000000
Neg Pred Value	0.965777	0.7895	0.996594
Prevalence	0.036054	0.4469	0.003401
Detection Rate	0.002041	0.3435	0.000000
Detection Prevalence	0.006122	0.5088	0.001361
Balanced Accuracy	0.526185	0.7349	0.499317

```
> results_rf_over <- data.frame(Actual = test_data2$grade, Predicted = predict(rf_
up5, test_data_new2, type = "prob"))
> head(results_rf_over)
      Actual Predicted.Average Predicted.Excellent Predicted.Good Predicted.Great
5  MoreThanAvg             0.164               0.000          0.034           0.004
7  MoreThanAvg             0.820               0.000          0.018           0.000
8  MoreThanAvg             0.220               0.000          0.040           0.000
9  MoreThanAvg             0.214               0.000          0.014           0.002
12     Average             0.250               0.002          0.052           0.004
14        Good             0.084               0.000          0.306           0.282
   Predicted.LessThanAvg Predicted.MoreThanAvg Predicted.NotAccept
5                  0.002                 0.796               0.000
7                  0.006                 0.156               0.000
8                  0.002                 0.738               0.000
9                  0.024                 0.746               0.000
12                 0.082                 0.584               0.026
14                 0.002                 0.314               0.012
> results_rf_over$predicted_grade <- ifelse(results_rf_over$Predicted.Average > 0.5,
"Average",
+         ifelse(results_rf_over$Predicted.Excellent > 0.5, "Excellent",
+           ifelse(results_rf_over$Predicted.Good > 0.5, "Good",
+             ifelse(results_rf_over$Predicted.Great > 0.5, "Great",
+               ifelse(results_rf_over$Predicted.LessThanAvg > 0.5, "LessThanAvg",
+                 ifelse(results_rf_over$Predicted.MoreThanAvg > 0.5, "MoreThanAvg",
+                   ifelse(results_rf_over$Predicted.NotAccept > 0.5, "NotAccept",
+                     '')))))))
```

```
> results_rf_over$predicted_grade <- factor(results_rf_over$predicted_grade,
levels=levels(results_rf_over$Actual))
>
> cm_over <- confusionMatrix(results_rf_over$predicted_grade, test_data2$grade)
> cm_over
Confusion Matrix and Statistics
```

```
              Reference
Prediction    Average Excellent Good Great LessThanAvg MoreThanAvg NotAccept
  Average         268         0    3     0          20          54         0
  Excellent         0         0    0     0           0           0         0
  Good              1         0  122     3           0          26         0
  Great             0         0    0    18           0           1         0
  LessThanAvg       0         0    0     0           2           0         0
  MoreThanAvg      56         0   39     4           5         317         1
  NotAccept         0         0    0     0           1           0         0
```

Overall Statistics

```
               Accuracy : 0.7726
                 95% CI : (0.7444, 0.799)
    No Information Rate : 0.423
    P-Value [Acc > NIR] : < 2.2e-16

                  Kappa : 0.6528
 Mcnemar's Test P-Value : NA
```

Statistics by Class:

	Class: Average	Class: Excellent	Class: Good	Class: Great
Sensitivity	0.8246	NA	0.7439	0.72000
Specificity	0.8750	1	0.9614	0.99891
Pos Pred Value	0.7768	NA	0.8026	0.94737
Neg Pred Value	0.9044	NA	0.9468	0.99241
Prevalence	0.3454	0	0.1743	0.02657
Detection Rate	0.2848	0	0.1296	0.01913
Detection Prevalence	0.3666	0	0.1615	0.02019
Balanced Accuracy	0.8498	NA	0.8526	0.85945

	Class: LessThanAvg	Class: MoreThanAvg	Class: NotAccept
Sensitivity	0.071429	0.7965	0.000000
Specificity	1.000000	0.8066	0.998936
Pos Pred Value	1.000000	0.7512	0.000000
Neg Pred Value	0.972311	0.8439	0.998936
Prevalence	0.029756	0.4230	0.001063
Detection Rate	0.002125	0.3369	0.000000
Detection Prevalence	0.002125	0.4485	0.001063
Balanced Accuracy	0.535714	0.8016	0.499468

```
> # Measure model performance with ROCR and AUC
> library(ROCR)
Loading required package: gplots
```

```
Attaching package: 'gplots'

The following object is masked from 'package:stats':

    lowess

Warning messages:
1: package 'ROCR' was built under R version 3.4.4
2: package 'gplots' was built under R version 3.4.4
> # Calculate the probability of new observations belonging to each class
> # grade_pred_up_ROC_AUC will be a matrix with dimensions (data_set_size x
number_of_classes)
> grade_pred_up_ROC_AUC <- predict(rf_up5,test_data_new2,type="prob")
> # Use colors for roc curves for the classes (one for each grade measure):
> colors <- c("green","orange","purple","yellow","blue","black","red")
> # Specify the different classes
> ROC_AUC_classes <- levels(test_data2$grade)
> # For each class
> for (i in 1:7)
+ {
+ # Define observations belonging to each class i.e., class[i]
+ Actualgrade_values <- ifelse(test_data2$grade==ROC_AUC_classes[i],1,0)
+ # Assess the performance of classifier for class[i]
+ pred <- prediction(grade_pred_up_ROC_AUC[,i],Actualgrade_values)
+ perf <- performance(pred, "tpr", "fpr")
+     pdf(paste("Random_Forest_up_ROC_Curve_for_",ROC_AUC_classes[i],".pdf"))
+     plot(perf,main=paste("Random Forest up ROC Curve for ",
      ROC_AUC_classes[i]),col=colors[i])
+     dev.off()
+ # Calculate the AUC and print it to screen
+ auc.perf <- performance(pred, measure = "auc")
+ print(paste("Random_Forest_up_AUC for ",ROC_AUC_classes[i],":",auc.perf@y.
values))
+ }
[1] "Random_Forest_up_AUC for  Average : 0.895005286167386"
[1] "Random_Forest_up_AUC for  Excellent : 0.993192648059905"
[1] "Random_Forest_up_AUC for  Good : 0.897973434103432"
[1] "Random_Forest_up_AUC for  Great : 0.887855634864783"
[1] "Random_Forest_up_AUC for  LessThanAvg : 0.876040265775422"
[1] "Random_Forest_up_AUC for  MoreThanAvg : 0.818323251725668"
[1] "Random_Forest_up_AUC for  NotAccept : 0.678907849829351"
> pairs(table(rf_up5_pred, test_data2$grade), main="Wine Quality Classification")
> models2 <- list(original = model_rf, over = rf_up5)
> resampling <- resamples(models2)
> bwplot(resampling)
```

The following points are noteworthy:

- *The feature with greatest importance changed from "alcohol" to "free.sulphur.dioxide."*
- *The confusion matrix shows more less data instances in classes being misclassified as well as having an improved Kappa value of > 65 as compared to that of the original random forest model, which was a little over 60.*
- *The ROC Curves show less overfitting compared to the original model.*
- *The ROC AUC performance is improved compared to the original model.*

Figures 4.19–4.28 show the variable importance plot of the improved model along with the ROC curves for each class and the bwplot comparing the original model with the improved model, taking accuracy and Kappa values into consideration and the pairs plot of the wine quality classification.

As can be seen, the "over" or "up" sampling model has a higher Kappa value than that of the original model.

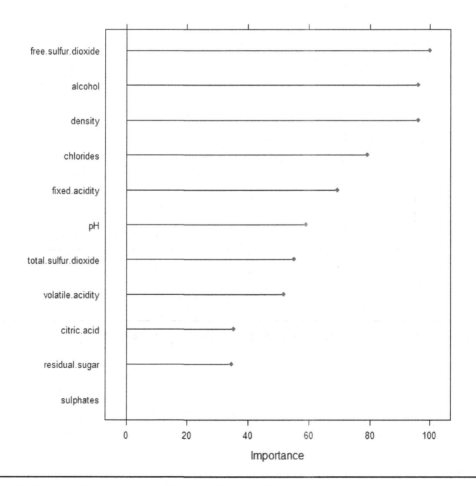

Figure 4.19   Variable importance plot of an improved random forest model.

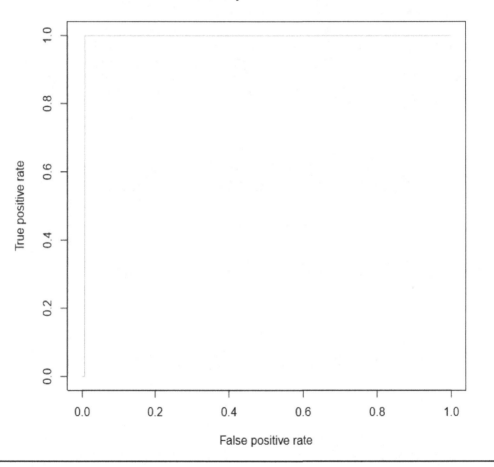

Figure 4.20   Random Forest ROC Curve using "up" sampling for Excellent.

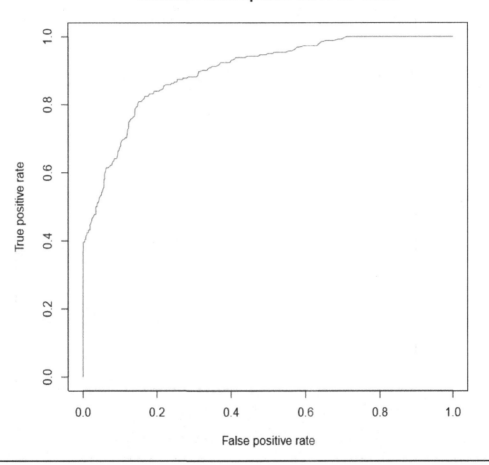

Figure 4.21   Random Forest ROC Curve using "up" sampling for Good.

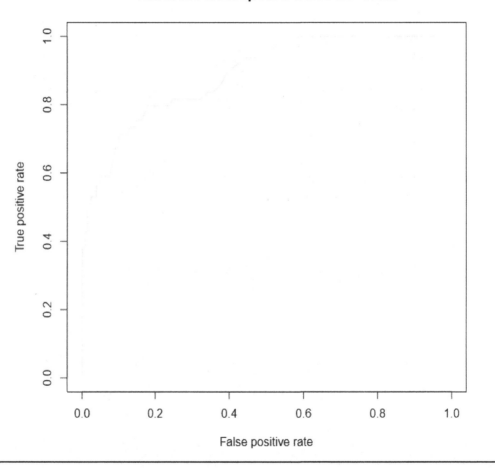

Figure 4.22   Random Forest ROC Curve using "up" sampling for Great.

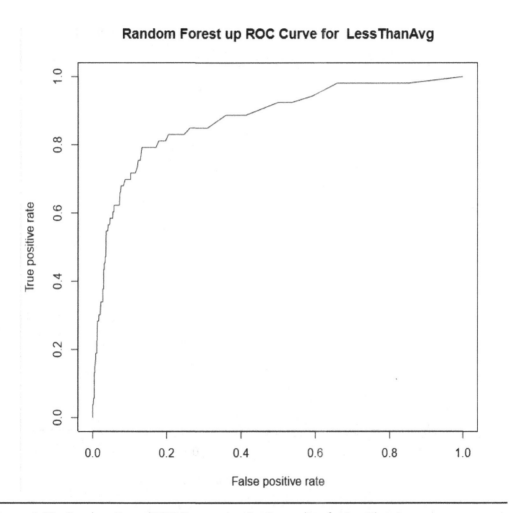

Figure 4.23 Random Forest ROC Curve using "up" sampling for LessThanAvg.

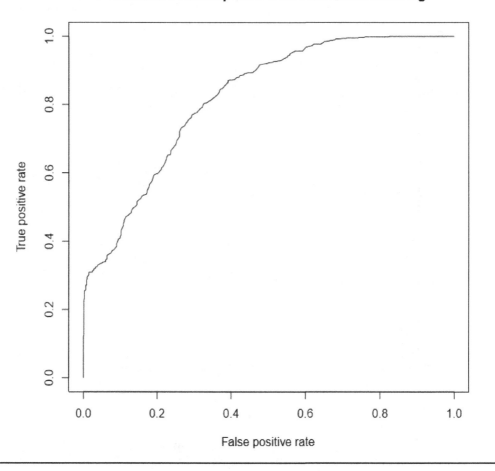

Figure 4.24 Random Forest ROC Curve using "up" sampling for MoreThanAvg.

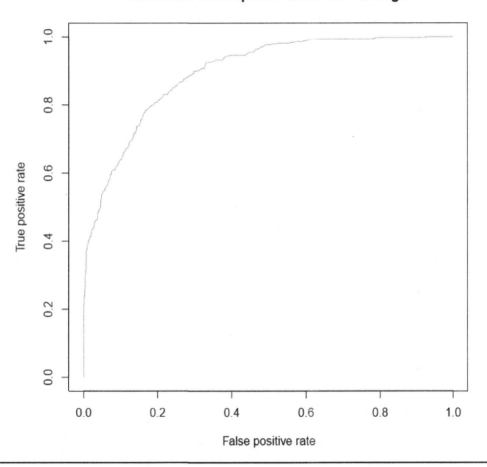

Figure 4.25   Random Forest ROC Curve using "up" sampling for Average.

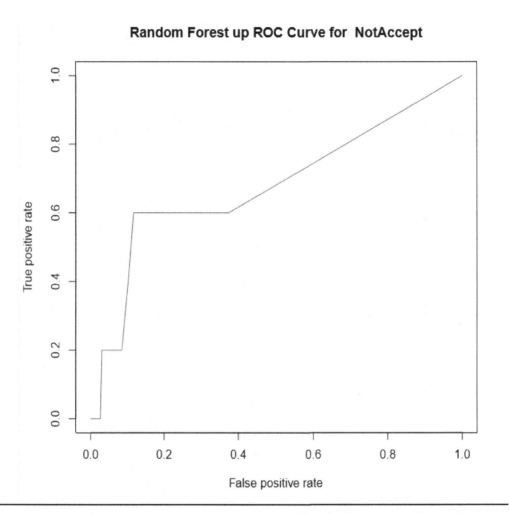

Figure 4.26   Random Forest ROC Curve using "up" sampling for NotAccept.

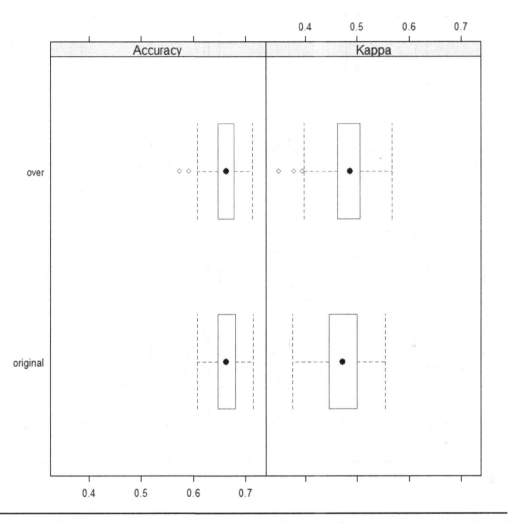

Figure 4.27 Comparison plot of original vs. improved random forest model showing Accuracy and Kappa values.

Wine Quality Classification

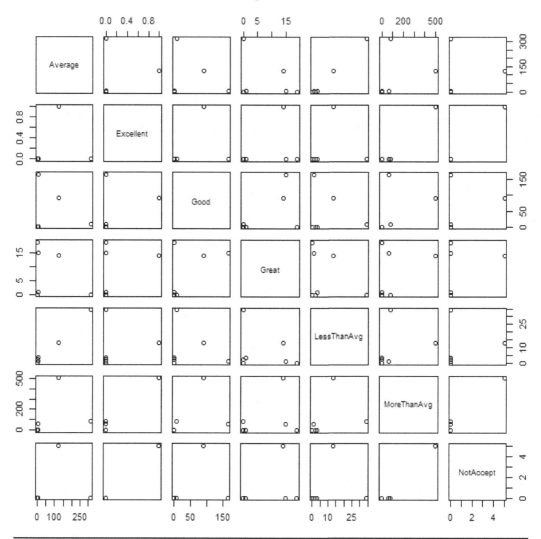

Figure 4.28   Pairs plot of improved random forest model for the Wine Grade Classification.

4.2.2 The BI-Enablement and Its Impact on the Enterprise

As seen from the figures **for both Random Forests and Decision Trees, the most important variable is alcohol for the wine grade classification. This must be kept in mind when conducting a business analysis for the procurement and sale of wines in a competitive market.** Also, the Kappa value accuracy of the classification into the seven classes is better in the case of a random forest implementation as opposed to a decision tree implementation. However, using the "up" sampling technique to improve the classification performance because of unbalanced data in each class in the training set indicates that it suffices to choose as much available data as possible in each class so as to balance the dataset.

4.3 Predicting Commodity Prices in Advance

In this section, we describe a case study in metallurgy by way of predicting precious metal prices based on monthly data available. We start by describing the purpose of the use case from a technical standpoint and then detail the implementation specifics.

4.3.1 The AI-Methodology—Predictive Analytics—Using Neural Networks

4.3.1.1 Purpose of Use Case

- Goal
  To predict precious metal prices. This is one of the primary applications in the metal industry. This enables the bullion rates to be fixed accordingly in various currencies and different parts of the world. It can also be used to study the impact of bullion prices in the market.

- Technology
  AI and ML using deep neural networks (DNNs).

- Implementation
  Using keras library with Tensorflow® framework in R.

- Input Dataset
  Bullion rates at the beginning of each month from 1950 to 2019 in a .csv file having Date and Price as fields.

4.3.1.2 Brief Introduction to Machine Learning–Based Neural and Deep Neural Networks

A neural network, also called an artificial neural network (ANN), is a machine learning (ML)–based algorithm/model/system that mimics the pattern of the human brain and processes and learns from data to solve complex problems. In other words, it is trained by feeding data resulting in knowledge that the system stores and uses while solving problems in context. It is structured as tiers of nodes similar to neurons in the human brain. The more data it is fed, the more it learns and stores the output from one layer to another, resulting in a final output that is an implementation of the solution. Figure 4.29 depicts the structure of an ANN.

A neural network model is as good as the data it learns from.

ANNs are composed of the following components:

1. Input layer nodes (that hold input values).
2. Weights (that get randomly initialized) at model learning time. In AI, the neural network model–based algorithm initializes and randomly assigns the weights without the need to programmatically do so.
3. Intermediate layers, also called hidden layers.
4. A bias term for each node in the intermediate layers and the output layer. The bias is used to shift the output value to the desired optimum output value.
5. Activation functions that trigger each of the intermediate neurons to perform computations. The activation functions accept the weighted sum (i.e., inputs*weights) plus the bias term for each hidden neuron.
6. Optimizers that work to improve the accuracy of the model (during the forward-propagation and computation phases).

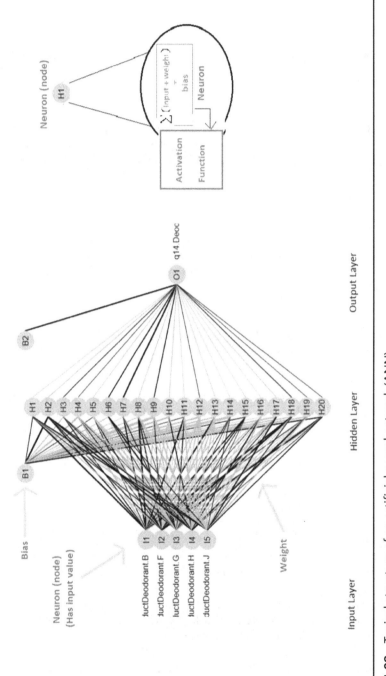

Figure 4.29 Typical structure of an artificial neural network (ANN).

7. Loss functions that are used to minimize the error rate in the learning phase (i.e., build and train, during the back-propagation phase).
8. Output layer (with one or more output neurons). For a regression problem, the output layer has a single node representing a binary value, and for classification problems, it has the number of nodes equal to the number of classes.

Deep neural networks (DNNs) are neural networks that consist of **hidden layer(s) (>1)** between the input and output layer. Figure 4.30 shows a typical DNN.

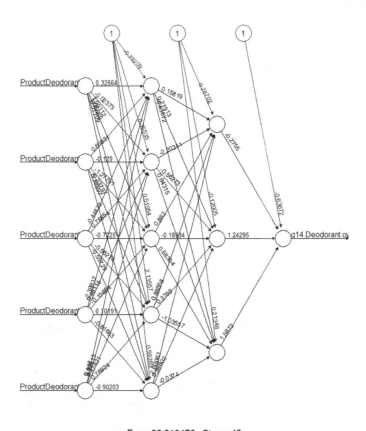

Error: 96.613473   Steps: 45

Figure 4.30   A typical deep neural network (DNN).

Figure 4.30 shows the different phases of the workings of an ANN. The primary phases are as follows:

1. Build and train the model using training data. In this phase, the ANN learns the various features and correlations between the data patterns, as observed in the input. Most importantly, it also extracts the nonlinearities in the data. This involves building, compiling the mode (specifying optimizer and loss functions), and fitting the model using the training and/or validation data in batches. The fitting is done in iterations called *epochs*.
2. Validate the model built using validation data. This is used to verify the trained model on samples of data in steps, to ascertain if it is able to provide the desired output or solution.

3. Score the model on new (or test data). This involves predicting the output (for regression problems) or the classes (for classification problems).
4. K-fold validation on the training and test sets in k-folds (i.e., iterations) to arrive at the optimized accuracy and to minimize loss. This is to measure the predictive performance of the model.

This involves the following:

- Splitting the data into train, test sets
- Building and fitting the model to the train set
- Scoring (predicting) the model on the test set
- Computing the prediction error (MSE or RMSE)
- Repeating the above process for K times
- Computing the average error of performance

Figure 4.31 shows the primary functions of an ANN.

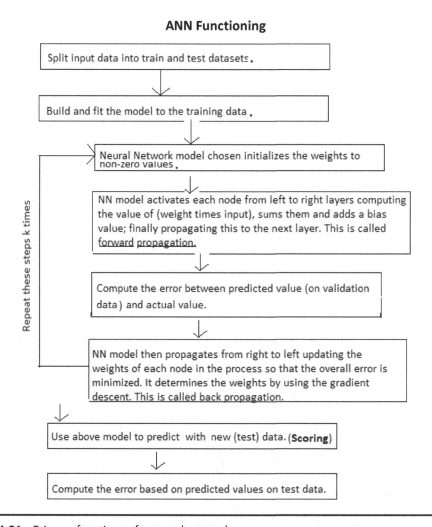

Figure 4.31   Primary functions of a neural network.

When done after the scoring phase using the test data as the dataset and splitting it randomly into train and test sets k times and computing the performance of the model for each fold followed by computing the average performance, k-fold validation gives an idea of how well the performance increased or not.

Listed below are some business applications of deep neural networks:

- Prescriptive analytics—recommending products based on their "user ratings"
- Natural language generation and querying
- Image recognition—as in Facebook™ image tagging
- Weather prediction
- Contextual speech-to-text processing
- Genetic applications

BI can have DNN solutions embedded within its implementation stack to realize competitive results. For example, for predicting weather, the output of a DNN system can be leveraged to forecast an incoming weather pattern such as a storm or snow blast.

4.3.1.3 Implementation Pragmatics

We will be using keras-based deep neural networks in R to implement the model.

- Keras—An open-source machine learning library originally made available in Python® and subsequently written in R.
- Keras is a high-level API that requires only a few lines of code and works on top of a framework called TensorFlow®. It can also use other frameworks such as Theano.
- Using keras, the neural network model is constructed by starting sequentially and adding additional layers on top of it. The model can be built using a training dataset, compiled (using loss function = M(ean)S(quared)E(rror) and optimizer (= "*adam*"—for learning rate)), fit to and evaluated, and then scored on new data.
- Output of recommendation can be visually integrated in BI dashboards for actionable insight (e.g., Tableau® Dashboard, Oracle® BI, Microsoft® BI, etc.)

Here are the steps involved in implementing the model:

- It uses a deep neural network ML model built by training itself based on price in correlation with the year and the first day of each month.
- This use case uses the data from the monthly_csv.csv file to predict the "Price." This file has the date in the format Date, Price, with the Date as the string value "YYYY-MM."
- Prepare the input data and make sure that the inputs are normalized (to ensure better accuracy). We convert the Date string into a date value in the format YYYY-MM-DD with DD, as always as "01"—the first day of each month using the *ymd()* function in the lubridate R library.
- Start with calling the *keras_model_sequential()* initialization function.
- Add a dense layer to establish the connection to the intermediate layers. It takes an input shape and an activation of '*relu*'.
- Add two additional dense layers using activation '*relu*'. These serve as the hidden layers (with 12 and 8 neurons, respectively).

- Add an output layer (with one node) and 'linear' activation that becomes the response "Price" variable. Since we are predicting only one response variable, the "Price," the number of neurons in the output layer is 1 and the activation function is 'softmax', for the float value "Price" (as opposed to a binary value prediction in which the activation function used would be 'sigmoid').
- Fit the data by applying the predicted model output against test data. The predictor variables used are Year, Month, and 1st day of each month, and the response variable used is "Price."
- Score the model on a new (test) dataset to get the predicted "Price."

Structure of Built and Trained Keras-Based DNN

summary(dnnFinal)

Layer (type)	Output Shape	Param #
dense_1 (Dense)	(None, 12)	48
dense_2 (Dense)	(None, 8)	104
dense_3 (Dense)	(None, 1)	9

Total params: 161
Trainable params: 161
Non-trainable params: 0

4.3.1.4 R Program That Implements the DNN

Listing 4.7 shows the R code to implement the model and score it on new data.

Listing 4.7 R Program to Implement DNN for Predicting Precious Metal Prices

```
setwd("<directory-name>")
dataset <- read.csv("monthly_csv.csv")
library(tidyverse)
library(keras)
library(lubridate)
date1 <- paste0(dataset[, 1],"-01")
date1.date <- ymd(date1)
date1.date.df <- as.data.frame(date1.date)
head(date1.date.df)
df_with_DateVal <- cbind(date1.date.df, dataset[, 2])
colnames(df_with_DateVal) <- c("Date", "Price")
df_with_DateVal$Year <- as.numeric(substr(as.character(df_with_DateVal[, 1]),0,4))
df_with_DateVal$Month <- as.numeric(substr(as.character(df_with_DateVal[, 1]),6,7))
df_with_DateVal$Day <- as.numeric(substr(as.character(df_with_DateVal[, 1]),9, 10))
head(cbind(df_with_DateVal$Date, df_with_DateVal$Year, df_with_DateVal$Month, df_
with_DateVal$Day, df_with_DateVal$Price))
head(df_with_DateVal)
dfFinal <- df_with_DateVal[, c(1, 3:5,2)]
head(dfFinal)
```

```
maxminnorm <- function(x) {
return ((x-min(x)) / (max(x) - min(x))) }

scaleddfFinal <- as.data.frame(lapply(dfFinal[, c(2,3,5)], maxminnorm))
head(scaleddfFinal)
attach(scaleddfFinal)
train_index <- sample(1:nrow(scaleddfFinal), 0.8 * nrow(scaleddfFinal))
test_index <- setdiff(1:nrow(scaleddfFinal), train_index)
X_train <- as.matrix(scaleddfFinal[train_index, -15])
y_train <- as.matrix(scaleddfFinal[train_index, "Price"])
X_test <- as.matrix(scaleddfFinal[test_index, -15])
y_test <- as.matrix(scaleddfFinal[test_index, "Price"])
dnnFinal <- keras_model_sequential()
dnnFinal %>%
layer_dense(units = 12, activation = 'relu',
kernel_initializer='RandomNormal',
input_shape = c(3)) %>%
layer_dense(units = 8, activation = 'relu') %>%
layer_dense(units = 1, activation = 'linear')
summary(dnnFinal)
dnnFinal %>% compile(
loss = 'mean_squared_error',
optimizer = 'adam',
metrics = c('mae')
)
dnnFinal.fit <- dnnFinal %>% fit(
X_train, y_train,
epochs = 150, batch_size = 50,
validation_split = 0.2
)
dnnFinal %>% evaluate(X_test, y_test)
$loss
$mean_absolute_error
dnnFinal.pred <- data.frame(y = predict(dnnFinal, as.matrix(X_test)))
dfFinal2 <-data.frame(dnnFinal.pred,X_test)
attach(dfFinal2)
dfFinal2$y[1]
X_test.df <- as.data.frame(X_test)
y_test.df <- as.data.frame(y_test)
dfFinal2$y[1]
dfFinal2$Price[1]
dfFinal2$y[1] - dfFinal2$Price[1]
dfFinal2$Year[1]
dfFinal2$Month[1]
head(dfFinal2)
plot(dfFinal2$Price, dfFinal2$y, col='green',
```

```
main='Actual vs. Predicted Price using DNN (keras)',
xlab='dfFinal2$Price (Actual)', ylab='dfFinal2$y (Predicted)',
pch=20,cex=1)
abline(0,1,lwd=0.5)
legend('bottomright',legend='Actual vs. Predicted Price - DNN (keras)',pch=20,
col='green',bty='n')

pred_price<- dfFinal2$y*(max(dfFinal$Price) - min(dfFinal$Price))+min(dfFinal$Price)
actual_price <- dfFinal2$Price*(max(dfFinal$Price) - min(dfFinal$Price))+min(dfFinal$Price)
MSE.nn <- sum((actual_price-pred_price)^2)/nrow(X_test)
MSE.nn
[1] 1.571772
plot(actual_price, pred_price, col='green',
main='Actual vs. Predicted Price
using DNN (keras)',
xlab='actual_price (Actual)', ylab='pred_price (Predicted)',
pch=20,cex=1)
abline(0,1,lwd=0.5)
legend('bottomright',legend='Actual vs. Predicted Price - DNN (keras)'
,pch=20,col='green',bty='n')

# Comparing pred with y_test or the Price response variable
dfFinal4 <- data.frame(dnnFinal.pred,y_test)
dfFinal4$y[1]
head(dfFinal4)
pred_price<- dfFinal4$y*(max(dfFinal$Price) - min(dfFinal$Price))+min(dfFinal$Price)
y_test[1]
# [1] 0.0001374446
actual_price <- y_test*(max(dfFinal$Price) - min(dfFinal$Price))+min(dfFinal$Price)
plot(actual_price, pred_price, col='green',
main='Actual vs. Predicted Price
using DNN (keras)',
xlab='actual_price (Actual)',
ylab='pred_price (Predicted)',
pch=20,cex=1)
abline(0,1,lwd=0.5)
legend('bottomright',legend='Actual vs. Predicted Price - DNN (keras)',pch=20,
col='green',bty='n')
MSE1 <- sum((actual_price-pred_price)^2)/nrow(y_test)
MSE1
# [1] 0.16877
MSE2 <- sum((actual_price-pred_price)^2)/nrow(X_test)
MSE2
# [1] 0.16877
```

Figure 4.32 provides the R plot of the actual vs. predicted value of price.

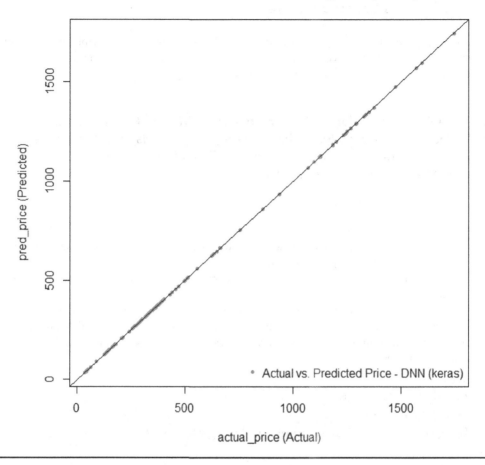

Figure 4.32   Fitted DNN plot—Actual vs. Predicted Price.

4.3.2 The BI-Enablement and Its Impact on the Enterprise

4.3.2.1 Recommendation Analysis from an AI Meets BI Standpoint

Figure 4.32 suggests the accuracy of fitted DNN, showing the actual versus predicted product price with a MSE of 0.16. On the basis of the fitted DNN plot integrated into a BI platform, enterprises can conduct an analysis to determine optimal prices for salability and related business process analytics.

4.3.2.2 Deduction for the BI Analyst

Figure 4.32 shows that the newly predicted price aligns along the line of best fit and, hence, almost closely with true (actual) price. Although there is some overfitting, this means that the model can generalize on new data, especially larger datasets, thereby improving the accuracy of the price predictions.

This allows the bullion rates to be fixed in various currencies in different parts of the world. This suggests that the model is quite accurate and can be used to study the impact of bullion prices in the market.

4.4 Recommender Systems to Suggest Optimal Choices Based on Score

In this section, we present a case of prescriptive analytics by recommending viable product sources based on score prediction, followed by predicting "how the product fares in the market" based on the recommended choices—a case of predictive analytics, both using DNNs.

4.4.1 The AI-Methodology—Prescriptive Analytics by Recommending Viable Sources Based on Score Prediction (using DNNs) and Predictive Analytics by Predicting "How the Product Fares in the Market" Based on the Recommended Choices

4.4.1.1 Purpose of Use Case

- Goal
  Part 1—Recommending viable products based on the ranking of each product on a scale from 1 to 10—a prescriptive analytics **solution.**
  Part 2—Predicting how the recommended product fares in the market based on its "likes"—**a** predictive analytics **solution.**
  Predictive and prescriptive analytics constitute one of the primary applications of AI in real life and are used in various industries wherever products such as retail, financial (financial instruments, etc.), entertainment (movies, television series, etc.), and many more are a subject of business or BI interest.

- Technology
  AI and ML using deep neural networks (DNNs).

- Implementation
  Using *neuralnet()* library and visualization library *ggplot2()* in R.

- Input Dataset
  The input dataset is a Kaggle dataset consisting of five deodorants and their various attributes and customer-usage based ranking. Source data for training is in the file Data_train_reduced. csv, which is available online. Test data for scoring and predicting the scale is in the file test_data. csv, also available online (https://www.kaggle.com/ramkumar/deodorant-instant-liking-data/).

4.4.1.2 Implementation Pragmatics

Here are the primary steps involved for Parts 1 and 2 as stated in the purpose of the use case above:

- Recommending viable products based on their ranking on a scale from 1 to 10 deals with first predicting scale analyzing the data based on Product as a primary predictor.
- The products having the highest scale are output as the recommended ones.
- Scale is predicted by using a deep neural network and then using the value to determine the outcome and recommend that product.
- For prescriptive analytics this enables to recommend viable products for maximizing sales.
- Taking a step further we predict how the product fares in the market based on the recommended product (predictive analytics).

Further pragmatics can be defined by way of cognition and recommend the "optimal" product for maximizing sales and thereby boosting competition. This introduces "cognition" into the model and trains it using a cognitive computing–based recommender model for decision making in terms of outputting the "most optimal product" to be used—as well as "comprehend" why the particular source is optimal to be used (i.e., the next best action)—from decision support to decision making.

The following two sections describe the implementation details of prescriptive and predictive analytics solutions.

4.4.1.3 Prescriptive Analytics Solution

As stated earlier, this consists of predicting Product score on a scale of 1 to 10 based on Product—building an AI-based deep neural network model using R-based *neuralnet()*. Here are the steps involved:

- This uses the data from the Data_train_reduced.csv file to predict the "q14.Deodorant.overall. on.a.scale.from.1.to.10" and based on its value to recommend the Products.
- It uses a deep neural network ML model built by training itself based on data correlating five products with each of their scale.
- It then predicts the scale on test data and, based on the value, recommends that Product.
- A DNN with one input layer with five input nodes (neurons), two middle (hidden) layers (with five and three nodes, respectively) and an output layer (with one node) is built and trained.
- It then fits the data by applying the predicted model output against each of the five Products. The predictor variable used is 'Product', and the response variable used is scale.

The prescriptive analytics solution is implemented by using R *neuralnet()* model to build and train the DNN and then using the *compute()* function to predict the output and use it for recommendation. The plot of fitted DNN for prescriptive analytics is shown in Figure 4.33.

Listings 4.8 and 4.9 give the R code and its output for this solution.

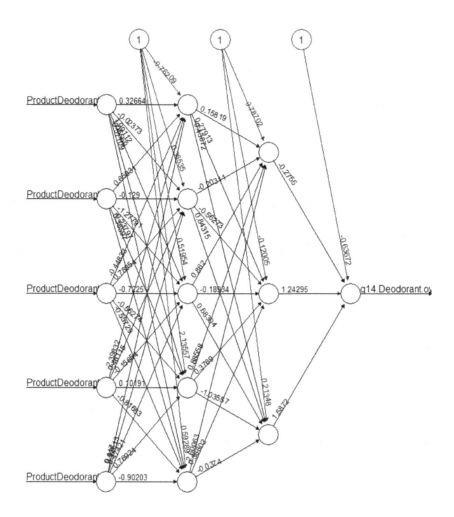

Error: 96.613473   Steps: 45

Figure 4.33   Plot of DNN for Prescriptive Analytics

Listing 4.8 R code Prescriptive Analytics Solution

```
setwd("<directory-name>")
product_data <- read.csv("Data_train_reduced.csv")
names(product_data)
test_data <- read.csv("<directory-name>test_data.csv")
names(test_data)
nrow(product_data)
nrow(test_data)
head(product_data)
product_dataF <- product_data[, c(1:3,5:37,39,42:44,47:64)]
Product.matrix <-model.matrix( ~Product - 1, data = product_dataF)
product_dataF <- data.frame(product_dataF, Product.matrix)
```

```
head(product_dataF)
ncol(product_dataF)
maxs <- apply(product_dataF[, c(1:2,4:58)], 2, max)
mins <- apply(product_dataF[, c(1:2,4:58)], 2, min)
scaled <- as.data.frame(scale(product_dataF[, c(1:2,4:58)], center = mins, scale =
maxs - mins))
scaledF <- as.data.frame(cbind(scaled, product_dataF[, c(59:63)]))
set.seed(500)
library(neuralnet)
library(ggplot2)
head(scaledF) # had some NA and NaN
scaledFF <- scaledF[, c(1:32,34:35,37,39:40,42:48,50:62)]
head(scaledFF)
ncol(scaledFF) # 57 # 43rd column is scale1.to.10
scaledFF <- scaledFF[, c(1:42,44:57,43)]
ncol(scaledFF) #57
head(scaledFF) # last column (57th) is scale1.to.10
n <- names(scaledFF)
f <- as.formula(q14.Deodorant.overall.on.a.scale.from.1.to.10 ~ ProductDeodorant.B +
 + ProductDeodorant.F + ProductDeodorant.G + ProductDeodorant.H +
 + ProductDeodorant.J)
f
DNNf3 <- neuralnet(f, data = scaledFF, hidden=c(5,3), linear.output=TRUE)
plot(DNNf3)
ncol(scaledFF) # 57
head(test_data)
nrow(test_data)
test.Product.matrix <-model.matrix( ~Product - 1, data = test_data)
test_dataF <- data.frame(test_data, test.Product.matrix)
ncol(test_dataF) # 63
head(test_dataF)
maxs <- apply(test_dataF[, c(1:2,4:58)], 2, max)
mins <- apply(test_dataF[, c(1:2,4:58)], 2, min)
scaledTest <- as.data.frame(scale(test_dataF[,c(1:2, 4:58)], center = mins, scale =
maxs - mins))
set.seed(500)
n1 <- names(scaledTest)
head(scaledTest)
ncol(scaledTest) # 57
scaledTestF <- as.data.frame(cbind(scaledTest, test_dataF[, c(59:63)]))
ncol(scaledTestF)
scaledTestFF <- scaledTestF[, c(1:32, 34:35, 37,39:40,42:48,50:57,58:62)]
ncol(scaledTestFF)
n2 <- names(scaledTestFF)
head(test_data)
head(scaledTestFF)
pr.DNNf3 <- compute(DNNf3, scaledTestFF[, c(53:57)])
```

```
pr.DNNf3_r <- pr.DNNf3$net.result*(max(test_data$q14.Deodorant.overall.
on.a.scale.from.1.to.10)-min(test_data$q14.Deodorant.overall.on.a.scale.
from.1.to.10))+min(test_data$q14.Deodorant.overall.on.a.scale.from.1.to.10)

test_data_r <- (scaledTestFF$q14.Deodorant.overall.on.a.scale.
from.1.to.10)*(max(test_data$q14.Deodorant.overall.on.a.scale.from.1.to.10)-
min(test_data$q14.Deodorant.overall.on.a.scale.from.1.to.10))+min(test_data$q14.
Deodorant.overall.on.a.scale.from.1.to.10)

MSE.DNNf3 <- sum((test_data_r - pr.DNNf3_r)^2)/nrow(scaledTestFF)

MSE.DNNf3

# [1] 6.400654791

plot(test_data$q14.Deodorant.overall.on.a.scale.from.1.to.10, pr.DNNf3_r,col='red',
main='Actual vs predicted DNN',pch=18,cex=0.7)

abline(0,1,lwd=2)

legend('bottomright',legend='DNN',pch=18,col='red',bty='n')

pr.DNNf3_r2 <- pr.DNNf3$net.result

pdf(" Plots ProductDeodorants vs Predicted.pdf")

plot(test_dataF$ProductDeodorant.B, pr.DNNf3_r2, col='green',main='Product
Deodorant B vs Predicted', xlab='Product Deodorant B',pch=18,cex=2)

abline(0,1,lwd=2)

legend('bottom',legend='Product Deodorant B vs Predicted',pch=2,col='green',bty='n')

plot(test_dataF$ProductDeodorant.F, pr.DNNf3_r2, col='green',main='Product
Deodorant F vs Predicted', xlab='Product Deodorant F',pch=18,cex=2)

abline(0,1,lwd=2)

legend('bottom',legend='Product Deodorant F vs Predicted',pch=2,col='green',bty='n')

plot(test_dataF$ProductDeodorant.G, pr.DNNf3_r2, col='green',main='Product
Deodorant G vs Predicted', xlab='Product Deodorant G',pch=18,cex=2)

abline(0,1,lwd=2)

legend('bottom',legend='Product Deodorant G vs Predicted',pch=2,col='green',bty='n')

plot(test_dataF$ProductDeodorant.H, pr.DNNf3_r2, col='green',main='Product Deodorant
H vs Predicted', xlab='Product Deodorant H',pch=18,cex=2)

abline(0,1,lwd=2)

legend('bottom',legend='Product Deodorant H vs Predicted',pch=2,col='green',bty='n')

plot(test_dataF$ProductDeodorant.J, pr.DNNf3_r2, col='green',main='Product Deodorant
J vs Predicted', xlab='Product Deodorant J',pch=18,cex=2)

abline(0,1,lwd=2)

legend('bottom',legend='Product Deodorant J vs Predicted',pch=2,col='green',bty='n')

dev.off()
```

Listing 4.9 Output of R Code in Listing 4.8

```
> setwd("<directory-name>")
> product_data <- read.csv("Data_train_reduced.csv")
> names(product_data)
 [1] "Respondent.ID"
 [2] "Product.ID"
 [3] "Product"
 [4] "Instant.Liking"
 [5] "q1_1.personal.opinion.of.this.Deodorant"
```

```
 [6]  "q2_all.words"
 [7]  "q3_1.strength.of.the.Deodorant"
 [8]  "q4_1.artificial.chemical"
 [9]  "q4_2.attractive"
[10]  "q4_3.bold"
[11]  "q4_4.boring"
[12]  "q4_5.casual"
[13]  "q4_6.cheap"
[14]  "q4_7.clean"
[15]  "q4_8.easy.to.wear"
[16]  "q4_9.elegant"
[17]  "q4_10.feminine"
[18]  "q4_11.for.someone.like.me"
[19]  "q4_12.heavy"
[20]  "q4_13.high.quality"
[21]  "q4_14.long.lasting"
[22]  "q4_15.masculine"
[23]  "q4_16.memorable"
[24]  "q4_17.natural"
[25]  "q4_18.old.fashioned"
[26]  "q4_19.ordinary"
[27]  "q4_20.overpowering"
[28]  "q4_21.sharp"
[29]  "q4_22.sophisticated"
[30]  "q4_23.upscale"
[31]  "q4_24.well.rounded"
[32]  "q5_1.Deodorant.is.addictive"
[33]  "q7"
[34]  "q8.1"
[35]  "q8.2"
[36]  "q8.5"
[37]  "q8.6"
[38]  "q8.7"
[39]  "q8.8"
[40]  "q8.9"
[41]  "q8.10"
[42]  "q8.11"
[43]  "q8.12"
[44]  "q8.13"
[45]  "q8.17"
[46]  "q8.18"
[47]  "q8.19"
[48]  "q8.20"
[49]  "q9.how.likely.would.you.be.to.purchase.this.Deodorant"
[50]  "q10.prefer.this.Deodorant.or.your.usual.Deodorant"
[51]  "q11.time.of.day.would.this.Deodorant.be.appropriate"
```

```
[52] "q12.which.occasions.would.this.Deodorant.be.appropriate"
[53] "Q13_Liking.after.30.minutes"
[54] "q14.Deodorant.overall.on.a.scale.from.1.to.10"
[55] "ValSegb"
[56] "s7.involved.in.the.selection.of.the.cosmetic.products"
[57] "s8.ethnic.background"
[58] "s9.education"
[59] "s10.income"
[60] "s11.marital.status"
[61] "s12.working.status"
[62] "s13.2"
[63] "s13a.b.most.often"
[64] "s13b.bottles.of.Deodorant.do.you.currently.own"
> test_data <- read.csv("<directory-name>test_data.csv")
> names(test_data)
 [1] "Respondent.ID"
 [2] "Product.ID"
 [3] "Product"
 [4] "q1_1.personal.opinion.of.this.Deodorant"
 [5] "q2_all.words"
 [6] "q3_1.strength.of.the.Deodorant"
 [7] "q4_1.artificial.chemical"
 [8] "q4_2.attractive"
 [9] "q4_3.bold"
[10] "q4_4.boring"
[11] "q4_5.casual"
[12] "q4_6.cheap"
[13] "q4_7.clean"
[14] "q4_8.easy.to.wear"
[15] "q4_9.elegant"
[16] "q4_10.feminine"
[17] "q4_11.for.someone.like.me"
[18] "q4_12.heavy"
[19] "q4_13.high.quality"
[20] "q4_14.long.lasting"
[21] "q4_15.masculine"
[22] "q4_16.memorable"
[23] "q4_17.natural"
[24] "q4_18.old.fashioned"
[25] "q4_19.ordinary"
[26] "q4_20.overpowering"
[27] "q4_21.sharp"
[28] "q4_22.sophisticated"
[29] "q4_23.upscale"
[30] "q4_24.well.rounded"
[31] "q5_1.Deodorant.is.addictive"
```

```
[32] "q7"
[33] "q8.1"
[34] "q8.2"
[35] "q8.5"
[36] "q8.6"
[37] "q8.8"
[38] "q8.11"
[39] "q8.12"
[40] "q8.13"
[41] "q8.19"
[42] "q8.20"
[43] "q9.how.likely.would.you.be.to.purchase.this.Deodorant"
[44] "q10.prefer.this.Deodorant.or.your.usual.Deodorant"
[45] "q11.time.of.day.would.this.Deodorant.be.appropriate"
[46] "q12.which.occasions.would.this.Deodorant.be.appropriate"
[47] "Q13_Liking.after.30.minutes"
[48] "q14.Deodorant.overall.on.a.scale.from.1.to.10"
[49] "ValSegb"
[50] "s7.involved.in.the.selection.of.the.cosmetic.products"
[51] "s8.ethnic.background"
[52] "s9.education"
[53] "s10.income"
[54] "s11.marital.status"
[55] "s12.working.status"
[56] "s13.2"
[57] "s13a.b.most.often"
[58] "s13b.bottles.of.Deodorant.do.you.currently.own"
> nrow(product_data)
[1] 2500
> nrow(test_data)
[1] 5105
> head(product_data)
  Respondent.ID Product.ID    Product Instant.Liking
1          3800        121 Deodorant B              1
2          3801        121 Deodorant B              0
3          3802        121 Deodorant B              0
4          3803        121 Deodorant B              1
5          3804        121 Deodorant B              1
6          3805        121 Deodorant B              0
  q1_1.personal.opinion.of.this.Deodorant q2_all.words
1                                       4            1
2                                       5            1
3                                       6            1
4                                       4            0
5                                       4            1
6                                       5            1
```

	q3_1.strength.of.the.Deodorant	q4_1.artificial.chemical	q4_2.attractive
1	4	2	5
2	4	4	2
3	3	2	5
4	4	5	5
5	2	1	3
6	5	5	5

	q4_3.bold	q4_4.boring	q4_5.casual	q4_6.cheap	q4_7.clean	q4_8.easy.to.wear
1	4	2	3	5	5	5
2	2	1	3	2	4	4
3	2	4	2	4	3	5
4	4	3	5	2	5	3
5	1	1	3	3	5	3
6	2	1	4	5	5	2

	q4_9.elegant	q4_10.feminine	q4_11.for.someone.like.me	q4_12.heavy
1	4	5	3	1
2	4	3	1	1
3	4	4	4	3
4	5	5	5	1
5	5	5	5	1
6	4	4	3	2

	q4_13.high.quality	q4_14.long.lasting	q4_15.masculine	q4_16.memorable
1	5	1	2	4
2	3	4	4	5
3	1	2	1	4
4	4	3	3	5
5	4	4	2	3
6	4	5	2	3

	q4_17.natural	q4_18.old.fashioned	q4_19.ordinary	q4_20.overpowering
1	5	4	5	1
2	3	3	4	2
3	2	4	3	2
4	5	4	2	5
5	5	1	2	4
6	4	2	2	3

	q4_21.sharp	q4_22.sophisticated	q4_23.upscale	q4_24.well.rounded
1	1	4	1	4
2	2	5	4	4
3	5	4	4	3
4	3	3	5	4
5	2	3	1	5
6	1	5	5	4

	q5_1.Deodorant.is.addictive	q7	q8.1	q8.2	q8.5	q8.6	q8.7	q8.8	q8.9	q8.10	q8.11
1	1	1	0	0	0	0	NA	1	NA	NA	0
2	4	4	0	0	0	1	NA	0	NA	NA	0
3	4	3	0	0	0	0	NA	0	NA	NA	0

4					4	3	0	0	0	0	NA	0	NA	NA	0
5					3	2	0	0	0	0	NA	0	NA	NA	0
6					1	3	0	0	0	0	NA	0	NA	NA	0

	q8.12	q8.13	q8.17	q8.18	q8.19	q8.20
1	0	0	NA	NA	0	0
2	0	0	NA	NA	0	0
3	0	0	NA	NA	0	0
4	0	0	NA	NA	0	0
5	0	0	NA	NA	0	0
6	0	0	NA	NA	0	0

	q9.how.likely.would.you.be.to.purchase.this.Deodorant
1	2
2	3
3	5
4	5
5	5
6	5

	q10.prefer.this.Deodorant.or.your.usual.Deodorant
1	1
2	5
3	1
4	4
5	3
6	4

	q11.time.of.day.would.this.Deodorant.be.appropriate
1	1
2	3
3	3
4	1
5	3
6	2

	q12.which.occasions.would.this.Deodorant.be.appropriate
1	2
2	3
3	3
4	3
5	2
6	2

	Q13_Liking.after.30.minutes	q14.Deodorant.overall.on.a.scale.from.1.to.10
1	1	7
2	3	8
3	2	5
4	6	8
5	5	4
6	6	7

```
    ValSegb s7.involved.in.the.selection.of.the.cosmetic.products
1      7                                                         4
2      6                                                         4
3      7                                                         4
4      1                                                         4
5      4                                                         4
6      7                                                         4
    s8.ethnic.background s9.education s10.income s11.marital.status
1                      1            4          3                  1
2                      1            4          3                  1
3                      1            3          5                  1
4                      1            4          9                  1
5                      1            3          5                  1
6                      1            4          5                  2
    s12.working.status s13.2 s13a.b.most.often
1                    1     0                  0
2                    1     0                  0
3                    1     0                  0
4                    3     0                  0
5                    2     0                  0
6                    2     0                  0
    s13b.bottles.of.Deodorant.do.you.currently.own
1                                             3
2                                             4
3                                             2
4                                             3
5                                             3
6                                             2
> product_dataF <- product_data[, c(1:3,5:37,39,42:44,47:64)]
> Product.matrix <-model.matrix( ~Product - 1, data = product_dataF)
> product_dataF <- data.frame(product_dataF, Product.matrix)
> head(product_dataF)
  Respondent.ID Product.ID    Product q1_1.personal.opinion.of.this.Deodorant
1          3800        121 Deodorant B                                      4
2          3801        121 Deodorant B                                      5
3          3802        121 Deodorant B                                      6
4          3803        121 Deodorant B                                      4
5          3804        121 Deodorant B                                      4
6          3805        121 Deodorant B                                      5
   q2_all.words q3_1.strength.of.the.Deodorant q4_1.artificial.chemical
1             1                              4                        2
2             1                              4                        4
3             1                              3                        2
4             0                              4                        5
5             1                              2                        1
6             1                              5                        5
```

	q4_2.attractive	q4_3.bold	q4_4.boring	q4_5.casual	q4_6.cheap	q4_7.clean
1	5	4	2	3	5	5
2	2	2	1	3	2	4
3	5	2	4	2	4	3
4	5	4	3	5	2	5
5	3	1	1	3	3	5
6	5	2	1	4	5	5

	q4_8.easy.to.wear	q4_9.elegant	q4_10.feminine	q4_11.for.someone.like.me
1	5	4	5	3
2	4	4	3	1
3	5	4	4	4
4	3	5	5	5
5	3	5	5	5
6	2	4	4	3

	q4_12.heavy	q4_13.high.quality	q4_14.long.lasting	q4_15.masculine
1	1	5	1	2
2	1	3	4	4
3	3	1	2	1
4	1	4	3	3
5	1	4	4	2
6	2	4	5	2

	q4_16.memorable	q4_17.natural	q4_18.old.fashioned	q4_19.ordinary
1	4	5	4	5
2	5	3	3	4
3	4	2	4	3
4	5	5	4	2
5	3	5	1	2
6	3	4	2	2

	q4_20.overpowering	q4_21.sharp	q4_22.sophisticated	q4_23.upscale
1	1	1	4	1
2	2	2	5	4
3	2	5	4	4
4	5	3	3	5
5	4	2	3	1
6	3	1	5	5

	q4_24.well.rounded	q5_1.Deodorant.is.addictive	q7	q8.1	q8.2	q8.5	q8.6	q8.8
1	4	1	1	0	0	0	0	1
2	4	4	4	0	0	0	1	0
3	3	4	3	0	0	0	0	0
4	4	4	3	0	0	0	0	0
5	5	3	2	0	0	0	0	0
6	4	1	3	0	0	0	0	0

	q8.11	q8.12	q8.13	q8.19	q8.20
1	0	0	0	0	0
2	0	0	0	0	0
3	0	0	0	0	0

4	0	0	0	0	0
5	0	0	0	0	0
6	0	0	0	0	0

q9.how.likely.would.you.be.to.purchase.this.Deodorant

1	2
2	3
3	5
4	5
5	5
6	5

q10.prefer.this.Deodorant.or.your.usual.Deodorant

1	1
2	5
3	1
4	4
5	3
6	4

q11.time.of.day.would.this.Deodorant.be.appropriate

1	1
2	3
3	3
4	1
5	3
6	2

q12.which.occasions.would.this.Deodorant.be.appropriate

1	2
2	3
3	3
4	3
5	2
6	2

	Q13_Liking.after.30.minutes	q14.Deodorant.overall.on.a.scale.from.1.to.10
1	1	7
2	3	8
3	2	5
4	6	8
5	5	4
6	6	7

	ValSegb	s7.involved.in.the.selection.of.the.cosmetic.products
1	7	4
2	6	4
3	7	4
4	1	4
5	4	4
6	7	4

```
   s8.ethnic.background s9.education s10.income s11.marital.status
1                     1           4         3                  1
2                     1           4         3                  1
3                     1           3         5                  1
4                     1           4         9                  1
5                     1           3         5                  1
6                     1           4         5                  2
  s12.working.status s13.2 s13a.b.most.often
1                  1     0                  0
2                  1     0                  0
3                  1     0                  0
4                  3     0                  0
5                  2     0                  0
6                  2     0                  0
  s13b.bottles.of.Deodorant.do.you.currently.own ProductDeodorant.B
1                                               3                  1
2                                               4                  1
3                                               2                  1
4                                               3                  1
5                                               3                  1
6                                               2                  1
  ProductDeodorant.F ProductDeodorant.G ProductDeodorant.H ProductDeodorant.J
1                  0                  0                  0                  0
2                  0                  0                  0                  0
3                  0                  0                  0                  0
4                  0                  0                  0                  0
5                  0                  0                  0                  0
6                  0                  0                  0                  0
> ncol(product_dataF)
[1] 63
> maxs <- apply(product_dataF[, c(1:2,4:58)], 2, max)
> mins <- apply(product_dataF[, c(1:2,4:58)], 2, min)
> scaled <- as.data.frame(scale(product_dataF[, c(1:2,4:58)], center = mins, scale
= maxs - mins))
> scaledF <- as.data.frame(cbind(scaled, product_dataF[, c(59:63)]))
> set.seed(500)
> library(neuralnet)
Warning message:
package 'neuralnet' was built under R version 3.5.0
> library(ggplot2)
Warning message:
package 'ggplot2' was built under R version 3.4.4
> head(scaledF) # had some NA and NaN
  Respondent.ID Product.ID q1_1.personal.opinion.of.this.Deodorant q2_all.words
1  0.000000e+00          0                               0.5000000          0.2
2  9.709681e-05          0                               0.6666667          0.2
3  1.941936e-04          0                               0.8333333          0.2
```

4	2.912904e-04	0	0.5000000	0.0
5	3.883872e-04	0	0.5000000	0.2
6	4.854840e-04	0	0.6666667	0.2

	q3_1.strength.of.the.Deodorant	q4_1.artificial.chemical	q4_2.attractive
1	0.75	0.25	1.00
2	0.75	0.75	0.25
3	0.50	0.25	1.00
4	0.75	1.00	1.00
5	0.25	0.00	0.50
6	1.00	1.00	1.00

	q4_3.bold	q4_4.boring	q4_5.casual	q4_6.cheap	q4_7.clean	q4_8.easy.to.wear
1	0.75	0.25	0.50	1.00	1.00	1.00
2	0.25	0.00	0.50	0.25	0.75	0.75
3	0.25	0.75	0.25	0.75	0.50	1.00
4	0.75	0.50	1.00	0.25	1.00	0.50
5	0.00	0.00	0.50	0.50	1.00	0.50
6	0.25	0.00	0.75	1.00	1.00	0.25

	q4_9.elegant	q4_10.feminine	q4_11.for.someone.like.me	q4_12.heavy
1	0.75	1.00	0.50	0.00
2	0.75	0.50	0.00	0.00
3	0.75	0.75	0.75	0.50
4	1.00	1.00	1.00	0.00
5	1.00	1.00	1.00	0.00
6	0.75	0.75	0.50	0.25

	q4_13.high.quality	q4_14.long.lasting	q4_15.masculine	q4_16.memorable
1	1.00	0.00	0.25	0.75
2	0.50	0.75	0.75	1.00
3	0.00	0.25	0.00	0.75
4	0.75	0.50	0.50	1.00
5	0.75	0.75	0.25	0.50
6	0.75	1.00	0.25	0.50

	q4_17.natural	q4_18.old.fashioned	q4_19.ordinary	q4_20.overpowering
1	1.00	0.75	1.00	0.00
2	0.50	0.50	0.75	0.25
3	0.25	0.75	0.50	0.25
4	1.00	0.75	0.25	1.00
5	1.00	0.00	0.25	0.75
6	0.75	0.25	0.25	0.50

	q4_21.sharp	q4_22.sophisticated	q4_23.upscale	q4_24.well.rounded
1	0.00	0.75	0.00	0.75
2	0.25	1.00	0.75	0.75
3	1.00	0.75	0.75	0.50
4	0.50	0.50	1.00	0.75
5	0.25	0.50	0.00	1.00
6	0.00	1.00	1.00	0.75

```
   q5_1.Deodorant.is.addictive       q7 q8.1 q8.2 q8.5 q8.6 q8.8 q8.11 q8.12
1                           0.00 0.4545455    0   NA    0    0   NA     0   NA
2                           0.75 0.7272727    0   NA    0    1   NA     0   NA
3                           0.75 0.6363636    0   NA    0    0   NA     0   NA
4                           0.75 0.6363636    0   NA    0    0   NA     0   NA
5                           0.50 0.5454545    0   NA    0    0   NA     0   NA
6                           0.00 0.6363636    0   NA    0    0   NA     0   NA
  q8.13 q8.19 q8.20 q9.how.likely.would.you.be.to.purchase.this.Deodorant
1     0     0    NA                                                    0.25
2     0     0    NA                                                    0.50
3     0     0    NA                                                    1.00
4     0     0    NA                                                    1.00
5     0     0    NA                                                    1.00
6     0     0    NA                                                    1.00
  q10.prefer.this.Deodorant.or.your.usual.Deodorant
1                                               0.00
2                                               1.00
3                                               0.00
4                                               0.75
5                                               0.50
6                                               0.75
  q11.time.of.day.would.this.Deodorant.be.appropriate
1                                                  0.0
2                                                  1.0
3                                                  1.0
4                                                  0.0
5                                                  1.0
6                                                  0.5
  q12.which.occasions.would.this.Deodorant.be.appropriate
1                                                      0.5
2                                                      1.0
3                                                      1.0
4                                                      1.0
5                                                      0.5
6                                                      0.5
  Q13_Liking.after.30.minutes q14.Deodorant.overall.on.a.scale.from.1.to.10
1                   0.0000000                                      0.6666667
2                   0.3333333                                      0.7777778
3                   0.1666667                                      0.4444444
4                   0.8333333                                      0.7777778
5                   0.6666667                                      0.3333333
6                   0.8333333                                      0.6666667
    ValSegb s7.involved.in.the.selection.of.the.cosmetic.products
1 1.0000000                                                    NaN
2 0.8333333                                                    NaN
3 1.0000000                                                    NaN
```

```
4 0.0000000                                               NaN
5 0.5000000                                               NaN
6 1.0000000                                               NaN
  s8.ethnic.background s9.education s10.income s11.marital.status
1                    0          0.4      0.125               0.00
2                    0          0.4      0.125               0.00
3                    0          0.2      0.375               0.00
4                    0          0.4      0.875               0.00
5                    0          0.2      0.375               0.00
6                    0          0.4      0.375               0.25
  s12.working.status s13.2 s13a.b.most.often
1          0.0000000     0                  0
2          0.0000000     0                  0
3          0.0000000     0                  0
4          0.3333333     0                  0
5          0.1666667     0                  0
6          0.1666667     0                  0
  s13b.bottles.of.Deodorant.do.you.currently.own ProductDeodorant.B
1                                            0.4                   1
2                                            0.6                   1
3                                            0.2                   1
4                                            0.4                   1
5                                            0.4                   1
6                                            0.2                   1
  ProductDeodorant.F ProductDeodorant.G ProductDeodorant.H ProductDeodorant.J
1                  0                  0                  0                  0
2                  0                  0                  0                  0
3                  0                  0                  0                  0
4                  0                  0                  0                  0
5                  0                  0                  0                  0
6                  0                  0                  0                  0
> scaledFF <- scaledF[, c(1:32,34:35,37,39:40,42:48,50:62)]
> head(scaledFF)
  Respondent.ID Product.ID q1_1.personal.opinion.of.this.Deodorant q2_all.words
1  0.000000e+00          0                               0.5000000          0.2
2  9.709681e-05          0                               0.6666667          0.2
3  1.941936e-04          0                               0.8333333          0.2
4  2.912904e-04          0                               0.5000000          0.0
5  3.883872e-04          0                               0.5000000          0.2
6  4.854840e-04          0                               0.6666667          0.2
  q3_1.strength.of.the.Deodorant q4_1.artificial.chemical q4_2.attractive
1                           0.75                     0.25            1.00
2                           0.75                     0.75            0.25
3                           0.50                     0.25            1.00
4                           0.75                     1.00            1.00
5                           0.25                     0.00            0.50
6                           1.00                     1.00            1.00
```

	q4_3.bold	q4_4.boring	q4_5.casual	q4_6.cheap	q4_7.clean	q4_8.easy.to.wear
1	0.75	0.25	0.50	1.00	1.00	1.00
2	0.25	0.00	0.50	0.25	0.75	0.75
3	0.25	0.75	0.25	0.75	0.50	1.00
4	0.75	0.50	1.00	0.25	1.00	0.50
5	0.00	0.00	0.50	0.50	1.00	0.50
6	0.25	0.00	0.75	1.00	1.00	0.25

	q4_9.elegant	q4_10.feminine	q4_11.for.someone.like.me	q4_12.heavy
1	0.75	1.00	0.50	0.00
2	0.75	0.50	0.00	0.00
3	0.75	0.75	0.75	0.50
4	1.00	1.00	1.00	0.00
5	1.00	1.00	1.00	0.00
6	0.75	0.75	0.50	0.25

	q4_13.high.quality	q4_14.long.lasting	q4_15.masculine	q4_16.memorable
1	1.00	0.00	0.25	0.75
2	0.50	0.75	0.75	1.00
3	0.00	0.25	0.00	0.75
4	0.75	0.50	0.50	1.00
5	0.75	0.75	0.25	0.50
6	0.75	1.00	0.25	0.50

	q4_17.natural	q4_18.old.fashioned	q4_19.ordinary	q4_20.overpowering
1	1.00	0.75	1.00	0.00
2	0.50	0.50	0.75	0.25
3	0.25	0.75	0.50	0.25
4	1.00	0.75	0.25	1.00
5	1.00	0.00	0.25	0.75
6	0.75	0.25	0.25	0.50

	q4_21.sharp	q4_22.sophisticated	q4_23.upscale	q4_24.well.rounded
1	0.00	0.75	0.00	0.75
2	0.25	1.00	0.75	0.75
3	1.00	0.75	0.75	0.50
4	0.50	0.50	1.00	0.75
5	0.25	0.50	0.00	1.00
6	0.00	1.00	1.00	0.75

	q5_1.Deodorant.is.addictive	q7	q8.1	q8.5	q8.6	q8.11	q8.13	q8.19
1	0.00	0.4545455	0	0	0	0	0	0
2	0.75	0.7272727	0	0	1	0	0	0
3	0.75	0.6363636	0	0	0	0	0	0
4	0.75	0.6363636	0	0	0	0	0	0
5	0.50	0.5454545	0	0	0	0	0	0
6	0.00	0.6363636	0	0	0	0	0	0

	q9.how.likely.would.you.be.to.purchase.this.Deodorant
1	0.25
2	0.50
3	1.00

4	1.00
5	1.00
6	1.00

	q10.prefer.this.Deodorant.or.your.usual.Deodorant
1	0.00
2	1.00
3	0.00
4	0.75
5	0.50
6	0.75

	q11.time.of.day.would.this.Deodorant.be.appropriate
1	0.0
2	1.0
3	1.0
4	0.0
5	1.0
6	0.5

	q12.which.occasions.would.this.Deodorant.be.appropriate
1	0.5
2	1.0
3	1.0
4	1.0
5	0.5
6	0.5

	Q13_Liking.after.30.minutes	q14.Deodorant.overall.on.a.scale.from.1.to.10
1	0.0000000	0.6666667
2	0.3333333	0.7777778
3	0.1666667	0.4444444
4	0.8333333	0.7777778
5	0.6666667	0.3333333
6	0.8333333	0.6666667

	ValSegb	s8.ethnic.background	s9.education	s10.income	s11.marital.status
1	1.0000000	0	0.4	0.125	0.00
2	0.8333333	0	0.4	0.125	0.00
3	1.0000000	0	0.2	0.375	0.00
4	0.0000000	0	0.4	0.875	0.00
5	0.5000000	0	0.2	0.375	0.00
6	1.0000000	0	0.4	0.375	0.25

	s12.working.status	s13.2	s13a.b.most.often
1	0.0000000	0	0
2	0.0000000	0	0
3	0.0000000	0	0
4	0.3333333	0	0
5	0.1666667	0	0
6	0.1666667	0	0

```
  s13b.bottles.of.Deodorant.do.you.currently.own ProductDeodorant.B
1                                             0.4                    1
2                                             0.6                    1
3                                             0.2                    1
4                                             0.4                    1
5                                             0.4                    1
6                                             0.2                    1
  ProductDeodorant.F ProductDeodorant.G ProductDeodorant.H ProductDeodorant.J
1                  0                  0                  0                  0
2                  0                  0                  0                  0
3                  0                  0                  0                  0
4                  0                 .0                  0                  0
5                  0                  0                  0                  0
6                  0                  0                  0                  0
> ncol(scaledFF) # 57 # 43rd column is scale1.to.10
[1] 57
> scaledFF <- scaledFF[, c(1:42,44:57,43)]
> ncol(scaledFF) #57
[1] 57
> head(scaledFF) # last column (57th) is scale1.to.10
  Respondent.ID Product.ID q1_1.personal.opinion.of.this.Deodorant q2_all.words
1  0.000000e+00          0                               0.5000000          0.2
2  9.709681e-05          0                               0.6666667          0.2
3  1.941936e-04          0                               0.8333333          0.2
4  2.912904e-04          0                               0.5000000          0.0
5  3.883872e-04          0                               0.5000000          0.2
6  4.854840e-04          0                               0.6666667          0.2
  q3_1.strength.of.the.Deodorant q4_1.artificial.chemical q4_2.attractive
1                           0.75                     0.25            1.00
2                           0.75                     0.75            0.25
3                           0.50                     0.25            1.00
4                           0.75                     1.00            1.00
5                           0.25                     0.00            0.50
6                           1.00                     1.00            1.00
  q4_3.bold q4_4.boring q4_5.casual q4_6.cheap q4_7.clean q4_8.easy.to.wear
1      0.75        0.25        0.50       1.00       1.00              1.00
2      0.25        0.00        0.50       0.25       0.75              0.75
3      0.25        0.75        0.25       0.75       0.50              1.00
4      0.75        0.50        1.00       0.25       1.00              0.50
5      0.00        0.00        0.50       0.50       1.00              0.50
6      0.25        0.00        0.75       1.00       1.00              0.25
  q4_9.elegant q4_10.feminine q4_11.for.someone.like.me q4_12.heavy
1         0.75           1.00                      0.50        0.00
2         0.75           0.50                      0.00        0.00
3         0.75           0.75                      0.75        0.50
```

4	1.00	1.00	1.00	0.00
5	1.00	1.00	1.00	0.00
6	0.75	0.75	0.50	0.25

	q4_13.high.quality	q4_14.long.lasting	q4_15.masculine	q4_16.memorable
1	1.00	0.00	0.25	0.75
2	0.50	0.75	0.75	1.00
3	0.00	0.25	0.00	0.75
4	0.75	0.50	0.50	1.00
5	0.75	0.75	0.25	0.50
6	0.75	1.00	0.25	0.50

	q4_17.natural	q4_18.old.fashioned	q4_19.ordinary	q4_20.overpowering
1	1.00	0.75	1.00	0.00
2	0.50	0.50	0.75	0.25
3	0.25	0.75	0.50	0.25
4	1.00	0.75	0.25	1.00
5	1.00	0.00	0.25	0.75
6	0.75	0.25	0.25	0.50

	q4_21.sharp	q4_22.sophisticated	q4_23.upscale	q4_24.well.rounded
1	0.00	0.75	0.00	0.75
2	0.25	1.00	0.75	0.75
3	1.00	0.75	0.75	0.50
4	0.50	0.50	1.00	0.75
5	0.25	0.50	0.00	1.00
6	0.00	1.00	1.00	0.75

	q5_1.Deodorant.is.addictive	q7	q8.1	q8.5	q8.6	q8.11	q8.13	q8.19
1	0.00	0.4545455	0	0	0	0	0	0
2	0.75	0.7272727	0	0	1	0	0	0
3	0.75	0.6363636	0	0	0	0	0	0
4	0.75	0.6363636	0	0	0	0	0	0
5	0.50	0.5454545	0	0	0	0	0	0
6	0.00	0.6363636	0	0	0	0	0	0

	q9.how.likely.would.you.be.to.purchase.this.Deodorant
1	0.25
2	0.50
3	1.00
4	1.00
5	1.00
6	1.00

	q10.prefer.this.Deodorant.or.your.usual.Deodorant
1	0.00
2	1.00
3	0.00
4	0.75
5	0.50
6	0.75

```
    q11.time.of.day.would.this.Deodorant.be.appropriate
1                                                       0.0
2                                                       1.0
3                                                       1.0
4                                                       0.0
5                                                       1.0
6                                                       0.5
    q12.which.occasions.would.this.Deodorant.be.appropriate
1                                                   0.5
2                                                   1.0
3                                                   1.0
4                                                   1.0
5                                                   0.5
6                                                   0.5
    Q13_Liking.after.30.minutes   ValSegb s8.ethnic.background s9.education
1                   0.0000000 1.0000000                 0          0.4
2                   0.3333333 0.8333333                 0          0.4
3                   0.1666667 1.0000000                 0          0.2
4                   0.8333333 0.0000000                 0          0.4
5                   0.6666667 0.5000000                 0          0.2
6                   0.8333333 1.0000000                 0          0.4
    s10.income s11.marital.status s12.working.status s13.2 s13a.b.most.often
1      0.125              0.00          0.0000000     0                 0
2      0.125              0.00          0.0000000     0                 0
3      0.375              0.00          0.0000000     0                 0
4      0.875              0.00          0.3333333     0                 0
5      0.375              0.00          0.1666667     0                 0
6      0.375              0.25          0.1666667     0                 0
    s13b.bottles.of.Deodorant.do.you.currently.own ProductDeodorant.B
1                                            0.4                 1
2                                            0.6                 1
3                                            0.2                 1
4                                            0.4                 1
5                                            0.4                 1
6                                            0.2                 1
    ProductDeodorant.F ProductDeodorant.G ProductDeodorant.H ProductDeodorant.J
1                  0                  0                  0                  0
2                  0                  0                  0                  0
3                  0                  0                  0                  0
4                  0                  0                  0                  0
5                  0                  0                  0                  0
6                  0                  0                  0                  0
    q14.Deodorant.overall.on.a.scale.from.1.to.10
1                                     0.6666667
2                                     0.7777778
3                                     0.4444444
```

```
4                                   0.7777778
5                                   0.3333333
6                                   0.6666667
> n <- names(scaledFF)
> f <- as.formula(q14.Deodorant.overall.on.a.scale.from.1.to.10 ~ ProductDeodorant.B +
+ + + ProductDeodorant.F + ProductDeodorant.G + ProductDeodorant.H +
+ + + ProductDeodorant.J)
> f
q14.Deodorant.overall.on.a.scale.from.1.to.10 ~ ProductDeodorant.B +
    ++ProductDeodorant.F + ProductDeodorant.G + ProductDeodorant.H +
    ++ProductDeodorant.J
> DNNf3 <- neuralnet(f, data = scaledFF, hidden=c(5,3), linear.output=TRUE)
> plot(DNNf3)
> ncol(scaledFF) # 57
[1] 57
> head(test_data)
  Respondent.ID Product.ID    Product q1_1.personal.opinion.of.this.Deodorant
1         4300        121 Deodorant B                                       7
2         4301        121 Deodorant B                                       6
3         4302        121 Deodorant B                                       6
4         4303        121 Deodorant B                                       5
5         4304        121 Deodorant B                                       6
6         4305        121 Deodorant B                                       7
  q2_all.words q3_1.strength.of.the.Deodorant q4_1.artificial.chemical
1            2                              3                        3
2            0                              3                        2
3            1                              3                        3
4            1                              5                        3
5            2                              3                        2
6            4                              3                        2
  q4_2.attractive q4_3.bold q4_4.boring q4_5.casual q4_6.cheap q4_7.clean
1               1         4           2           3          3          5
2               4         2           1           4          4          5
3               5         3           3           5          4          5
4               4         5           2           5          2          4
5               4         3           1           2          1          3
6               4         4           2           5          1          4
  q4_8.easy.to.wear q4_9.elegant q4_10.feminine q4_11.for.someone.like.me
1                 2            1              5                         3
2                 5            3              2                         1
3                 3            5              5                         5
4                 5            3              4                         4
5                 4            5              5                         3
6                 1            4              4                         5
```

```
   q4_12.heavy q4_13.high.quality q4_14.long.lasting q4_15.masculine
1            2                  3                  5                1
2            3                  5                  4                1
3            3                  5                  5                1
4            5                  5                  5                1
5            3                  4                  3                1
6            5                  3                  4                1
   q4_16.memorable q4_17.natural q4_18.old.fashioned q4_19.ordinary
1                4             4                   4              2
2                3             1                   1              5
3                5             4                   1              1
4                5             4                   4              4
5                5             5                   5              2
6                4             3                   2              1
   q4_20.overpowering q4_21.sharp q4_22.sophisticated q4_23.upscale
1                   3           2                   3             4
2                   1           4                   3             2
3                   4           5                   3             5
4                   2           3                   5             3
5                   4           4                   4             4
6                   4           5                   5             5
   q4_24.well.rounded q5_1.Deodorant.is.addictive q7 q8.1 q8.2 q8.5 q8.6 q8.8
1                   4                              5  1    0    0    0    0    0
2                   3                              4  2    0    0    0    0    0
3                   3                              1  4    0    0    0    1    0
4                   4                              4  1    0    0    0    0    0
5                   4                              4  3    0    0    0    0    0
6                   2                              5  2    0    0    0    0    0
   q8.11 q8.12 q8.13 q8.19 q8.20
1     0     0     0     0     0
2     0     1     0     0     0
3     0     0     0     0     0
4     0     0     0     0     0
5     0     0     0     0     0
6     0     0     0     0     0
   q9.how.likely.would.you.be.to.purchase.this.Deodorant
1                                                       4
2                                                       4
3                                                       5
4                                                       5
5                                                       2
6                                                       4
   q10.prefer.this.Deodorant.or.your.usual.Deodorant
1                                                   1
2                                                   4
3                                                   3
```

	q11.time.of.day.would.this.Deodorant.be.appropriate
4	3
5	5
6	3

q11.time.of.day.would.this.Deodorant.be.appropriate

1	3
2	3
3	2
4	3
5	3
6	3

q12.which.occasions.would.this.Deodorant.be.appropriate

1	2
2	3
3	3
4	3
5	3
6	1

Q13_Liking.after.30.minutes q14.Deodorant.overall.on.a.scale.from.1.to.10

	Q13_Liking.after.30.minutes	q14.Deodorant.overall.on.a.scale.from.1.to.10
1	1	5
2	3	10
3	6	1
4	6	8
5	6	4
6	4	7

ValSegb s7.involved.in.the.selection.of.the.cosmetic.products

	ValSegb	s7.involved.in.the.selection.of.the.cosmetic.products
1	7	4
2	1	4
3	6	4
4	2	4
5	5	4
6	2	4

s8.ethnic.background s9.education s10.income s11.marital.status

	s8.ethnic.background	s9.education	s10.income	s11.marital.status
1	2	3	2	2
2	1	4	4	1
3	1	3	3	1
4	2	3	10	1
5	1	2	3	3
6	2	3	2	2

s12.working.status s13.2 s13a.b.most.often

	s12.working.status	s13.2	s13a.b.most.often
1	1	0	0
2	1	0	0
3	1	0	0
4	1	0	0
5	1	0	0
6	1	0	0

```
   s13b.bottles.of.Deodorant.do.you.currently.own
1                                                 4
2                                                 1
3                                                 6
4                                                 4
5                                                 4
6                                                 1
> nrow(test_data)
[1] 5105
> test.Product.matrix <-model.matrix( ~Product - 1, data = test_data)
> test_dataF <- data.frame(test_data, test.Product.matrix)
> ncol(test_dataF) # 63
[1] 63
> head(test_dataF)
  Respondent.ID Product.ID    Product q1_1.personal.opinion.of.this.Deodorant
1          4300        121 Deodorant B                                       7
2          4301        121 Deodorant B                                       6
3          4302        121 Deodorant B                                       6
4          4303        121 Deodorant B                                       5
5          4304        121 Deodorant B                                       6
6          4305        121 Deodorant B                                       7
  q2_all.words q3_1.strength.of.the.Deodorant q4_1.artificial.chemical
1            2                              3                        3
2            0                              3                        2
3            1                              3                        3
4            1                              5                        3
5            2                              3                        2
6            4                              3                        2
  q4_2.attractive q4_3.bold q4_4.boring q4_5.casual q4_6.cheap q4_7.clean
1               1         4           2           3          3          5
2               4         2           1           4          4          5
3               5         3           3           5          4          5
4               4         5           2           5          2          4
5               4         3           1           2          1          3
6               4         4           2           5          1          4
  q4_8.easy.to.wear q4_9.elegant q4_10.feminine q4_11.for.someone.like.me
1                 2            1              5                         3
2                 5            3              2                         1
3                 3            5              5                         5
4                 5            3              4                         4
5                 4            5              5                         3
6                 1            4              4                         5
  q4_12.heavy q4_13.high.quality q4_14.long.lasting q4_15.masculine
1           2                  3                  5               1
2           3                  5                  4               1
3           3                  5                  5               1
```

4	5	5	5	1
5	3	4	3	1
6	5	3	4	1

	q4_16.memorable	q4_17.natural	q4_18.old.fashioned	q4_19.ordinary
1	4	4	4	2
2	3	1	1	5
3	5	4	1	1
4	5	4	4	4
5	5	5	5	2
6	4	3	2	1

	q4_20.overpowering	q4_21.sharp	q4_22.sophisticated	q4_23.upscale
1	3	2	3	4
2	1	4	3	2
3	4	5	3	5
4	2	3	5	3
5	4	4	4	4
6	4	5	5	5

	q4_24.well.rounded	q5_1.Deodorant.is.addictive	q7	q8.1	q8.2	q8.5	q8.6	q8.8
1	4		5	1	0	0	0	0	0
2	3		4	2	0	0	0	0	0
3	3		1	4	0	0	0	1	0
4	4		4	1	0	0	0	0	0
5	4		4	3	0	0	0	0	0
6	2		5	2	0	0	0	0	0

	q8.11	q8.12	q8.13	q8.19	q8.20
1	0	0	0	0	0
2	0	1	0	0	0
3	0	0	0	0	0
4	0	0	0	0	0
5	0	0	0	0	0
6	0	0	0	0	0

	q9.how.likely.would.you.be.to.purchase.this.Deodorant
1	4
2	4
3	5
4	5
5	2
6	4

	q10.prefer.this.Deodorant.or.your.usual.Deodorant
1	1
2	4
3	3
4	3
5	5
6	3

	q11.time.of.day.would.this.Deodorant.be.appropriate
1	3
2	3
3	2
4	3
5	3
6	3

	q12.which.occasions.would.this.Deodorant.be.appropriate
1	2
2	3
3	3
4	3
5	3
6	1

	Q13_Liking.after.30.minutes	q14.Deodorant.overall.on.a.scale.from.1.to.10
1	1	5
2	3	10
3	6	1
4	6	8
5	6	4
6	4	7

	ValSegb	s7.involved.in.the.selection.of.the.cosmetic.products
1	7	4
2	1	4
3	6	4
4	2	4
5	5	4
6	2	4

	s8.ethnic.background	s9.education	s10.income	s11.marital.status
1	2	3	2	2
2	1	4	4	1
3	1	3	3	1
4	2	3	10	1
5	1	2	3	3
6	2	3	2	2

	s12.working.status	s13.2	s13a.b.most.often
1	1	0	0
2	1	0	0
3	1	0	0
4	1	0	0
5	1	0	0
6	1	0	0

	s13b.bottles.of.Deodorant.do.you.currently.own	ProductDeodorant.B
1	4	1
2	1	1
3	6	1

```
4                                                    4                    1
5                                                    4                    1
6                                                    1                    1
  ProductDeodorant.F ProductDeodorant.G ProductDeodorant.H ProductDeodorant.J
1                  0                 0                 0                 0
2                  0                 0                 0                 0
3                  0                 0                 0                 0
4                  0                 0                 0                 0
5                  0                 0                 0                 0
6                  0                 0                 0                 0
> maxs <- apply(test_dataF[, c(1:2,4:58)], 2, max)
> mins <- apply(test_dataF[, c(1:2,4:58)], 2, min)
> scaledTest <- as.data.frame(scale(test_dataF[,c(1:2, 4:58)], center = mins, scale
= maxs - mins))
> set.seed(500)
> n1 <- names(scaledTest)
> head(scaledTest)
     Respondent.ID Product.ID q1_1.personal.opinion.of.this.Deodorant
1 0.00000000000000          0                            1.0000000000
2 0.00008392077878          0                            0.8333333333
3 0.00016784155757          0                            0.8333333333
4 0.00025176233635          0                            0.6666666667
5 0.00033568311514          0                            0.8333333333
6 0.00041960389392          0                            1.0000000000
  q2_all.words q3_1.strength.of.the.Deodorant q4_1.artificial.chemical
1          0.4                            0.5                     0.50
2          0.0                            0.5                     0.25
3          0.2                            0.5                     0.50
4          0.2                            1.0                     0.50
5          0.4                            0.5                     0.25
6          0.8                            0.5                     0.25
  q4_2.attractive q4_3.bold q4_4.boring q4_5.casual q4_6.cheap q4_7.clean
1            0.00      0.75        0.25        0.50       0.50       1.00
2            0.75      0.25        0.00        0.75       0.75       1.00
3            1.00      0.50        0.50        1.00       0.75       1.00
4            0.75      1.00        0.25        1.00       0.25       0.75
5            0.75      0.50        0.00        0.25       0.00       0.50
6            0.75      0.75        0.25        1.00       0.00       0.75
  q4_8.easy.to.wear q4_9.elegant q4_10.feminine q4_11.for.someone.like.me
1              0.25         0.00           1.00                      0.50
2              1.00         0.50           0.25                      0.00
3              0.50         1.00           1.00                      1.00
4              1.00         0.50           0.75                      0.75
5              0.75         1.00           1.00                      0.50
6              0.00         0.75           0.75                      1.00
```

	q4_12.heavy	q4_13.high.quality	q4_14.long.lasting	q4_15.masculine
1	0.25	0.50	1.00	0
2	0.50	1.00	0.75	0
3	0.50	1.00	1.00	0
4	1.00	1.00	1.00	0
5	0.50	0.75	0.50	0
6	1.00	0.50	0.75	0

	q4_16.memorable	q4_17.natural	q4_18.old.fashioned	q4_19.ordinary
1	0.75	0.75	0.75	0.25
2	0.50	0.00	0.00	1.00
3	1.00	0.75	0.00	0.00
4	1.00	0.75	0.75	0.75
5	1.00	1.00	1.00	0.25
6	0.75	0.50	0.25	0.00

	q4_20.overpowering	q4_21.sharp	q4_22.sophisticated	q4_23.upscale
1	0.50	0.25	0.50	0.75
2	0.00	0.75	0.50	0.25
3	0.75	1.00	0.50	1.00
4	0.25	0.50	1.00	0.50
5	0.75	0.75	0.75	0.75
6	0.75	1.00	1.00	1.00

	q4_24.well.rounded	q5_1.Deodorant.is.addictive	q7	q8.1	q8.2	q8.5
1	0.75	1.00	0.4166666667	0	0	0
2	0.50	0.75	0.5000000000	0	0	0
3	0.50	0.00	0.6666666667	0	0	0
4	0.75	0.75	0.4166666667	0	0	0
5	0.75	0.75	0.5833333333	0	0	0
6	0.25	1.00	0.5000000000	0	0	0

	q8.6	q8.8	q8.11	q8.12	q8.13	q8.19	q8.20
1	0	0	0	0	0	0	0
2	0	0	0	1	0	0	0
3	1	0	0	0	0	0	0
4	0	0	0	0	0	0	0
5	0	0	0	0	0	0	0
6	0	0	0	0	0	0	0

	q9.how.likely.would.you.be.to.purchase.this.Deodorant
1	0.75
2	0.75
3	1.00
4	1.00
5	0.25
6	0.75

	q10.prefer.this.Deodorant.or.your.usual.Deodorant
1	0.00
2	0.75
3	0.50

4	0.50
5	1.00
6	0.50

q11.time.of.day.would.this.Deodorant.be.appropriate

1	1.0
2	1.0
3	0.5
4	1.0
5	1.0
6	1.0

q12.which.occasions.would.this.Deodorant.be.appropriate

1	0.5
2	1.0
3	1.0
4	1.0
5	1.0
6	0.0

	Q13_Liking.after.30.minutes	q14.Deodorant.overall.on.a.scale.from.1.to.10
1	0.0000000000	0.4444444444
2	0.3333333333	1.0000000000
3	0.8333333333	0.0000000000
4	0.8333333333	0.7777777778
5	0.8333333333	0.3333333333
6	0.5000000000	0.6666666667

	ValSegb	s7.involved.in.the.selection.of.the.cosmetic.products
1	1.0000000000	1
2	0.0000000000	1
3	0.8333333333	1
4	0.1666666667	1
5	0.6666666667	1
6	0.1666666667	1

	s8.ethnic.background	s9.education	s10.income	s11.marital.status
1	0.25	0.2	0.000	0.25
2	0.00	0.4	0.250	0.00
3	0.00	0.2	0.125	0.00
4	0.25	0.2	1.000	0.00
5	0.00	0.0	0.125	0.50
6	0.25	0.2	0.000	0.25

	s12.working.status	s13.2	s13a.b.most.often
1	0	0	0
2	0	0	0
3	0	0	0
4	0	0	0
5	0	0	0
6	0	0	0

```
  s13b.bottles.of.Deodorant.do.you.currently.own
1                                              0.6
2                                              0.0
3                                              1.0
4                                              0.6
5                                              0.6
6                                              0.0
> ncol(scaledTest) # 57
[1] 57
> scaledTestF <- as.data.frame(cbind(scaledTest, test_dataF[, c(59:63)]))
> ncol(scaledTestF)
[1] 62
> scaledTestFF <- scaledTestF[, c(1:32, 34:35, 37,39:40,42:48,50:57,58:62)]
> ncol(scaledTestFF)
[1] 57
> n2 <- names(scaledTestFF)
> head(test_data)
  Respondent.ID Product.ID    Product q1_1.personal.opinion.of.this.Deodorant
1          4300        121 Deodorant B                                      7
2          4301        121 Deodorant B                                      6
3          4302        121 Deodorant B                                      6
4          4303        121 Deodorant B                                      5
5          4304        121 Deodorant B                                      6
6          4305        121 Deodorant B                                      7
  q2_all.words q3_1.strength.of.the.Deodorant q4_1.artificial.chemical
1            2                              3                        3
2            0                              3                        2
3            1                              3                        3
4            1                              5                        3
5            2                              3                        2
6            4                              3                        2
  q4_2.attractive q4_3.bold q4_4.boring q4_5.casual q4_6.cheap q4_7.clean
1               1         4           2           3          3          5
2               4         2           1           4          4          5
3               5         3           3           5          4          5
4               4         5           2           5          2          4
5               4         3           1           2          1          3
6               4         4           2           5          1          4
  q4_8.easy.to.wear q4_9.elegant q4_10.feminine q4_11.for.someone.like.me
1                 2            1              5                         3
2                 5            3              2                         1
3                 3            5              5                         5
4                 5            3              4                         4
5                 4            5              5                         3
6                 1            4              4                         5
```

```
   q4_12.heavy q4_13.high.quality q4_14.long.lasting q4_15.masculine
1            2                  3                  5                1
2            3                  5                  4                1
3            3                  5                  5                1
4            5                  5                  5                1
5            3                  4                  3                1
6            5                  3                  4                1
   q4_16.memorable q4_17.natural q4_18.old.fashioned q4_19.ordinary
1              4              4                   4              2
2              3              1                   1              5
3              5              4                   1              1
4              5              4                   4              4
5              5              5                   5              2
6              4              3                   2              1
   q4_20.overpowering q4_21.sharp q4_22.sophisticated q4_23.upscale
1                  3            2                   3             4
2                  1            4                   3             2
3                  4            5                   3             5
4                  2            3                   5             3
5                  4            4                   4             4
6                  4            5                   5             5
   q4_24.well.rounded q5_1.Deodorant.is.addictive q7 q8.1 q8.2 q8.5 q8.6 q8.8
1                  4                             5   1    0    0    0    0    0
2                  3                             4   2    0    0    0    0    0
3                  3                             1   4    0    0    0    1    0
4                  4                             4   1    0    0    0    0    0
5                  4                             4   3    0    0    0    0    0
6                  2                             5   2    0    0    0    0    0
   q8.11 q8.12 q8.13 q8.19 q8.20
1      0     0     0     0     0
2      0     1     0     0     0
3      0     0     0     0     0
4      0     0     0     0     0
5      0     0     0     0     0
6      0     0     0     0     0
   q9.how.likely.would.you.be.to.purchase.this.Deodorant
1                                                       4
2                                                       4
3                                                       5
4                                                       5
5                                                       2
6                                                       4
   q10.prefer.this.Deodorant.or.your.usual.Deodorant
1                                                   1
2                                                   4
3                                                   3
```

4	3
5	5
6	3

q11.time.of.day.would.this.Deodorant.be.appropriate

1	3
2	3
3	2
4	3
5	3
6	3

q12.which.occasions.would.this.Deodorant.be.appropriate

1	2
2	3
3	3
4	3
5	3
6	1

	Q13_Liking.after.30.minutes	q14.Deodorant.overall.on.a.scale.from.1.to.10
1	1	5
2	3	10
3	6	1
4	6	8
5	6	4
6	4	7

	ValSegb	s7.involved.in.the.selection.of.the.cosmetic.products
1	7	4
2	1	4
3	6	4
4	2	4
5	5	4
6	2	4

	s8.ethnic.background	s9.education	s10.income	s11.marital.status
1	2	3	2	2
2	1	4	4	1
3	1	3	3	1
4	2	3	10	1
5	1	2	3	3
6	2	3	2	2

	s12.working.status	s13.2	s13a.b.most.often
1	1	0	0
2	1	0	0
3	1	0	0
4	1	0	0
5	1	0	0
6	1	0	0

```
      s13b.bottles.of.Deodorant.do.you.currently.own
1                                                   4
2                                                   1
3                                                   6
4                                                   4
5                                                   4
6                                                   1
> head(scaledTestFF)
     Respondent.ID Product.ID q1_1.personal.opinion.of.this.Deodorant
1 0.00000000000000          0                                1.0000000000
2 0.00008392077878          0                                0.8333333333
3 0.00016784155757          0                                0.8333333333
4 0.00025176233635          0                                0.6666666667
5 0.00033568311514          0                                0.8333333333
6 0.00041960389392          0                                1.0000000000
  q2_all.words q3_1.strength.of.the.Deodorant q4_1.artificial.chemical
1          0.4                             0.5                     0.50
2          0.0                             0.5                     0.25
3          0.2                             0.5                     0.50
4          0.2                             1.0                     0.50
5          0.4                             0.5                     0.25
6          0.8                             0.5                     0.25
  q4_2.attractive q4_3.bold q4_4.boring q4_5.casual q4_6.cheap q4_7.clean
1            0.00      0.75        0.25        0.50       0.50       1.00
2            0.75      0.25        0.00        0.75       0.75       1.00
3            1.00      0.50        0.50        1.00       0.75       1.00
4            0.75      1.00        0.25        1.00       0.25       0.75
5            0.75      0.50        0.00        0.25       0.00       0.50
6            0.75      0.75        0.25        1.00       0.00       0.75
  q4_8.easy.to.wear q4_9.elegant q4_10.feminine q4_11.for.someone.like.me
1              0.25         0.00           1.00                       0.50
2              1.00         0.50           0.25                       0.00
3              0.50         1.00           1.00                       1.00
4              1.00         0.50           0.75                       0.75
5              0.75         1.00           1.00                       0.50
6              0.00         0.75           0.75                       1.00
  q4_12.heavy q4_13.high.quality q4_14.long.lasting q4_15.masculine
1        0.25               0.50               1.00               0
2        0.50               1.00               0.75               0
3        0.50               1.00               1.00               0
4        1.00               1.00               1.00               0
5        0.50               0.75               0.50               0
6        1.00               0.50               0.75               0
  q4_16.memorable q4_17.natural q4_18.old.fashioned q4_19.ordinary
1            0.75          0.75                0.75           0.25
2            0.50          0.00                0.00           1.00
3            1.00          0.75                0.00           0.00
```

4	1.00	0.75	0.75	0.75
5	1.00	1.00	1.00	0.25
6	0.75	0.50	0.25	0.00

	q4_20.overpowering	q4_21.sharp	q4_22.sophisticated	q4_23.upscale
1	0.50	0.25	0.50	0.75
2	0.00	0.75	0.50	0.25
3	0.75	1.00	0.50	1.00
4	0.25	0.50	1.00	0.50
5	0.75	0.75	0.75	0.75
6	0.75	1.00	1.00	1.00

	q4_24.well.rounded	q5_1.Deodorant.is.addictive	q7	q8.1	q8.5	q8.6
1	0.75	1.00	0.4166666667	0	0	0
2	0.50	0.75	0.5000000000	0	0	0
3	0.50	0.00	0.6666666667	0	0	1
4	0.75	0.75	0.4166666667	0	0	0
5	0.75	0.75	0.5833333333	0	0	0
6	0.25	1.00	0.5000000000	0	0	0

	q8.11	q8.13	q8.19	q9.how.likely.would.you.be.to.purchase.this.Deodorant
1	0	0	0	0.75
2	0	0	0	0.75
3	0	0	0	1.00
4	0	0	0	1.00
5	0	0	0	0.25
6	0	0	0	0.75

	q10.prefer.this.Deodorant.or.your.usual.Deodorant
1	0.00
2	0.75
3	0.50
4	0.50
5	1.00
6	0.50

	q11.time.of.day.would.this.Deodorant.be.appropriate
1	1.0
2	1.0
3	0.5
4	1.0
5	1.0
6	1.0

	q12.which.occasions.would.this.Deodorant.be.appropriate
1	0.5
2	1.0
3	1.0
4	1.0
5	1.0
6	0.0

	Q13_Liking.after.30.minutes	q14.Deodorant.overall.on.a.scale.from.1.to.10
1	0.0000000000	0.4444444444
2	0.3333333333	1.0000000000
3	0.8333333333	0.0000000000
4	0.8333333333	0.7777777778
5	0.8333333333	0.3333333333
6	0.5000000000	0.6666666667

	ValSegb	s8.ethnic.background	s9.education	s10.income	s11.marital.status
1	1.0000000000	0.25	0.2	0.000	0.25
2	0.0000000000	0.00	0.4	0.250	0.00
3	0.8333333333	0.00	0.2	0.125	0.00
4	0.1666666667	0.25	0.2	1.000	0.00
5	0.6666666667	0.00	0.0	0.125	0.50
6	0.1666666667	0.25	0.2	0.000	0.25

	s12.working.status	s13.2	s13a.b.most.often
1	0	0	0
2	0	0	0
3	0	0	0
4	0	0	0
5	0	0	0
6	0	0	0

	s13b.bottles.of.Deodorant.do.you.currently.own	ProductDeodorant.B
1	0.6	1
2	0.0	1
3	1.0	1
4	0.6	1
5	0.6	1
6	0.0	1

	ProductDeodorant.F	ProductDeodorant.G	ProductDeodorant.H	ProductDeodorant.J
1	0	0	0	0
2	0	0	0	0
3	0	0	0	0
4	0	0	0	0
5	0	0	0	0
6	0	0	0	0

```
> pr.DNNf3 <- compute(DNNf3, scaledTestFF[, c(53:57)])

> pr.DNNf3_r <- pr.DNNf3$net.result*(max(test_data$q14.Deodorant.overall.
on.a.scale.from.1.to.10)-min(test_data$q14.Deodorant.overall.on.a.scale.
from.1.to.10))+min(test_data$q14.Deodorant.overall.on.a.scale.from.1.to.10)

> test_data_r <- (scaledTestFF$q14.Deodorant.overall.on.a.scale.
from.1.to.10)*(max(test_data$q14.Deodorant.overall.on.a.scale.from.1.to.10)-
min(test_data$q14.Deodorant.overall.on.a.scale.from.1.to.10))+min(test_data$q14.
Deodorant.overall.on.a.scale.from.1.to.10)

> MSE.DNNf3 <- sum((test_data_r - pr.DNNf3_r)^2)/nrow(scaledTestFF)

> MSE.DNNf3

[1] 6.400654791

> # [1] 6.400654791

> plot(test_data$q14.Deodorant.overall.on.a.scale.from.1.to.10, pr.DNNf3_r,col='red
',main='Actual vs predicted DNN',pch=18,cex=0.7)
```

```
> abline(0,1,lwd=2)
> legend('bottomright',legend='DNN',pch=18,col='red',bty='n')
> pr.DNNf3_r2 <- pr.DNNf3$net.result
> pdf(" Plots ProductDeodorants vs Predicted.pdf")
> plot(test_dataF$ProductDeodorant.B, pr.DNNf3_r2, col='green',main='Product
Deodorant B vs Predicted', xlab='Product Deodorant B',pch=18,cex=2)
> abline(0,1,lwd=2)
> legend('bottom',legend='Product Deodorant B vs Predicted',pch=2,col='green',bty='n')
> plot(test_dataF$ProductDeodorant.F, pr.DNNf3_r2, col='green',main='Product
Deodorant F vs Predicted', xlab='Product Deodorant F',pch=18,cex=2)
> abline(0,1,lwd=2)
> legend('bottom',legend='Product Deodorant F vs Predicted',pch=2,col='green',bty='n')
> plot(test_dataF$ProductDeodorant.G, pr.DNNf3_r2, col='green',main='Product
Deodorant G vs Predicted', xlab='Product Deodorant G',pch=18,cex=2)
> abline(0,1,lwd=2)
> legend('bottom',legend='Product Deodorant G vs Predicted',pch=2,col='green',bty='n')
> plot(test_dataF$ProductDeodorant.H, pr.DNNf3_r2, col='green',main='Product
Deodorant H vs Predicted', xlab='Product Deodorant H',pch=18,cex=2)
> abline(0,1,lwd=2)
> legend('bottom',legend='Product Deodorant H vs Predicted',pch=2,col='green',bty='n')
> plot(test_dataF$ProductDeodorant.J, pr.DNNf3_r2, col='green',main='Product
Deodorant J vs Predicted', xlab='Product Deodorant J',pch=18,cex=2)
> abline(0,1,lwd=2)
> legend('bottom',legend='Product Deodorant J vs Predicted',pch=2,col='green',bty='n')
> dev.off()
windows
      2
>
```

4.4.1.4 Predictive Analytics Solution

This involves predicting instant liking based on Product and Scale as predictor variables—building a similar AI-based deep neural network model using R-based *neuralnet()*. The steps involved are as follows:

- It uses the data from the Data_train_reduced.csv file to predict the "Instant Liking" based on "Product" and "q14.Deodorant.overall.on.a.scale.from.1.to.10".
- It uses a deep neural network ML model built by training itself based on data correlating five products with each of their scales.
- It then predicts the scale on test data and based on the value recommends that Product.
- A DNN with one input layer with six input nodes (neurons), two middle (hidden) layers (with five and three nodes, respectively) and an output layer (with one node) is built and trained.
- It then fits the data by applying the predicted model output against each of the five Products and their scale. The response variable used is Instant.Liking
- It is implemented by using the R-based *neuralnet()* model to build and train the DNN and then using the *compute()* function to predict the output and use it for recommendation.

The DNN-based output plot along with the fitted output plot are shown in Figure 4.34.
Listing 4.10 gives the R code and its output for the predictive analytics solution.

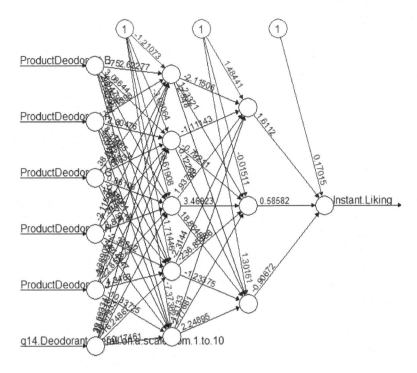

Error: 229.625047   Steps: 45475

Figure 4.34   DNN for Predictive Analytics.

Listing 4.10 R Code for Predictive Analytics Solution

```
> setwd("<directory-name>")
> product_data <- read.csv("Data_train_reduced.csv")
> names(product_data)
 [1] "Respondent.ID"
 [2] "Product.ID"
 [3] "Product"
 [4] "Instant.Liking"
 [5] "q1_1.personal.opinion.of.this.Deodorant"
 [6] "q2_all.words"
 [7] "q3_1.strength.of.the.Deodorant"
 [8] "q4_1.artificial.chemical"
 [9] "q4_2.attractive"
[10] "q4_3.bold"
[11] "q4_4.boring"
[12] "q4_5.casual"
[13] "q4_6.cheap"
[14] "q4_7.clean"
[15] "q4_8.easy.to.wear"
```

```
[16] "q4_9.elegant"
[17] "q4_10.feminine"
[18] "q4_11.for.someone.like.me"
[19] "q4_12.heavy"
[20] "q4_13.high.quality"
[21] "q4_14.long.lasting"
[22] "q4_15.masculine"
[23] "q4_16.memorable"
[24] "q4_17.natural"
[25] "q4_18.old.fashioned"
[26] "q4_19.ordinary"
[27] "q4_20.overpowering"
[28] "q4_21.sharp"
[29] "q4_22.sophisticated"
[30] "q4_23.upscale"
[31] "q4_24.well.rounded"
[32] "q5_1.Deodorant.is.addictive"
[33] "q7"
[34] "q8.1"
[35] "q8.2"
[36] "q8.5"
[37] "q8.6"
[38] "q8.7"
[39] "q8.8"
[40] "q8.9"
[41] "q8.10"
[42] "q8.11"
[43] "q8.12"
[44] "q8.13"
[45] "q8.17"
[46] "q8.18"
[47] "q8.19"
[48] "q8.20"
[49] "q9.how.likely.would.you.be.to.purchase.this.Deodorant"
[50] "q10.prefer.this.Deodorant.or.your.usual.Deodorant"
[51] "q11.time.of.day.would.this.Deodorant.be.appropriate"
[52] "q12.which.occasions.would.this.Deodorant.be.appropriate"
[53] "Q13_Liking.after.30.minutes"
[54] "q14.Deodorant.overall.on.a.scale.from.1.to.10"
[55] "ValSegb"
[56] "s7.involved.in.the.selection.of.the.cosmetic.products"
[57] "s8.ethnic.background"
[58] "s9.education"
[59] "s10.income"
[60] "s11.marital.status"
[61] "s12.working.status"
```

```
 [62] "s13.2"
 [63] "s13a.b.most.often"
 [64] "s13b.bottles.of.Deodorant.do.you.currently.own"
> test_data <- read.csv("<directory-name>test_data.csv")
> names(test_data)
 [1] "Respondent.ID"
 [2] "Product.ID"
 [3] "Product"
 [4] "q1_1.personal.opinion.of.this.Deodorant"
 [5] "q2_all.words"
 [6] "q3_1.strength.of.the.Deodorant"
 [7] "q4_1.artificial.chemical"
 [8] "q4_2.attractive"
 [9] "q4_3.bold"
[10] "q4_4.boring"
[11] "q4_5.casual"
[12] "q4_6.cheap"
[13] "q4_7.clean"
[14] "q4_8.easy.to.wear"
[15] "q4_9.elegant"
[16] "q4_10.feminine"
[17] "q4_11.for.someone.like.me"
[18] "q4_12.heavy"
[19] "q4_13.high.quality"
[20] "q4_14.long.lasting"
[21] "q4_15.masculine"
[22] "q4_16.memorable"
[23] "q4_17.natural"
[24] "q4_18.old.fashioned"
[25] "q4_19.ordinary"
[26] "q4_20.overpowering"
[27] "q4_21.sharp"
[28] "q4_22.sophisticated"
[29] "q4_23.upscale"
[30] "q4_24.well.rounded"
[31] "q5_1.Deodorant.is.addictive"
[32] "q7"
[33] "q8.1"
[34] "q8.2"
[35] "q8.5"
[36] "q8.6"
[37] "q8.8"
[38] "q8.11"
[39] "q8.12"
[40] "q8.13"
[41] "q8.19"
[42] "q8.20"
```

```
[43] "q9.how.likely.would.you.be.to.purchase.this.Deodorant"
[44] "q10.prefer.this.Deodorant.or.your.usual.Deodorant"
[45] "q11.time.of.day.would.this.Deodorant.be.appropriate"
[46] "q12.which.occasions.would.this.Deodorant.be.appropriate"
[47] "Q13_Liking.after.30.minutes"
[48] "q14.Deodorant.overall.on.a.scale.from.1.to.10"
[49] "ValSegb"
[50] "s7.involved.in.the.selection.of.the.cosmetic.products"
[51] "s8.ethnic.background"
[52] "s9.education"
[53] "s10.income"
[54] "s11.marital.status"
[55] "s12.working.status"
[56] "s13.2"
[57] "s13a.b.most.often"
[58] "s13b.bottles.of.Deodorant.do.you.currently.own"
> nrow(product_data)
[1] 2500
> nrow(test_data)
[1] 5105
> head(product_data)
  Respondent.ID Product.ID    Product Instant.Liking
1         3800        121 Deodorant B              1
2         3801        121 Deodorant B              0
3         3802        121 Deodorant B              0
4         3803        121 Deodorant B              1
5         3804        121 Deodorant B              1
6         3805        121 Deodorant B              0
  q1_1.personal.opinion.of.this.Deodorant q2_all.words
1                                       4            1
2                                       5            1
3                                       6            1
4                                       4            0
5                                       4            1
6                                       5            1
  q3_1.strength.of.the.Deodorant q4_1.artificial.chemical q4_2.attractive
1                              4                        2               5
2                              4                        4               2
3                              3                        2               5
4                              4                        5               5
5                              2                        1               3
6                              5                        5               5
  q4_3.bold q4_4.boring q4_5.casual q4_6.cheap q4_7.clean q4_8.easy.to.wear
1         4           2           3          5          5                 5
2         2           1           3          2          4                 4
3         2           4           2          4          3                 5
```

4	4	3	5	2	5	3
5	1	1	3	3	5	3
6	2	1	4	5	5	2

	q4_9.elegant	q4_10.feminine	q4_11.for.someone.like.me	q4_12.heavy
1	4	5	3	1
2	4	3	1	1
3	4	4	4	3
4	5	5	5	1
5	5	5	5	1
6	4	4	3	2

	q4_13.high.quality	q4_14.long.lasting	q4_15.masculine	q4_16.memorable
1	5	1	2	4
2	3	4	4	5
3	1	2	1	4
4	4	3	3	5
5	4	4	2	3
6	4	5	2	3

	q4_17.natural	q4_18.old.fashioned	q4_19.ordinary	q4_20.overpowering
1	5	4	5	1
2	3	3	4	2
3	2	4	3	2
4	5	4	2	5
5	5	1	2	4
6	4	2	2	3

	q4_21.sharp	q4_22.sophisticated	q4_23.upscale	q4_24.well.rounded
1	1	4	1	4
2	2	5	4	4
3	5	4	4	3
4	3	3	5	4
5	2	3	1	5
6	1	5	5	4

	q5_1.Deodorant.is.addictive	q7	q8.1	q8.2	q8.5	q8.6	q8.7	q8.8	q8.9	q8.10	q8.11
1	1	1	0	0	0	0	NA	1	NA	NA	0
2	4	4	0	0	0	1	NA	0	NA	NA	0
3	4	3	0	0	0	0	NA	0	NA	NA	0
4	4	3	0	0	0	0	NA	0	NA	NA	0
5	3	2	0	0	0	0	NA	0	NA	NA	0
6	1	3	0	0	0	0	NA	0	NA	NA	0

	q8.12	q8.13	q8.17	q8.18	q8.19	q8.20
1	0	0	NA	NA	0	0
2	0	0	NA	NA	0	0
3	0	0	NA	NA	0	0
4	0	0	NA	NA	0	0
5	0	0	NA	NA	0	0
6	0	0	NA	NA	0	0

```
   q9.how.likely.would.you.be.to.purchase.this.Deodorant
1                                                        2
2                                                        3
3                                                        5
4                                                        5
5                                                        5
6                                                        5
   q10.prefer.this.Deodorant.or.your.usual.Deodorant
1                                                   1
2                                                   5
3                                                   1
4                                                   4
5                                                   3
6                                                   4
   q11.time.of.day.would.this.Deodorant.be.appropriate
1                                                     1
2                                                     3
3                                                     3
4                                                     1
5                                                     3
6                                                     2
   q12.which.occasions.would.this.Deodorant.be.appropriate
1                                                         2
2                                                         3
3                                                         3
4                                                         3
5                                                         2
6                                                         2
   Q13_Liking.after.30.minutes q14.Deodorant.overall.on.a.scale.from.1.to.10
1                            1                                              7
2                            3                                              8
3                            2                                              5
4                            6                                              8
5                            5                                              4
6                            6                                              7
   ValSegb s7.involved.in.the.selection.of.the.cosmetic.products
1       7                                                       4
2       6                                                       4
3       7                                                       4
4       1                                                       4
5       4                                                       4
6       7                                                       4
   s8.ethnic.background s9.education s10.income s11.marital.status
1                     1            4          3                  1
2                     1            4          3                  1
3                     1            3          5                  1
```

```
4                        1              4              9                        1
5                        1              3              5                        1
6                        1              4              5                        2
  s12.working.status s13.2 s13a.b.most.often
1                    1     0                    0
2                    1     0                    0
3                    1     0                    0
4                    3     0                    0
5                    2     0                    0
6                    2     0                    0
  s13b.bottles.of.Deodorant.do.you.currently.own
1                                              3
2                                              4
3                                              2
4                                              3
5                                              3
6                                              2
> product_dataF <- product_data[, c(1:3,5:37,39,42:44,47:64)]
> Product.matrix <-model.matrix( ~Product - 1, data = product_dataF)
> product_dataF <- data.frame(product_dataF, Product.matrix)
> head(product_dataF)
  Respondent.ID Product.ID      Product q1_1.personal.opinion.of.this.Deodorant
1          3800         121 Deodorant B                                       4
2          3801         121 Deodorant B                                       5
3          3802         121 Deodorant B                                       6
4          3803         121 Deodorant B                                       4
5          3804         121 Deodorant B                                       4
6          3805         121 Deodorant B                                       5
  q2_all.words q3_1.strength.of.the.Deodorant q4_1.artificial.chemical
1            1                              4                        2
2            1                              4                        4
3            1                              3                        2
4            0                              4                        5
5            1                              2                        1
6            1                              5                        5
  q4_2.attractive q4_3.bold q4_4.boring q4_5.casual q4_6.cheap q4_7.clean
1               5         4           2           3          5          5
2               2         2           1           3          2          4
3               5         2           4           2          4          3
4               5         4           3           5          2          5
5               3         1           1           3          3          5
6               5         2           1           4          5          5
  q4_8.easy.to.wear q4_9.elegant q4_10.feminine q4_11.for.someone.like.me
1                 5            4              5                         3
2                 4            4              3                         1
3                 5            4              4                         4
```

4	3	5	5	5
5	3	5	5	5
6	2	4	4	3

	q4_12.heavy	q4_13.high.quality	q4_14.long.lasting	q4_15.masculine
1	1	5	1	2
2	1	3	4	4
3	3	1	2	1
4	1	4	3	3
5	1	4	4	2
6	2	4	5	2

	q4_16.memorable	q4_17.natural	q4_18.old.fashioned	q4_19.ordinary
1	4	5	4	5
2	5	3	3	4
3	4	2	4	3
4	5	5	4	2
5	3	5	1	2
6	3	4	2	2

	q4_20.overpowering	q4_21.sharp	q4_22.sophisticated	q4_23.upscale
1	1	1	4	1
2	2	2	5	4
3	2	5	4	4
4	5	3	3	5
5	4	2	3	1
6	3	1	5	5

	q4_24.well.rounded	q5_1.Deodorant.is.addictive	q7	q8.1	q8.2	q8.5	q8.6	q8.8
1	4		1	1	0	0	0	0	1
2	4		4	4	0	0	0	1	0
3	3		4	3	0	0	0	0	0
4	4		4	3	0	0	0	0	0
5	5		3	2	0	0	0	0	0
6	4		1	3	0	0	0	0	0

	q8.11	q8.12	q8.13	q8.19	q8.20
1	0	0	0	0	0
2	0	0	0	0	0
3	0	0	0	0	0
4	0	0	0	0	0
5	0	0	0	0	0
6	0	0	0	0	0

	q9.how.likely.would.you.be.to.purchase.this.Deodorant
1	2
2	3
3	5
4	5
5	5
6	5

```
    q10.prefer.this.Deodorant.or.your.usual.Deodorant
1                                                    1
2                                                    5
3                                                    1
4                                                    4
5                                                    3
6                                                    4
    q11.time.of.day.would.this.Deodorant.be.appropriate
1                                                    1
2                                                    3
3                                                    3
4                                                    1
5                                                    3
6                                                    2
    q12.which.occasions.would.this.Deodorant.be.appropriate
1                                                    2
2                                                    3
3                                                    3
4                                                    3
5                                                    2
6                                                    2
    Q13_Liking.after.30.minutes q14.Deodorant.overall.on.a.scale.from.1.to.10
1                             1                                              7
2                             3                                              8
3                             2                                              5
4                             6                                              8
5                             5                                              4
6                             6                                              7
    ValSegb s7.involved.in.the.selection.of.the.cosmetic.products
1       7                                                        4
2       6                                                        4
3       7                                                        4
4       1                                                        4
5       4                                                        4
6       7                                                        4
    s8.ethnic.background s9.education s10.income s11.marital.status
1                      1            4          3                  1
2                      1            4          3                  1
3                      1            3          5                  1
4                      1            4          9                  1
5                      1            3          5                  1
6                      1            4          5                  2
    s12.working.status s13.2 s13a.b.most.often
1                    1     0                  0
2                    1     0                  0
3                    1     0                  0
```

```
4                3    0            0
5                2    0            0
6                2    0            0
  s13b.bottles.of.Deodorant.do.you.currently.own ProductDeodorant.B
1                                     .                3                1
2                                                      4                1
3                                                      2                1
4                                                      3                1
5                                                      3                1
6                                                      2                1
  ProductDeodorant.F ProductDeodorant.G ProductDeodorant.H ProductDeodorant.J
1                 0                  0                  0                  0
2                 0                  0                  0                  0
3                 0                  0                  0                  0
4                 0                  0                  0                  0
5                 0                  0                  0                  0
6                 0                  0                  0                  0
> ncol(product_dataF)
[1] 63
> maxs <- apply(product_dataF[, c(1:2,4:58)], 2, max)
> mins <- apply(product_dataF[, c(1:2,4:58)], 2, min)
> scaled <- as.data.frame(scale(product_dataF[, c(1:2,4:58)], center = mins, scale
= maxs - mins))
> scaledF <- as.data.frame(cbind(scaled, product_dataF[, c(59:63)]))
> set.seed(500)
> library(neuralnet)
Warning message:
package 'neuralnet' was built under R version 3.5.0
> library(ggplot2)
Warning message:
package 'ggplot2' was built under R version 3.4.4
> head(scaledF) # had some NA and NaN
  Respondent.ID Product.ID q1_1.personal.opinion.of.this.Deodorant q2_all.words
1   0.000000e+00          0                                0.5000000          0.2
2   9.709681e-05          0                                0.6666667          0.2
3   1.941936e-04          0                                0.8333333          0.2
4   2.912904e-04          0                                0.5000000          0.0
5   3.883872e-04          0                                0.5000000          0.2
6   4.854840e-04          0                                0.6666667          0.2
  q3_1.strength.of.the.Deodorant q4_1.artificial.chemical q4_2.attractive
1                           0.75                     0.25            1.00
2                           0.75                     0.75            0.25
3                           0.50                     0.25            1.00
4                           0.75                     1.00            1.00
5                           0.25                     0.00            0.50
6                           1.00                     1.00            1.00
```

	q4_3.bold	q4_4.boring	q4_5.casual	q4_6.cheap	q4_7.clean	q4_8.easy.to.wear
1	0.75	0.25	0.50	1.00	1.00	1.00
2	0.25	0.00	0.50	0.25	0.75	0.75
3	0.25	0.75	0.25	0.75	0.50	1.00
4	0.75	0.50	1.00	0.25	1.00	0.50
5	0.00	0.00	0.50	0.50	1.00	0.50
6	0.25	0.00	0.75	1.00	1.00	0.25

	q4_9.elegant	q4_10.feminine	q4_11.for.someone.like.me	q4_12.heavy
1	0.75	1.00	0.50	0.00
2	0.75	0.50	0.00	0.00
3	0.75	0.75	0.75	0.50
4	1.00	1.00	1.00	0.00
5	1.00	1.00	1.00	0.00
6	0.75	0.75	0.50	0.25

	q4_13.high.quality	q4_14.long.lasting	q4_15.masculine	q4_16.memorable
1	1.00	0.00	0.25	0.75
2	0.50	0.75	0.75	1.00
3	0.00	0.25	0.00	0.75
4	0.75	0.50	0.50	1.00
5	0.75	0.75	0.25	0.50
6	0.75	1.00	0.25	0.50

	q4_17.natural	q4_18.old.fashioned	q4_19.ordinary	q4_20.overpowering
1	1.00	0.75	1.00	0.00
2	0.50	0.50	0.75	0.25
3	0.25	0.75	0.50	0.25
4	1.00	0.75	0.25	1.00
5	1.00	0.00	0.25	0.75
6	0.75	0.25	0.25	0.50

	q4_21.sharp	q4_22.sophisticated	q4_23.upscale	q4_24.well.rounded
1	0.00	0.75	0.00	0.75
2	0.25	1.00	0.75	0.75
3	1.00	0.75	0.75	0.50
4	0.50	0.50	1.00	0.75
5	0.25	0.50	0.00	1.00
6	0.00	1.00	1.00	0.75

	q5_1.Deodorant.is.addictive	q7	q8.1	q8.2	q8.5	q8.6	q8.8	q8.11	q8.12
1	0.00	0.4545455	0	NA	0	0	NA	0	NA
2	0.75	0.7272727	0	NA	0	1	NA	0	NA
3	0.75	0.6363636	0	NA	0	0	NA	0	NA
4	0.75	0.6363636	0	NA	0	0	NA	0	NA
5	0.50	0.5454545	0	NA	0	0	NA	0	NA
6	0.00	0.6363636	0	NA	0	0	NA	0	NA

	q8.13	q8.19	q8.20	q9.how.likely.would.you.be.to.purchase.this.Deodorant
1	0	0	NA	0.25
2	0	0	NA	0.50
3	0	0	NA	1.00

4	0	0	NA	1.00
5	0	0	NA	1.00
6	0	0	NA	1.00

	q10.prefer.this.Deodorant.or.your.usual.Deodorant
1	0.00
2	1.00
3	0.00
4	0.75
5	0.50
6	0.75

	q11.time.of.day.would.this.Deodorant.be.appropriate
1	0.0
2	1.0
3	1.0
4	0.0
5	1.0
6	0.5

	q12.which.occasions.would.this.Deodorant.be.appropriate
1	0.5
2	1.0
3	1.0
4	1.0
5	0.5
6	0.5

	Q13_Liking.after.30.minutes	q14.Deodorant.overall.on.a.scale.from.1.to.10
1	0.0000000	0.6666667
2	0.3333333	0.7777778
3	0.1666667	0.4444444
4	0.8333333	0.7777778
5	0.6666667	0.3333333
6	0.8333333	0.6666667

	ValSegb	s7.involved.in.the.selection.of.the.cosmetic.products
1	1.0000000	NaN
2	0.8333333	NaN
3	1.0000000	NaN
4	0.0000000	NaN
5	0.5000000	NaN
6	1.0000000	NaN

	s8.ethnic.background	s9.education	s10.income	s11.marital.status
1	0	0.4	0.125	0.00
2	0	0.4	0.125	0.00
3	0	0.2	0.375	0.00
4	0	0.4	0.875	0.00
5	0	0.2	0.375	0.00
6	0	0.4	0.375	0.25

```
  s12.working.status s13.2 s13a.b.most.often
1         0.0000000     0               0
2         0.0000000     0               0
3         0.0000000     0               0
4         0.3333333     0               0
5         0.1666667     0               0
6         0.1666667     0               0
  s13b.bottles.of.Deodorant.do.you.currently.own ProductDeodorant.B
1                                             0.4                  1
2                                             0.6                  1
3                                             0.2                  1
4                                             0.4                  1
5                                             0.4                  1
6                                             0.2                  1
  ProductDeodorant.F ProductDeodorant.G ProductDeodorant.H ProductDeodorant.J
1                  0                  0                  0                  0
2                  0                  0                  0                  0
3                  0                  0                  0                  0
4                  0                  0                  0                  0
5                  0                  0                  0                  0
6                  0                  0                  0                  0
> scaledFF <- scaledF[, c(1:32,34:35,37,39:40,42:48,50:62)]
> head(scaledFF)
  Respondent.ID Product.ID q1_1.personal.opinion.of.this.Deodorant q2_all.words
1  0.000000e+00          0                                0.5000000          0.2
2  9.709681e-05          0                                0.6666667          0.2
3  1.941936e-04          0                                0.8333333          0.2
4  2.912904e-04          0                                0.5000000          0.0
5  3.883872e-04          0                                0.5000000          0.2
6  4.854840e-04          0                                0.6666667          0.2
  q3_1.strength.of.the.Deodorant q4_1.artificial.chemical q4_2.attractive
1                           0.75                      0.25            1.00
2                           0.75                      0.75            0.25
3                           0.50                      0.25            1.00
4                           0.75                      1.00            1.00
5                           0.25                      0.00            0.50
6                           1.00                      1.00            1.00
  q4_3.bold q4_4.boring q4_5.casual q4_6.cheap q4_7.clean q4_8.easy.to.wear
1      0.75        0.25        0.50       1.00       1.00              1.00
2      0.25        0.00        0.50       0.25       0.75              0.75
3      0.25        0.75        0.25       0.75       0.50              1.00
4      0.75        0.50        1.00       0.25       1.00              0.50
5      0.00        0.00        0.50       0.50       1.00              0.50
6      0.25        0.00        0.75       1.00       1.00              0.25
```

	q4_9.elegant	q4_10.feminine	q4_11.for.someone.like.me	q4_12.heavy
1	0.75	1.00	0.50	0.00
2	0.75	0.50	0.00	0.00
3	0.75	0.75	0.75	0.50
4	1.00	1.00	1.00	0.00
5	1.00	1.00	1.00	0.00
6	0.75	0.75	0.50	0.25

	q4_13.high.quality	q4_14.long.lasting	q4_15.masculine	q4_16.memorable
1	1.00	0.00	0.25	0.75
2	0.50	0.75	0.75	1.00
3	0.00	0.25	0.00	0.75
4	0.75	0.50	0.50	1.00
5	0.75	0.75	0.25	0.50
6	0.75	1.00	0.25	0.50

	q4_17.natural	q4_18.old.fashioned	q4_19.ordinary	q4_20.overpowering
1	1.00	0.75	1.00	0.00
2	0.50	0.50	0.75	0.25
3	0.25	0.75	0.50	0.25
4	1.00	0.75	0.25	1.00
5	1.00	0.00	0.25	0.75
6	0.75	0.25	0.25	0.50

	q4_21.sharp	q4_22.sophisticated	q4_23.upscale	q4_24.well.rounded
1	0.00	0.75	0.00	0.75
2	0.25	1.00	0.75	0.75
3	1.00	0.75	0.75	0.50
4	0.50	0.50	1.00	0.75
5	0.25	0.50	0.00	1.00
6	0.00	1.00	1.00	0.75

	q5_1.Deodorant.is.addictive	q7	q8.1	q8.5	q8.6	q8.11	q8.13	q8.19
1	0.00	0.4545455	0	0	0	0	0	0
2	0.75	0.7272727	0	0	1	0	0	0
3	0.75	0.6363636	0	0	0	0	0	0
4	0.75	0.6363636	0	0	0	0	0	0
5	0.50	0.5454545	0	0	0	0	0	0
6	0.00	0.6363636	0	0	0	0	0	0

	q9.how.likely.would.you.be.to.purchase.this.Deodorant
1	0.25
2	0.50
3	1.00
4	1.00
5	1.00
6	1.00

	q10.prefer.this.Deodorant.or.your.usual.Deodorant
1	0.00
2	1.00
3	0.00

4	0.75
5	0.50
6	0.75

	q11.time.of.day.would.this.Deodorant.be.appropriate
1	0.0
2	1.0
3	1.0
4	0.0
5	1.0
6	0.5

	q12.which.occasions.would.this.Deodorant.be.appropriate
1	0.5
2	1.0
3	1.0
4	1.0
5	0.5
6	0.5

	Q13_Liking.after.30.minutes	q14.Deodorant.overall.on.a.scale.from.1.to.10
1	0.0000000	0.6666667
2	0.3333333	0.7777778
3	0.1666667	0.4444444
4	0.8333333	0.7777778
5	0.6666667	0.3333333
6	0.8333333	0.6666667

	ValSegb	s8.ethnic.background	s9.education	s10.income	s11.marital.status
1	1.0000000	0	0.4	0.125	0.00
2	0.8333333	0	0.4	0.125	0.00
3	1.0000000	0	0.2	0.375	0.00
4	0.0000000	0	0.4	0.875	0.00
5	0.5000000	0	0.2	0.375	0.00
6	1.0000000	0	0.4	0.375	0.25

	s12.working.status	s13.2	s13a.b.most.often
1	0.0000000	0	0
2	0.0000000	0	0
3	0.0000000	0	0
4	0.3333333	0	0
5	0.1666667	0	0
6	0.1666667	0	0

	s13b.bottles.of.Deodorant.do.you.currently.own	ProductDeodorant.B
1	0.4	1
2	0.6	1
3	0.2	1
4	0.4	1
5	0.4	1
6	0.2	1

```
   ProductDeodorant.F ProductDeodorant.G ProductDeodorant.H ProductDeodorant.J
1                    0                  0                  0                  0
2                    0                  0                  0                  0
3                    0                  0                  0                  0
4                    0                  0                  0                  0
5                    0                  0                  0                  0
6                    0                  0                  0                  0
> ncol(scaledFF) # 57 # 43rd column is scale1.to.10
[1] 57
> scaledFF <- scaledFF[, c(1:42,44:57,43)]
> ncol(scaledFF) #57
[1] 57
> head(scaledFF) # last column (57th) is scale1.to.10
  Respondent.ID Product.ID q1_1.personal.opinion.of.this.Deodorant q2_all.words
1  0.000000e+00          0                               0.5000000          0.2
2  9.709681e-05          0                               0.6666667          0.2
3  1.941936e-04          0                               0.8333333          0.2
4  2.912904e-04          0                               0.5000000          0.0
5  3.883872e-04          0                               0.5000000          0.2
6  4.854840e-04          0                               0.6666667          0.2
  q3_1.strength.of.the.Deodorant q4_1.artificial.chemical q4_2.attractive
1                           0.75                     0.25            1.00
2                           0.75                     0.75            0.25
3                           0.50                     0.25            1.00
4                           0.75                     1.00            1.00
5                           0.25                     0.00            0.50
6                           1.00                     1.00            1.00
  q4_3.bold q4_4.boring q4_5.casual q4_6.cheap q4_7.clean q4_8.easy.to.wear
1      0.75        0.25        0.50       1.00       1.00              1.00
2      0.25        0.00        0.50       0.25       0.75              0.75
3      0.25        0.75        0.25       0.75       0.50              1.00
4      0.75        0.50        1.00       0.25       1.00              0.50
5      0.00        0.00        0.50       0.50       1.00              0.50
6      0.25        0.00        0.75       1.00       1.00              0.25
  q4_9.elegant q4_10.feminine q4_11.for.someone.like.me q4_12.heavy
1         0.75           1.00                      0.50        0.00
2         0.75           0.50                      0.00        0.00
3         0.75           0.75                      0.75        0.50
4         1.00           1.00                      1.00        0.00
5         1.00           1.00                      1.00        0.00
6         0.75           0.75                      0.50        0.25
  q4_13.high.quality q4_14.long.lasting q4_15.masculine q4_16.memorable
1               1.00               0.00            0.25            0.75
2               0.50               0.75            0.75            1.00
3               0.00               0.25            0.00            0.75
```

4	0.75	0.50	0.50	1.00
5	0.75	0.75	0.25	0.50
6	0.75	1.00	0.25	0.50

	q4_17.natural	q4_18.old.fashioned	q4_19.ordinary	q4_20.overpowering
1	1.00	0.75	1.00	0.00
2	0.50	0.50	0.75	0.25
3	0.25	0.75	0.50	0.25
4	1.00	0.75	0.25	1.00
5	1.00	0.00	0.25	0.75
6	0.75	0.25	0.25	0.50

	q4_21.sharp	q4_22.sophisticated	q4_23.upscale	q4_24.well.rounded
1	0.00	0.75	0.00	0.75
2	0.25	1.00	0.75	0.75
3	1.00	0.75	0.75	0.50
4	0.50	0.50	1.00	0.75
5	0.25	0.50	0.00	1.00
6	0.00	1.00	1.00	0.75

	q5_1.Deodorant.is.addictive	q7	q8.1	q8.5	q8.6	q8.11	q8.13	q8.19
1	0.00	0.4545455	0	0	0	0	0	0
2	0.75	0.7272727	0	0	1	0	0	0
3	0.75	0.6363636	0	0	0	0	0	0
4	0.75	0.6363636	0	0	0	0	0	0
5	0.50	0.5454545	0	0	0	0	0	0
6	0.00	0.6363636	0	0	0	0	0	0

	q9.how.likely.would.you.be.to.purchase.this.Deodorant
1	0.25
2	0.50
3	1.00
4	1.00
5	1.00
6	1.00

	q10.prefer.this.Deodorant.or.your.usual.Deodorant
1	0.00
2	1.00
3	0.00
4	0.75
5	0.50
6	0.75

	q11.time.of.day.would.this.Deodorant.be.appropriate
1	0.0
2	1.0
3	1.0
4	0.0
5	1.0
6	0.5

```
   q12.which.occasions.would.this.Deodorant.be.appropriate
1                                                        0.5
2                                                        1.0
3                                                        1.0
4                                                        1.0
5                                                        0.5
6                                                        0.5
```

	Q13_Liking.after.30.minutes	ValSegb	s8.ethnic.background	s9.education
1	0.0000000	1.0000000	0	0.4
2	0.3333333	0.8333333	0	0.4
3	0.1666667	1.0000000	0	0.2
4	0.8333333	0.0000000	0	0.4
5	0.6666667	0.5000000	0	0.2
6	0.8333333	1.0000000	0	0.4

	s10.income	s11.marital.status	s12.working.status	s13.2	s13a.b.most.often
1	0.125	0.00	0.0000000	0	0
2	0.125	0.00	0.0000000	0	0
3	0.375	0.00	0.0000000	0	0
4	0.875	0.00	0.3333333	0	0
5	0.375	0.00	0.1666667	0	0
6	0.375	0.25	0.1666667	0	0

	s13b.bottles.of.Deodorant.do.you.currently.own	ProductDeodorant.B
1	0.4	1
2	0.6	1
3	0.2	1
4	0.4	1
5	0.4	1
6	0.2	1

	ProductDeodorant.F	ProductDeodorant.G	ProductDeodorant.H	ProductDeodorant.J
1	0	0	0	0
2	0	0	0	0
3	0	0	0	0
4	0	0	0	0
5	0	0	0	0
6	0	0	0	0

```
   q14.Deodorant.overall.on.a.scale.from.1.to.10
1                                         0.6666667
2                                         0.7777778
3                                         0.4444444
4                                         0.7777778
5                                         0.3333333
6                                         0.6666667
> scaledFF_for_PA <- cbind(scaledFF, product_data[, c(4)])
> ncol(scaledFF_for_PA)
[1] 58
> names(scaledFF_for_PA)[58] <- "Instant.Liking"
> head(scaledFF_for_PA)
```

	Respondent.ID	Product.ID	q1_1.personal.opinion.of.this.Deodorant
1	0.00000000000000	0	0.5000000000
2	0.00009709680552	0	0.6666666667
3	0.00019419361103	0	0.8333333333
4	0.00029129041655	0	0.5000000000
5	0.00038838722206	0	0.5000000000
6	0.00048548402758	0	0.6666666667

	q2_all.words	q3_1.strength.of.the.Deodorant	q4_1.artificial.chemical
1	0.2	0.75	0.25
2	0.2	0.75	0.75
3	0.2	0.50	0.25
4	0.0	0.75	1.00
5	0.2	0.25	0.00
6	0.2	1.00	1.00

	q4_2.attractive	q4_3.bold	q4_4.boring	q4_5.casual	q4_6.cheap	q4_7.clean
1	1.00	0.75	0.25	0.50	1.00	1.00
2	0.25	0.25	0.00	0.50	0.25	0.75
3	1.00	0.25	0.75	0.25	0.75	0.50
4	1.00	0.75	0.50	1.00	0.25	1.00
5	0.50	0.00	0.00	0.50	0.50	1.00
6	1.00	0.25	0.00	0.75	1.00	1.00

	q4_8.easy.to.wear	q4_9.elegant	q4_10.feminine	q4_11.for.someone.like.me
1	1.00	0.75	1.00	0.50
2	0.75	0.75	0.50	0.00
3	1.00	0.75	0.75	0.75
4	0.50	1.00	1.00	1.00
5	0.50	1.00	1.00	1.00
6	0.25	0.75	0.75	0.50

	q4_12.heavy	q4_13.high.quality	q4_14.long.lasting	q4_15.masculine
1	0.00	1.00	0.00	0.25
2	0.00	0.50	0.75	0.75
3	0.50	0.00	0.25	0.00
4	0.00	0.75	0.50	0.50
5	0.00	0.75	0.75	0.25
6	0.25	0.75	1.00	0.25

	q4_16.memorable	q4_17.natural	q4_18.old.fashioned	q4_19.ordinary
1	0.75	1.00	0.75	1.00
2	1.00	0.50	0.50	0.75
3	0.75	0.25	0.75	0.50
4	1.00	1.00	0.75	0.25
5	0.50	1.00	0.00	0.25
6	0.50	0.75	0.25	0.25

	q4_20.overpowering	q4_21.sharp	q4_22.sophisticated	q4_23.upscale
1	0.00	0.00	0.75	0.00
2	0.25	0.25	1.00	0.75
3	0.25	1.00	0.75	0.75

4	1.00	0.50	0.50	1.00
5	0.75	0.25	0.50	0.00
6	0.50	0.00	1.00	1.00

	q4_24.well.rounded	q5_1.Deodorant.is.addictive	q7	q8.1	q8.5	q8.6
1	0.75	0.00 0.4545454545	0	0	0	
2	0.75	0.75 0.7272727273	0	0	1	
3	0.50	0.75 0.6363636364	0	0	0	
4	0.75	0.75 0.6363636364	0	0	0	
5	1.00	0.50 0.5454545455	0	0	0	
6	0.75	0.00 0.6363636364	0	0	0	

	q8.11	q8.13	q8.19	q9.how.likely.would.you.be.to.purchase.this.Deodorant
1	0	0	0	0.25
2	0	0	0	0.50
3	0	0	0	1.00
4	0	0	0	1.00
5	0	0	0	1.00
6	0	0	0	1.00

	q10.prefer.this.Deodorant.or.your.usual.Deodorant
1	0.00
2	1.00
3	0.00
4	0.75
5	0.50
6	0.75

	q11.time.of.day.would.this.Deodorant.be.appropriate
1	0.0
2	1.0
3	1.0
4	0.0
5	1.0
6	0.5

	q12.which.occasions.would.this.Deodorant.be.appropriate
1	0.5
2	1.0
3	1.0
4	1.0
5	0.5
6	0.5

	Q13_Liking.after.30.minutes	ValSegb	s8.ethnic.background	s9.education
1	0.0000000000	1.0000000000	0	0.4
2	0.3333333333	0.8333333333	0	0.4
3	0.1666666667	1.0000000000	0	0.2
4	0.8333333333	0.0000000000	0	0.4
5	0.6666666667	0.5000000000	0	0.2
6	0.8333333333	1.0000000000	0	0.4

```
     s10.income s11.marital.status s12.working.status s13.2 s13a.b.most.often
1        0.125             0.00       0.0000000000     0                    0
2        0.125             0.00       0.0000000000     0                    0
3        0.375             0.00       0.0000000000     0                    0
4        0.875             0.00       0.3333333333     0                    0
5        0.375             0.00       0.1666666667     0                    0
6        0.375             0.25       0.1666666667     0                    0
     s13b.bottles.of.Deodorant.do.you.currently.own ProductDeodorant.B
1                                                0.4                  1
2                                                0.6                  1
3                                                0.2                  1
4                                                0.4                  1
5                                                0.4                  1
6                                                0.2                  1
  ProductDeodorant.F ProductDeodorant.G ProductDeodorant.H ProductDeodorant.J
1                  0                  0                  0                  0
2                  0                  0                  0                  0
3                  0                  0                  0                  0
4                  0                  0                  0                  0
5                  0                  0                  0                  0
6                  0                  0                  0                  0
  q14.Deodorant.overall.on.a.scale.from.1.to.10 Instant.Liking
1                                  0.6666666667              1
2                                  0.7777777778              0
3                                  0.4444444444              0
4                                  0.7777777778              1
5                                  0.3333333333              1
6                                  0.6666666667              0
> n_for_PA <- names(scaledFF_for_PA)
> set.seed(456)
> f_for_PA <- as.formula(Instant.Liking ~ ProductDeodorant.B + ProductDeodorant.F
+ ProductDeodorant.G + ProductDeodorant.H + ProductDeodorant.J + q14.Deodorant.
overall.on.a.scale.from.1.to.10)
> f_for_PA
Instant.Liking ~ ProductDeodorant.B + ProductDeodorant.F + ProductDeodorant.G +
    ProductDeodorant.H + ProductDeodorant.J + q14.Deodorant.overall.on.a.scale.from.1.to.10
> DNNf3_for_PA <- neuralnet(f_for_PA, data = scaledFF_for_PA, hidden=c(5,3),
linear.output=TRUE)
> plot(DNNf3_for_PA)
> colnames(scaledFF_for_PA)
> predicted_scale_value <- pr.DNNf3_r2
> scaledTestFF <- scaledTestFF[, c(1:42, 44:52, 53:57, 43)]
> colnames(scaledTestFF)
> scaledTestFF_for_PA <- cbind(scaledTestFF, predicted_scale_value)
> colnames(scaledTestFF_for_PA)
> scaledTestFF_for_PA <- scaledTestFF_for_PA[, c(1:56, 58, 57)]
```

```
> pr.DNNf3_r2_for_PA <- compute(DNNf3_for_PA, scaledTestFF_for_PA[, c(52:57)])
> pr.DNNf3_r2_for_PA_r2 <- pr.DNNf3_r2_for_PA$net.result
> class(pr.DNNf3_r2_for_PA_r2)
[1] "matrix"
> dim(pr.DNNf3_r2_for_PA_r2)
[1] 5105    1
> head(pr.DNNf3_r2_for_PA_r2)
          [,1]
1 0.2462013271
2 0.2462013271
3 0.2462013271
4 0.2462013271
5 0.2462013271
6 0.2462013271
>
> plot(scaledTestFF_for_PA$ProductDeodorant.G,pr.DNNf3_r2_for_PA_
r2,col='green',main='Product Deodorant G vs Predicted',
+ xlab='Product Deodorant G',pch=18,cex=2)
> abline(0,1,lwd=2)
> legend('bottom',legend='Product Deodorant G vs Predicted',pch=2,col='green',bty='n')
> plot(scaledTestFF_for_PA$ProductDeodorant.H,pr.DNNf3_r2_for_PA_
r2,col='green',main='Product Deodorant H vs Predicted',
+ xlab='Product Deodorant H',pch=18,cex=2)
> abline(0,1,lwd=2)
> legend('bottom',legend='Product Deodorant H vs Predicted',pch=2,col='green',bty='n')
> colnames(scaledTestFF_for_PA)

> pr.DNNf3_r2_for_PA2 <- compute(DNNf3_for_PA, scaledTestFF_for_PA[, c(52:56, 58)])
> pr.DNNf3_r2_for_PA_r2_2 <- pr.DNNf3_r2_for_PA2$net.result
> dim(pr.DNNf3_r2_for_PA_r2_2)
[1] 5105    1
> head(pr.DNNf3_r2_for_PA_r2_2)
          [,1]
1 0.2327684731
2 0.2827996446
3 0.1303827389
4 0.2617500624
5 0.3360772057
6 0.2532206749
>
> plot(scaledTestFF_for_PA$ProductDeodorant.G, pr.DNNf3_r2_for_PA_r2_2,
+ col='green',main='Product Deodorant G vs Predicted',
+ xlab='Product Deodorant G',pch=18,cex=2)
> abline(0,1,lwd=2)
> legend('bottom',legend='Product Deodorant G vs Predicted',pch=2,col='green',bty='n')
> > plot(scaledTestFF_for_PA$ProductDeodorant.H, pr.DNNf3_r2_for_PA_r2_2,
```

```
+ col='green',main='Product Deodorant H  vs Predicted',
+ xlab='Product Deodorant G',pch=18,cex=2)
> abline(0,1,lwd=2)
> legend('bottom',legend='Product Deodorant H vs Predicted',pch=2,col='green',bty='n')
> plot(scaledTestFF_for_PA$ProductDeodorant.B, pr.DNNf3_r2_for_PA_r2_2,
+ col='green',main='Product Deodorant B  vs Predicted',
+ xlab='Product Deodorant B',pch=18,cex=2)
> abline(0,1,lwd=2)
> legend('bottom',legend='Product Deodorant B vs Predicted',pch=2,col='green',bty='n')
> plot(scaledTestFF_for_PA$ProductDeodorant.F, pr.DNNf3_r2_for_PA_r2_2,
+ col='green',main='Product Deodorant F  vs Predicted',
+ xlab='Product Deodorant F',pch=18,cex=2)
> abline(0,1,lwd=2)
> legend('bottom',legend='Product Deodorant F vs Predicted',pch=2,col='green',bty='n')
> plot(scaledTestFF_for_PA$ProductDeodorant.J, pr.DNNf3_r2_for_PA_r2_2,
+ col='green',main='Product Deodorant J  vs Predicted',
+ xlab='Product Deodorant J',pch=18,cex=2)
> abline(0,1,lwd=2)
> legend('bottom',legend='Product Deodorant J vs Predicted',pch=2,col='green',bty='n')
>
```

4.4.2 The BI-Enablement and Its Impact on the Enterprise

Output of recommendation can be visually integrated into BI dashboards for actionable insight (e.g., Tableau Dashboard, Oracle BI, Microsoft BI, etc.)

4.4.2.1 The BI-Enablement and Its Impact on the Enterprise (Prescriptive Analytics)

Output of recommendation can be visually integrated in BI dashboards for actionable insight (e.g., Tableau Dashboard, Oracle BI, Microsoft BI, etc.)

Figure 4.35 shows the fitted DNN plot—actual versus predicted scale. Five products are graphed here.

Prescriptive Analysis from an AI Meets BI Standpoint

Figure 4.35 suggests the accuracy of fitted DNN showing the actual versus predicted product scale with a MSE of 6.4.

The single almost vertical line parallel to the y-axis is the line of best fit for our DNN. The points to the right of this vertical line of fit mean that they represent higher actuals when compared to predicted. And those to the left of this line suggest that they represent lower actuals when compared to predicted. In addition, we realize that the average actual is 6.7, which is clearly demarking the higher and lower actuals around it for all five products.

The horizontal dotted lines suggest the following: Those dotted lines that are nearer to the x-axis represent a low predicted value and hence higher deviation compared to the actuals, and those dotted lines that are farther away from the x-axis represent a higher predicted value and hence lower deviation compared to the actuals.

The graphs for individual products versus prediction in Figures 4.35 to 4.40 can be interpreted as follows:

o In the graphs for products G and H (Figures 4.38 and 4.39), the points on the right of the vertical line represent high actuals-based—much less deviance from the actuals, as they are farther away from the y-axis and are highly predictable as well (farther away from x-axis). Therefore, they have high functionality and quality because of higher predictability.

o Other products have a much lower predictability (closer to the x-axis) and, hence, less quality and functionality.

o In general, the four points to the left of the vertical line have some linearity in the graphs, except those for products G and H, but represent less actuals even though they are aligned with the 0.0 on the x-axis. However, they can be predicted using mathematical, statistical, or information systems models.

o *In principle, for the best recommendation purposes we take only higher predictability values.* **In this use case, it happens to be the three categories from the top.**

o The plots in Figure 4.35 and the ones with individual versus predicted products (Figures 4.36 to 4.45) can be integrated with BI platforms such as Tableau dashboard, Oracle BI, Microsoft BI, etc. using either an R interface or SQL interface for further/supplemental analyses for business process purposes.

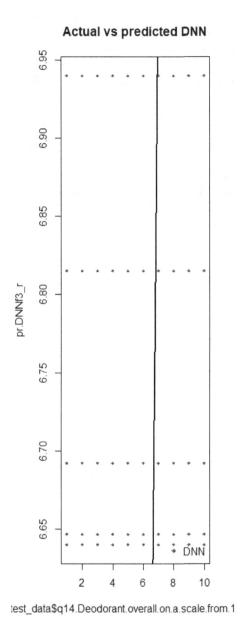

Figure 4.35   Accuracy of fitted DNN showing the actual vs. predicted product scale.

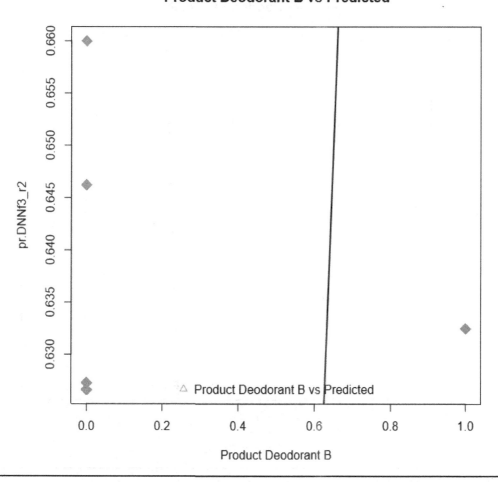

Figure 4.36   Product Deodorant B vs. Predicted.

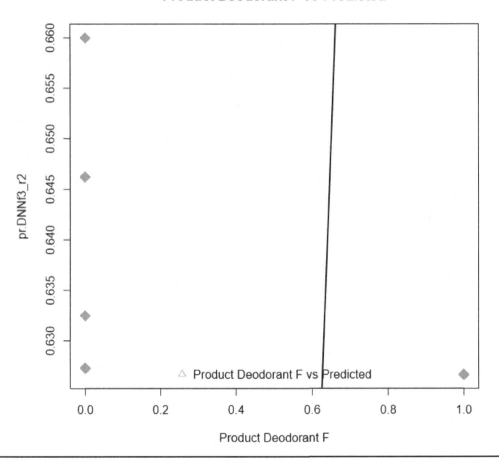

Figure 4.37   Product Deodorant F vs. Predicted.

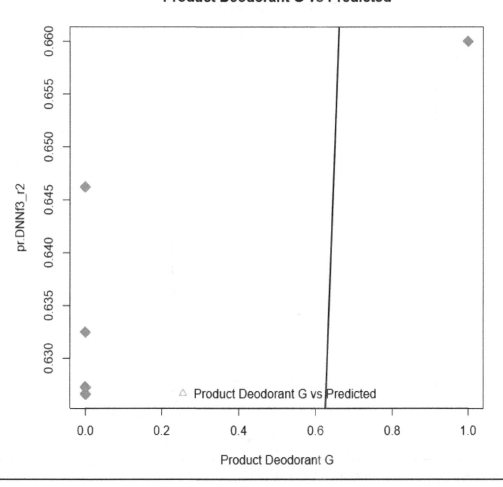

Figure 4.38 Product Deodorant G vs. Predicted.

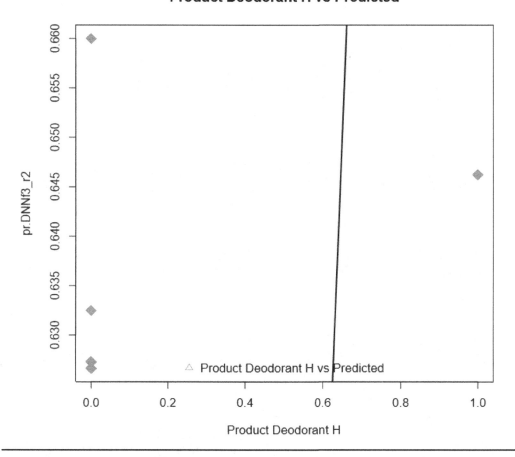

Figure 4.39   Product Deodorant H vs. Predicted.

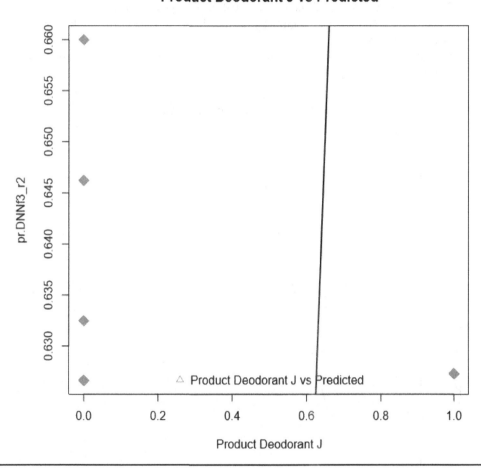

Figure 4.40   Product Deodorant J vs. Predicted.

4.4.2.2 The BI-Enablement and Its Impact on the Enterprise (Predictive Analytics)

The output of recommendation can be visually integrated in BI dashboards for actionable insight (e.g., Tableau Dashboard, Oracle BI, Microsoft BI, etc.)

The graphs for individual versus predicted products are shown in Figures 4.41 to 4.45.

- Among all the graphs, only G has high probability values at x = 1.0.
- In all graphs, at x = 0.0, G possesses less probability when compared to others.
  - The probability of instant likeness is very high at x = 1.0 only in G (not in the rest).
  - The probability of instant likeness is at x = 0.0 in all graphs except G.
- The points x = 0 and x = 1 are significant as they have the scale of the product from 1 to 10 factored into the prediction.
- Hence, among the recommended products G and H, Product G has the most instant liking. In other words, product G is the most preferred.

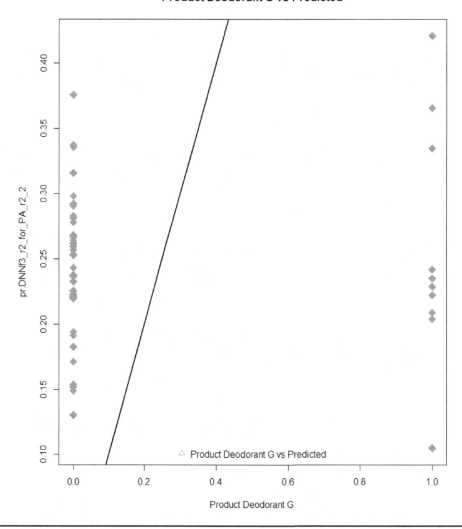

Figure 4.41   Product Deodorant G vs. Predicted (for Predictive Analytics).

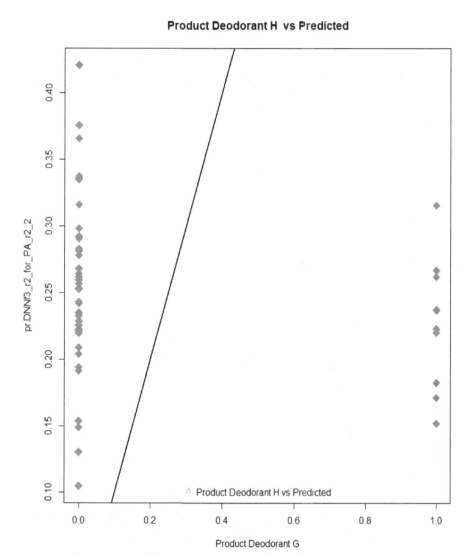

Figure 4.42   Product Deodorant H vs. Predicted (for Predictive Analytics).

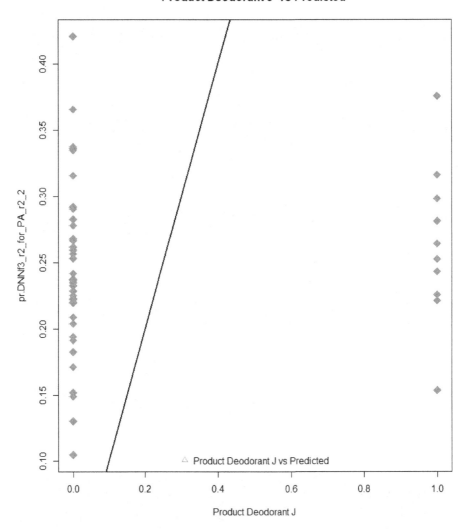

Figure 4.43   Product Deodorant J vs. Predicted (for Predictive Analytics).

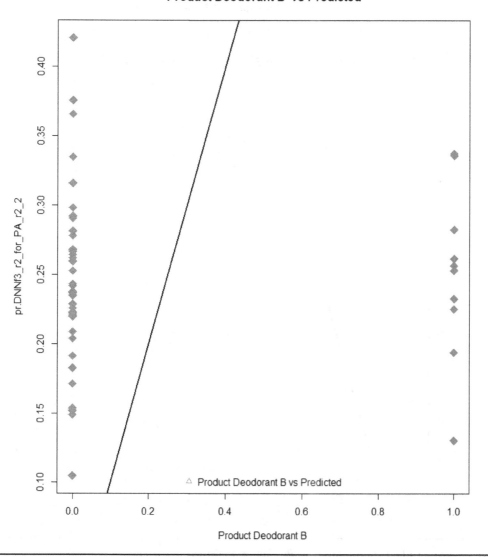

Figure 4.44   Product Deodorant B vs. Predicted (for Predictive Analytics).

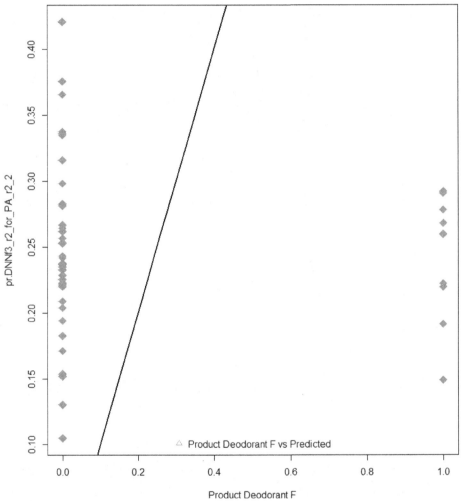

Figure 4.45　Product Deodorant F vs. Predicted (for Predictive Analytics).

4.5 Automatic Image Recognition

4.5.1 The AI-Methodology—Prescriptive and Augmented Analytics—Using Deep Learning–Based Convolutional Neural Networks for Classification

4.5.1.1 Purpose of Use Case

- Goal
  Image recognition using deep learning. This is one of the primary applications of AI in real life and is used for Facebook image tagging and automatic caption generation for images, etc.

- Technology
  AI and ML using deep neural networks (DNNs)—convolutional neural networks (CNNs), in particular.

- Implementation
  Using keras library with TensorFlow framework in R.

- Input Dataset
  Fashion MNIST dataset of images. Fashion MNIST is a dataset of 60,000 images in grayscale, 28 × 28 pixels each, along with a test set of 10,000 images. The class labels are encoded as 10 integers, ranging from 0 to 9, representing T-shirt/top, trouser, pullover, dress, coat, sandal, shirt, sneaker, sag, and ankle foot shoe.

  The dataset structure is such that it returns lists of training and test data: The x-part is an array of images with dimension (60000,28,28), and the y-part is an array of corresponding labels, ranging from 0 to 9, with dimension (10000).

4.5.1.2 An Outline of Convolutional Neural Networks (CNNs)

Figures 4.46 and 4.47 show an outline of a Convolutional Neural Network.

Figure 4.48 shows the structure of a CNN as obtained by the "Build" process. Figure 4.49 shows the representation of a CNN and its various layers.

An Outline of a CNN process

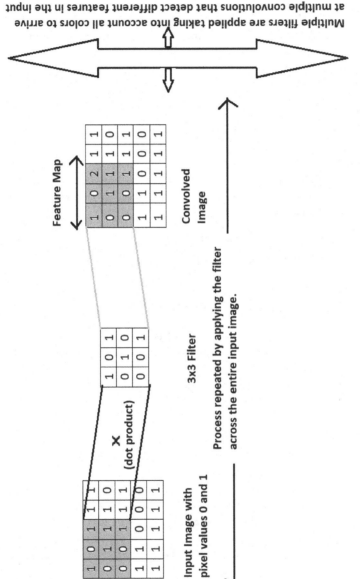

Input Image with
pixel values 0 and 1

x
(dot product)

3x3 Filter

Process repeated by applying the filter
across the entire input image.

Feature Map

Convolved
Image

Multiple filters are applied taking into account all colors to arrive
at multiple convolutions that detect different features in the input
image and finally arrive at an output class that classifies the
image as belonging to one of the class labels.
Repeat the above process by inputting images in batches till all
the images are classified.

Figure 4.46 An outline of a convolutional neural network (CNN) process.

How does a CNN see an image?—As a matrix of [number of rows of pixels × number of columns of pixels × number of color channels]

If the number of input images are factored into it, the above multiplication becomes:

[Numbers of input images × number of rows of pixels × number of columns of pixels × number of color channels]

What's a filter?—A filter is like a feature extractor that is specified by an m by n size, for example, 3 × 3. It is placed over a region of the image, and a matrix multiplication is done in this region and the filter.

Why a filter?—Since a filter is placed on a localized portion of the image and processed, it helps in extracting the specific details in the particular region of the image.

A larger size filter is more costly than a smaller filter in terms of the number of multiplications to be done.

Figure 4.47   A CNN explained in greater detail.

Structure of CNN model for Automatic Image Recognition

Layer (type)	Output Shape	Param #
conv2d_1 (Conv2D)	(None, 28, 28, 32)	320
activation_1 (Activation)	(None, 28, 28, 32)	0
conv2d_2 (Conv2D)	(None, 26, 26, 32)	9248
activation_2 (activation)	(None, 26, 26, 32)	0
max_pooling2d_1 (MaxPooling2D)	(None, 13, 13, 32)	0
dropout_1 (Dropout)	(None, 13, 13, 32)	0
conv2d_3 (Conv2D)	(None, 13, 13, 32)	9248
activation_3 (Activation)	(None, 13, 13, 32)	0
conv2d_4 (Conv2D)	(None, 11, 11, 32)	9248
activation_4 (Activation)	(None, 11, 11, 32)	0
max_pooling2d_2 (MaxPooling2D)	(None, 5, 5, 32)	0
dropout_2 (Dropout)	(None, 5, 5, 32)	0
flatten_1 (Flatten)	(None, 800)	0
dense_1 (Dense)	(None, 512)	410112
activation_5 (Activation)	(None, 512)	0
dropout_3 (Dropout)	(None, 512)	0
dense_2 (Dense)	(None, 10)	5130
activation_6 (Activation)	(None, 10)	0

Repeat above layers as needed

Repeat as needed

Output Layer (10 classes)

Total params: 443,306
Trainable params: 443,306
Non-trainable params: 0

Figure 4.48 Structure of CNN model used for automatic image recognition.

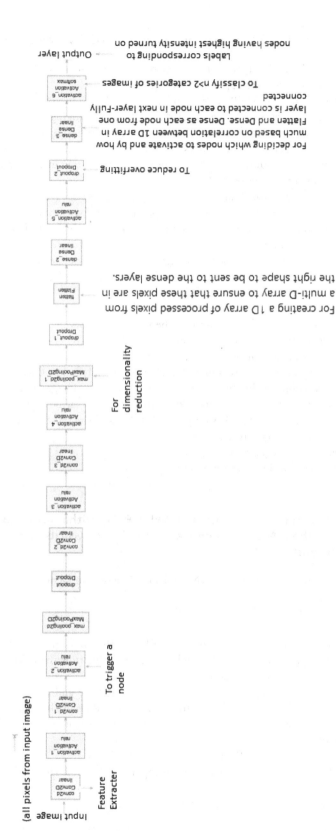

Figure 4.49 Representation of the CNN model built for Automatic Image Recognition and its various layers.

4.5.1.3 Using the Fashion MNIST Dataset and Keras-Based CNN Model in R

- Keras is a high-level API originally written in Python and now available in R as well. Both of the APIs use TensorFlow as the backend platform to run on.
- Fashion MNIST is a dataset of 60,000 images in grayscale, 28 × 28 pixels each, along with a test set of 10,000 images. The class labels are encoded as 10 integers, ranging from 0 to 9, representing T-shirt/top, trouser, pullover, dress, coat, sandal, shirt, sneaker, bag, and ankle foot shoe.
- The dataset structure is such that it returns lists of training and test data: The x-part is an array of images with dimension (60000,28,28), and the y-part is an array of corresponding labels, ranging from 0 to 9, with dimension (10000).
- The CNN model first trains with training data and then classifies the images in test data. This way, it recognizes the images in the test data by applying the AI-based model to it. The output of the classification (thereby recognition) is correctly determining the image label for any given image and checking the raster display of the same image in the test set. One example of this technique is the one used for automatic image tagging, as in Facebook, etc.
- The first step in proceeding further is preparing the image data so that it is in an acceptable format of the CNN model. This consists of:
  - o Reshaping the x-array into dimension of rank 4, that is, (num_samples, width in pixels, height in pixels, channels). Thus, we reshape the x-part as follows:
    train_images <- array_reshape(train x-part, c(60000,28,28,1))
    test_images <- array_reshape(test x-part, c(10000,28,28,1))
  - o Normalizing the x-data so that each image pixel lies in the interval [0,1] as opposed to original [0,255]. This is done by dividing the train_images and test_images by 255.
  - o One-hot encoding the train and test labels (the y-part). One-hot encoding means a label value is transformed into an array that has only one '1' value and the rest have '0' values. This is required for neural network target variables.
    train_labels <- to_categorical(train y-part)
    test_labels <- to_categorical(test y-part)

4.5.1.4 Building and Scoring a Model Using CNN in R Algorithm for Image Recognition Based on the MNIST Fashion Dataset Using Keras Library with TensorFlow Backend

The following are the steps needed to build a CNN model (code shown in Demo):

- Build a CNN architecture (adding a linear stack of layers).
  - o Add hidden layers.
- Add convolution(-al layer) specifying the number of filters, the size of each filter, and the shape (dimension) of the input format—width, height, channels. This runs the filter over the whole image, thus helping in feature extraction.
- Add activation (layer). This layer is used to reduce training time and uses the famous "*relu*" activation that replaces all negative values in the matrix to 0 and keeps all other values the same.
- Add pooling (layer) (to reduce the dimensionality of the features map and make the model less complex to compute).
- Add dropout (layer) (to avoid overfitting).
  - o Add layer to flatten input. (This is needed to input the layers already added to the dense layers.)
  - o Add dense layers. (Using this, the CNN classifies the inputs.)

- o Add output layer (using softmax activation to calculate categorical cross-entropy, since we have 10 classes that correspond to 10 images).
- Compile the CNN.
- Train the CNN by way of fitting it using the features (train x-part), targets (train y-part), number of epochs, batch size, and validation split.
- Plot the fitted output for loss and accuracy curves (shown in Figure 4.50).
- Evaluate the CNN on test dataset (test x-part, test y-part).
- Predict the classes using the model and the test images (test x-part).
- Test the validity of the model using a table of predicted and actual values (output of the prediction above and the test y-part). The output is a table comprising 10 rows and 10 columns.
- Check the values of the labels (predicted vs. actual) for any given label, that is, pred_test[1] and test y-part[1]. In addition, plot the raster image of original test x-part [1, ,] and see that its label matches with the predicted label number (class) (raster image shown in Figure 4.51)

Listing 4.11 gives the R code of this implementation along with its output.

Listing 4.11 R code of CNN Implementation for Automatic Image Classification

```
> library(keras)
Warning message:
package 'keras' was built under R version 3.5.0
> fashion_mnist <- dataset_fashion_mnist()
Using TensorFlow backend.
> train_images <- fashion_mnist$train$x
> train_labels <- fashion_mnist$train$y
> test_images <- fashion_mnist$test$x
> test_labels <- fashion_mnist$test$y
> str(fashion_mnist)
List of 2
 $ train:List of 2
  ..$ x: int [1:60000, 1:28, 1:28] 0 0 0 0 0 0 0 0 0 0 ...
  ..$ y: int [1:60000(1d)] 9 0 0 3 0 2 7 2 5 5 ...
 $ test :List of 2
  ..$ x: int [1:10000, 1:28, 1:28] 0 0 0 0 0 0 0 0 0 0 ...
  ..$ y: int [1:10000(1d)] 9 2 1 1 6 1 4 6 5 7 ...
> train_images[1, , ]
      [,1] [,2] [,3] [,4] [,5] [,6] [,7] [,8] [,9] [,10] [,11] [,12] [,13] [,14] [,15]
 [1,]    0    0    0    0    0    0    0    0    0     0     0     0     0     0     0
 [2,]    0    0    0    0    0    0    0    0    0     0     0     0     0     0     0
 [3,]    0    0    0    0    0    0    0    0    0     0     0     0     0     0     0
 [4,]    0    0    0    0    0    0    0    0    0     0     0     0     1     0     0
 [5,]    0    0    0    0    0    0    0    0    0     0     0     0     3     0    36
 [6,]    0    0    0    0    0    0    0    0    0     0     0     0     6     0   102
 [7,]    0    0    0    0    0    0    0    0    0     0     0     0     0     0   155
 [8,]    0    0    0    0    0    0    0    0    0     0     0     1     0    69   207
 [9,]    0    0    0    0    0    0    0    0    0     1     1     1     0   200   232
[10,]    0    0    0    0    0    0    0    0    0     0     0     0     0   183   225
```

	[,1]	[,2]	[,3]	[,4]	[,5]	[,6]	[,7]	[,8]	[,9]	[,10]	[,11]	[,12]	[,13]	[,14]	[,15]
[11,]	0	0	0	0	0	0	0	0	0	0	0	0	0	193	228
[12,]	0	0	0	0	0	0	0	0	0	1	3	0	12	219	220
[13,]	0	0	0	0	0	0	0	0	0	0	6	0	99	244	222
[14,]	0	0	0	0	0	0	0	0	0	4	0	0	55	236	228
[15,]	0	0	1	4	6	7	2	0	0	0	0	0	237	226	217
[16,]	0	3	0	0	0	0	0	0	0	62	145	204	228	207	213
[17,]	0	0	0	0	18	44	82	107	189	228	220	222	217	226	200
[18,]	0	57	187	208	224	221	224	208	204	214	208	209	200	159	245
[19,]	3	202	228	224	221	211	211	214	205	205	205	220	240	80	150
[20,]	98	233	198	210	222	229	229	234	249	220	194	215	217	241	65
[21,]	75	204	212	204	193	205	211	225	216	185	197	206	198	213	240
[22,]	48	203	183	194	213	197	185	190	194	192	202	214	219	221	220
[23,]	0	122	219	193	179	171	183	196	204	210	213	207	211	210	200
[24,]	0	0	74	189	212	191	175	172	175	181	185	188	189	188	193
[25,]	2	0	0	0	66	200	222	237	239	242	246	243	244	221	220
[26,]	0	0	0	0	0	0	0	40	61	44	72	41	35	0	0
[27,]	0	0	0	0	0	0	0	0	0	0	0	0	0	0	0
[28,]	0	0	0	0	0	0	0	0	0	0	0	0	0	0	0

	[,16]	[,17]	[,18]	[,19]	[,20]	[,21]	[,22]	[,23]	[,24]	[,25]	[,26]	[,27]	[,28]
[1,]	0	0	0	0	0	0	0	0	0	0	0	0	0
[2,]	0	0	0	0	0	0	0	0	0	0	0	0	0
[3,]	0	0	0	0	0	0	0	0	0	0	0	0	0
[4,]	13	73	0	0	1	4	0	0	0	0	1	1	0
[5,]	136	127	62	54	0	0	0	1	3	4	0	0	3
[6,]	204	176	134	144	123	23	0	0	0	0	12	10	0
[7,]	236	207	178	107	156	161	109	64	23	77	130	72	15
[8,]	223	218	216	216	163	127	121	122	146	141	88	172	66
[9,]	232	233	229	223	223	215	213	164	127	123	196	229	0
[10,]	216	223	228	235	227	224	222	224	221	223	245	173	0
[11,]	218	213	198	180	212	210	211	213	223	220	243	202	0
[12,]	212	218	192	169	227	208	218	224	212	226	197	209	52
[13,]	220	218	203	198	221	215	213	222	220	245	119	167	56
[14,]	230	228	240	232	213	218	223	234	217	217	209	92	0
[15,]	223	222	219	222	221	216	223	229	215	218	255	77	0
[16,]	221	218	208	211	218	224	223	219	215	224	244	159	0
[17,]	205	211	230	224	234	176	188	250	248	233	238	215	0
[18,]	193	206	223	255	255	221	234	221	211	220	232	246	0
[19,]	255	229	221	188	154	191	210	204	209	222	228	225	0
[20,]	73	106	117	168	219	221	215	217	223	223	224	229	29
[21,]	195	227	245	239	223	218	212	209	222	220	221	230	67
[22,]	236	225	216	199	206	186	181	177	172	181	205	206	115
[23,]	196	194	191	195	191	198	192	176	156	167	177	210	92
[24,]	198	204	209	210	210	211	188	188	194	192	216	170	0
[25,]	193	191	179	182	182	181	176	166	168	99	58	0	0
[26,]	0	0	0	0	0	0	0	0	0	0	0	0	0
[27,]	0	0	0	0	0	0	0	0	0	0	0	0	0
[28,]	0	0	0	0	0	0	0	0	0	0	0	0	0

```
> mage <- train_images[1, , ]
> image <- train_images[1, , ]
> plot(as.raster(image, max = 255))
> train_labels[1]
[1] 9
> train_images <- array_reshape(train_images, c(60000, 28, 28, 1))
> train_images <- train_images / 255
> test_images <- array_reshape(test_images, c(10000, 28, 28, 1))
> test_images <- test_images / 255
> train_labels <- to_categorical(train_labels)
> test_labels <- to_categorical(test_labels)
> train_y <- fashion_mnist$train$y
> test_y <- fashion_mnist$test$y
> model <- keras_model_sequential()
> model %>%
+ layer_conv_2d(
+ filter = 32, kernel_size = c(3,3), padding = "same",
+ input_shape = c(28, 28, 1)
+ ) %>%
+ layer_activation("relu") %>%
+ layer_conv_2d(filter = 32, kernel_size = c(3,3)) %>%
+ layer_activation("relu") %>%
+ layer_max_pooling_2d(pool_size = c(2,2)) %>%
+ layer_dropout(0.25) %>%
+ layer_conv_2d(filter = 32, kernel_size = c(3,3), padding = "same") %>%
+ layer_activation("relu") %>%
+ layer_conv_2d(filter = 32, kernel_size = c(3,3)) %>%
+ layer_activation("relu") %>%
+ layer_max_pooling_2d(pool_size = c(2,2)) %>%
+ layer_dropout(0.25) %>%
+ layer_flatten() %>%
+ layer_dense(512) %>%
+ layer_activation("relu") %>%
+ layer_dropout(0.5) %>%
+ layer_dense(10) %>%
+ layer_activation("softmax")
> str(model)
```

Model

Layer (type)	Output Shape	Param #
conv2d_1 (Conv2D)	(None, 28, 28, 32)	320
activation_1 (Activation)	(None, 28, 28, 32)	0
conv2d_2 (Conv2D)	(None, 26, 26, 32)	9248
activation_2 (Activation)	(None, 26, 26, 32)	0

max_pooling2d_1 (MaxPooling2D)	(None, 13, 13, 32)	0
dropout_1 (Dropout)	(None, 13, 13, 32)	0
conv2d_3 (Conv2D)	(None, 13, 13, 32)	9248
activation_3 (Activation)	(None, 13, 13, 32)	0
conv2d_4 (Conv2D)	(None, 11, 11, 32)	9248
activation_4 (Activation)	(None, 11, 11, 32)	0
max_pooling2d_2 (MaxPooling2D)	(None, 5, 5, 32)	0
dropout_2 (Dropout)	(None, 5, 5, 32)	0
flatten_1 (Flatten)	(None, 800)	0
dense_1 (Dense)	(None, 512)	410112
activation_5 (Activation)	(None, 512)	0
dropout_3 (Dropout)	(None, 512)	0
dense_2 (Dense)	(None, 10)	5130
activation_6 (Activation)	(None, 10)	0

```
=================================================================================
Total params: 443,306
Trainable params: 443,306
Non-trainable params: 0
```

```
> set.seed(1234)
> model %>% compile(
+ optimizer = "rmsprop",
+ loss = "categorical_crossentropy",
+ metrics = c("accuracy")
+ )
> model %>%
+ fit(train_images, train_labels, epochs=2, batch_size=128)
> model %>%
+ fit(train_images, train_labels, epochs=2, batch_size=128)
Epoch 1/2
60000/60000 [==========================] - 158s 3ms/step - loss: 0.5863 - acc: 0.7849
Epoch 2/2
60000/60000 [==========================] - 161s 3ms/step - loss: 0.3646 - acc: 0.8677
> model %>% evaluate(test_images, test_labels)
10000/10000 [==========================] - 8s 822us/step
$loss
[1] 0.3220585

$acc
[1] 0.8831

> pred_test <- model %>% predict_classes(test_images)
```

```
> str(pred_test)
 num [1:10000(1d)] 9 2 1 1 6 1 4 6 5 7 ...
> pred_test[1]
[1] 9
> test_y[1]
[1] 9
> table(Predicted = pred_test, Actual = test_y)
        Actual
Predicted   0   1   2   3   4   5   6   7   8   9
        0 911   1  14  32   1   0 226   0   4   0
        1   0 969   0   2   0   0   0   0   0   0
        2  23   1 916  22 133   0 137   0   9   0
        3  14  20   6 895  29   0  22   0   6   0
        4   6   5  38  30 796   0  98   0   1   0
        5   2   0   0   0   0 980   0  15   3  20
        6  38   2  26  17  40   0 502   0   7   0
        7   0   0   0   0   0  18   0 977   4  60
        8   6   2   0   2   1   0  15   0 965   0
        9   0   0   0   0   0   2   0   8   1 920
> test_x <- fashion_mnist$test$x
> plot(as.raster(test_x[1, , ], max = 255))
>
```

Figures 4.50 and 4.51 show loss and accuracy curves of the CNN model on training images and test images along with the raster plot of the recognized image from CNN—belonging to class 9—ankle foot shoe.

```
pred_test[1]
9
```

matches with that of

```
test_y[1]
9
```

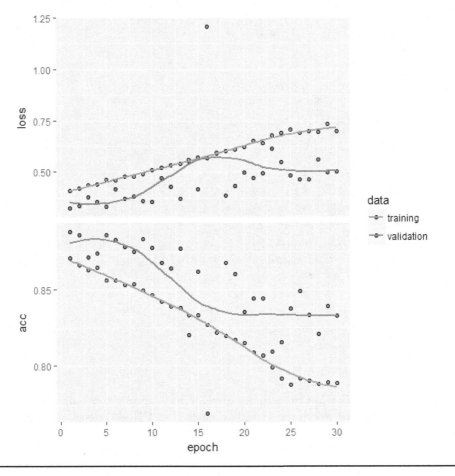

Figure 4.50 Plot of fitted CNN using keras and TensorFlow.

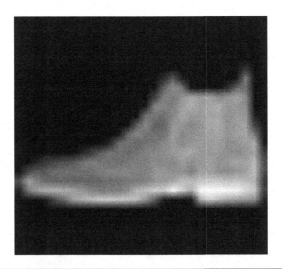

Figure 4.51 Image of predicted image using CNN (ankle foot shoe).

4.5.1.5 Summary of Built CNN Model

```
s
Model
```

Layer (type)	Output Shape	Param #
conv2d_1 (Conv2D)	(None, 28, 28, 32)	320
activation_1 (Activation)	(None, 28, 28, 32)	0
conv2d_2 (Conv2D)	(None, 26, 26, 32)	9248
activation_2 (Activation)	(None, 26, 26, 32)	0
max_pooling2d_1 (MaxPooling2D)	(None, 13, 13, 32)	0
dropout_1 (Dropout)	(None, 13, 13, 32)	0
conv2d_3 (Conv2D)	(None, 13, 13, 32)	9248
activation_3 (Activation)	(None, 13, 13, 32)	0
conv2d_4 (Conv2D)	(None, 11, 11, 32)	9248
activation_4 (Activation)	(None, 11, 11, 32)	0
max_pooling2d_2 (MaxPooling2D)	(None, 5, 5, 32)	0
dropout_2 (Dropout)	(None, 5, 5, 32)	0
flatten_1 (Flatten)	(None, 800)	0
dense_1 (Dense)	(None, 512)	410112
activation_5 (Activation)	(None, 512)	0
dropout_3 (Dropout)	(None, 512)	0
dense_2 (Dense)	(None, 10)	5130
activation_6 (Activation)	(None, 10)	0

```
Total params: 443,306
Trainable params: 443,306
Non-trainable params: 0
```

4.6 Summary

This chapter focused on using AI and its intersection with the 3rd generation of BI for multiple real-world use cases based on classifications using random forests, decision trees, and neural networks. It showed how AI solutions can be implemented using machine learning models and R code along with how decision making can be achieved for BI purposes. It also described the predictive capabilities of AI with use case predicting precious metal prices.

The following chapter focuses on what is next in the AI frontier in the 21st century and its advancements for use in BI, cognitive computing, and beyond.

4.7 References

1. Lan, H. (2017, August). "Decision Trees and Random Forests for Classification and Regression pt.1." Retrieved from https://towardsdatascience.com/decision-trees-and-random-forests-for-classification-and-regression-pt-1-dbb65a458df)
2. Lan, H. (2017, November)."Decision Trees and Random Forests for Classification and Regression pt.2." Retrieved from https://towardsdatascience.com/decision-trees-and-random-forests-for-classification-and-regression-pt-2-2b1fcd03e342)
3. Glander, S. (2017, April)."Dealing with Unbalanced Data in Machine Learning." Retrieved from https://shiring.github.io/machine_learning/2017/04/02/unbalanced)

Chapter 5

What's Next in AI Meets BI?

In This Chapter

5.1 Introduction
5.2 AI-Powered Cognitive Computing
5.3 Security and Governance in AI-Powered BI
5.4 The Trust Factor in AI-Powered BI
5.5 Summary

5.1 Introduction

This chapter outlines the next frontier in AI-powered BI. It begins with a description of AI-powered cognitive computing. It then highlights the security and governance aspects of AI-powered BI, followed by the ethical aspects of its adoption in enterprises.

5.2 AI-Powered Cognitive Computing

The next wave of AI-powered computing is cognitive computing, which involves the computing of context using AI techniques. Quoting directly from Chapter 2,

- *It [AI] has provided an area in which AI and cognitive computing can work together, resulting in an optimal autonomous, augmented, and adaptive intelligence platform.*
- *Through AI, cognitive computing can consist of the following technologies: natural language processing (NLP), machine learning with neural networks and deep neural networks, algorithms that learn and adapt with AI, deep learning, image recognition, reason and decision automation, and emotional intelligence.*
- *AI has become a convergence of three powerful technologies, namely, machine learning, natural language processing, and cognitive computing. This is where the future of AI is heading.*

- *Further, pragmatics can be defined by way of cognition and recommend the "optimal" choice, thereby boosting competition. This integrates "cognition" into the model and trains it using the cognitive computing–based recommender model for decision making in terms of outputting the "most optimal" choice to be used, as well as "comprehend" why the particular choice is optimal to be used (i.e., the next best action)—from decision support to insightful decision making.*
- *Typical levels of data analytics include descriptive analytics, diagnostic analytics, predictive analytics, prescriptive analytics, and cognitive computing. The fifth type of data analytics—cognitive computing—answers questions such as, What is the next best action that can be taken? This involves the computing of context with respect to the business use case.*

The capability of AI-powered systems that leverage big data, BI, AI, and deep learning resulting in cognitive and competitive intelligence working in parallel goes a long way in computing of context and the reasoning that comes out of it. Using cognitive computing, an enterprise BI system can benefit from actionable decision making—one that leverages augmented analytics. Enterprises that adopt AI-powered cognitive computing can use it for such use cases as AI-powered 360-degree customer experiences, chatbots, intelligent healthcare solutions such as cognitive behavioral therapy, and analytics—anytime, anywhere, and by anyone. Whereas AI systems enable machines to augment human thinking by using algorithms and techniques and provide results to a reasonable level of accuracy, AI-powered cognitive computing enables machines to reason in a manner similar to humans and resolve ambiguity and chaos involved in the process of providing solutions. A good example of an AI-powered system is image processing, whereas a good example of AI-powered cognitive computing is face recognition. This is further exemplified by the fact that the former can be used for speech recognition, whereas the latter can be used for sentiment analysis.

Whereas AI focuses on the right result(s), cognitive computing focuses on the best result using evidence-based reasoning. Both involve content analysis, but cognitive computing takes computing to a higher level.

The key functions of an AI-based cognitive system are:

1. Adaptive—It learns as data changes and as requirements evolve and from information based on user inputs.
2. Interactive—It allows human–computer interaction so that business users can custom define their goals and objectives, as well, while interacting with other systems. This way, they can learn from the user feedback that, in turn, can loop back into the cognitive system. This, in turn, enables the cognitive system to learn from the interactive feedback and evolve in its functionality.
3. Iterative and stateful—It has the capability of "memorizing" the user feedback it learned from the interaction so that it can output context-sensitive and custom-specific information at any point in time.
4. Contextual—It is context-aware by its ability to reason and extract context-specific information—the data domain, user's domain, and business domain—as it applies to the harnessing of inputs-based and knowledge-based data (which comprises all of the relevant data). The key here is relevance from all angles that pertain to such processing and may consist of information that is visual, voice-based, or otherwise—for example, providing a meaning to IoT data by way of thoughtful reasoning.
5. Integrable—It enables integration with other AI-powered systems to enable a solution that involves a best-case recommendation.

6. AI-powered—One that is based on deep learning, neural networks, natural language processing (NLP), and sentiment analysis in addition to using self-learning techniques, such as pattern recognition and intelligent data mining.

Real-world examples of cognitive computing systems include IBM Watson® for deep-dive content analysis and outcome optimization; concierge healthcare systems; and others involving multiple domains, such as those used for therapy, for studying disease patterns, SparkCognition™ for the industrialized world, and the like.

An AI-powered cognition framework can be built around prototyping the following:

1. Evidence-based reasoning and hypothesis generation that evolves using learned information, outcomes, and actions
2. Involvement by way of providing expert advice, as humans do
3. Discovery of knowledge by semantic synthesis of information that is varied and vast at the same time
4. Security and governance compliance that puts it ahead of the enterprise business benefits

5.3 Security and Governance in AI-Powered BI

As many experts put it,

$$AI = Data + Governance + Trust$$

A next-gen AI-powered BI system can be emphasized as

$$AI\text{-}Powered\ BI = Machine + Human + BI$$

An AI-powered BI system is as secure as the decisions it makes and the data that drives those decisions. This involves security across the end-to-end AI flow vis-à-vis the business process flow. The following depicts a few points to be considered from the security aspect of an AI-powered BI system:

1. Ensure that data rules are in place so as to support protection of important data, from on-premise to cloud deployments. In addition, ensure intelligent validations based on data and that these rules are in place at every step of the AI-powered BI solution.
2. It is important that data and decisions storage are secure on-premise or in the cloud and that there is no residual storage.
3. The system can support secure remote use in addition to being managed in place without loss of data, and it can retain the same security when the data and decisions flow bidirectionally from on-premise to cloud.
4. The system can handle the redundancy of data and decisions thereto.
5. The system can leverage all relevant data in the form of input without compromising the validity of the same.
6. The execution context of the AI-powered BI system aligns with that of the contextual business scenarios in an integrated manner.
7. The system passes the BI process impacts test as administered by the business.
8. The system provides insights from both positive and negative outputs.

9. The system takes into account query context and result set context, and allows for user input-based parameters.

10. The system can account for uncertainty and ambiguity of both data and output and the methods to expose them via special AI- or SQL-based queries.

11. The system is implemented to handle separation of duties when it comes to authorization and authenticity of use.

Regarding the aspect of governance of an AI-powered BI system, the following list comprises some implementation criteria:

1. Approvals:
   a. Ensure that a mechanism exists in place that enables approval of the information and analytics output by the system, as well as that augmented by authorized users—from a strategic perspective.
   b. Ensure that business rules as implemented by the system can be validated and approved based on its results.
   c. The system allows for validation in terms of both positive and negative results, along with the details of negative results and any exceptions in place.
   d. Approval processes are reusable by way of workflows built into the system.
   e. Such approvals can be communicable to the business user workspace by way of emails or on-the-fly reports.

2. Transparent data quality and getting users involved in defining the validations as well the approval of the same.

3. The system allows for auditing of data-to-decisions end to end, in a transparent manner, and makes the output of such auditing communicable via messaging.

4. The system can put the business process ownership in the hands of the contextual line-of-business without additional coding using embedded intelligence. The users must be able to request changes to the system that best describe the functionality.

5. The system provides consistency in terms of functionality across the entire user spectrum, with the ability to coexist with existing BI systems.

6. Any changes to the AI-powered BI system are driven by the users. For example, changes in rules are initiable by the users. and any technical changes to improve performance can be user driven, based on their usage of the system. Additionally, these changes are trackable in real time.

7. The governance team makes recommendations about the processes put in place, as listed above. It also makes sure that such recommendations are implemented for the system to conform to governance criteria. These criteria can pertain to usage segmentation, feedback, and reporting on compliance to standards on AI-powered systems in place, including the processes encompassed from request to response.

5.4 The Trust Factor in AI-Powered BI

The trust factor in AI-powered BI is based on data (and processed information) and whether inclusion of AI changes or augments existing business processes in place and the way users of such AI systems tend to work. A framework for trustable AI can involve the following:

1. AI-powered BI systems are explainable in that they do not replace existing systems but, rather, augment them by way of enhancement of decisions and precision of such decisions. This bridges the gap between business users of AI and the data scientists who are technically savvy about AI.

Hence, business users can have an explanation of how AI-powered BI is ethical in the enterprise and does not damage the brand of the business.

2. AI-powered data-driven insights and decision making to be made context specific. This means engaging the lob users in knowing that the AI-based BI solution is relevant in what it's meant to output as far as the business use case these users are dealing with is concerned.

3. AI-powered BI system allows for continuous loopback feedback from its users when trying to analyze or use the system's outcome. Machine-based analytics and insight can be ambiguous or inaccurate at times, and the more information in the form of feedback or reviews is fed into the AI meets BI system, the more it evolves in providing intelligent decisions. For example, to cater to consumers who prefer to see photos of those who bought a particular product, such as a suit, an image processing system that can identify those people's faces, as well as the color of and brand of suits they are wearing, and is integrated into BI, is more trustworthy if it can address how it arrived a particular decision as also *why* such a decision is optimal. If it predicts that increasing the production of a particular brand can optimize demand, telling the user that a particular campaign in place across business segments is the reason for the prediction enables the user to trust the prediction. In addition, how correlating to similar campaigns that have been in place has improved such demand suggests that the decision being made is correct, from both business and users' points of view. This way, combining both predictive and prescriptive analytics that answers the *how* and *why* aspects of decisions can infuse trust in business users for such a system.

4. Exploration of feedback that a BI user deems as fake can impact trust in a negative way. This downplays the trust factor in the AI-powered system. In such cases, AI-powered BI systems can generate content based on both negative and positive feedback that is interpretable by a BI user as more relatable to the decision in context. Interactions with users, feedback from them, and the ability to auto-send notifications based on them that contain data-driven AI-based output, as well as *currency* of the feedback, go a long way in protecting trust of the AI-powered system—from data input to decisions output.

5. The system is business context-aware and is secure across the AI flow, end to end.

6. And last but not least, datasets can be enhanced to include outcomes of AI-powered BI systems so that such systems can use them to improve decision making. These enhanced datasets can be made available to users as enhanced test data for them to test on their own and see the outcomes improve. This occurs because the datasets have been created with such user-based feedback.

5.5 Summary

This chapter explored aspects of the next wave of AI and AI-powered BI in terms of cognitive computing, security and governance, and the trust factor of an AI meets BI solution. It attempted to outline key considerations in each of these areas and demonstrate how an AI-powered BI system that encompasses cognitive computing and, at the same time, is secure, governance-enabled, and trustworthy is a proven solution that stands out as a powerful system of the future.

Index

360-degree customer experiences, 210

A

accuracy metric, 50, 51, 92
actionable insight, 16, 117, 182, 190
activation functions, 113
activation (layer), 46, 200
ad hoc reporting, 3
adam, 117, 119
adaptive intelligence, 9, 10, 209
agile analytics, 4
AI- and ML-based model classification
    performance, 20, 34
AI/ML-embedded BI platforms, 15
AI-powered analytics, 4, 8–10, 13–15, 17
AI-powered BI, 1, 4, 10, 11, 13, 15, 19, 209,
    211–213
algorithms, 7, 10, 14, 15, 49, 50, 92, 113, 200,
    209, 210
ambiguity, 210, 212
analyses, 3, 4, 7, 8, 13, 14, 16, 19, 21, 30, 33, 34,
    48, 112, 121, 182, 183, 210, 211
analytic dashboards, 19
analytics sphere, 9, 10, 12, 13
ankle foot shoe, 48, 195, 200, 205, 206
ANN. *See* artificial neural network
anomalies, 19, 20, 23, 26, 33, 34
approvals, 212
Area Under (ROC) Curve (AUC), 50, 51, 53, 54,
    72, 81, 94, 95, 101–103
ARIMA. *See* Auto-Regressive Integrated Moving
    Average
array of corresponding labels, 195, 200

array of images, 195, 200
artificial neural network (ANN), 113–116
attributes, 15, 19, 20, 23, 34, 48–50, 122
AUC. *See* Area Under (ROC) Curve
augmented analytics, 4, 10, 14, 15, 46, 48, 195,
    210
augmented data, 46
authenticity, 212
authorization, 212
autogenerate visuals, 15
automation of content-and-context, 4
autonomous, 4, 9, 13, 209
Auto-Regressive Integrated Moving Average
    (ARIMA), 34, 35, 37–39, 44, 45
auto-send notifications, 213

B

back propagation, 115
batchwise epochs, 47
best context, 21, 34
best result, 210
BI. *See* business intelligence
bias, 62, 113
BI-as-a-service, 7
BI dashboards, 3, 16, 46, 117, 182, 190
bidirectional(ly), 211
big data, 4, 7, 210
Big Data Discovery, 4, 7
BI platforms, 15, 17, 121, 183
BI process impacts test, 211
both positive and negative results, 212
brand, 213
business analyst, 3, 4, 7, 9, 19, 48

business analytics, 4, 7, 8, 13, 14
business continuity, 10
business decision making, 1, 7
business goal, 4, 7
business intelligence (BI), 1–11, 13–17, 19, 21,
    34, 46, 48, 49, 117, 121, 122, 182, 183, 190,
    207, 209–213
business process, 3, 4, 7, 8, 10, 19, 183, 211, 212
business process analytics, 121
business process ownership, 212
bwplot, 95, 102, 103

C

catalog, 10
categorical feature encoding, 51
changes are trackable, 212
chaos, 210
chatbots, 210
check the values of the labels, 201
citizen scientist, 9
classes, 20, 21, 23, 29, 30, 33, 34, 46, 48, 50–57,
    59, 61, 70–72, 74, 76, 78–81, 83, 92–97,
    100–103, 112, 115, 116, 181, 195, 200, 201,
    204, 205
classification, 14–16, 20, 23, 34, 46–48, 50–52,
    54, 61–63, 70, 73, 83, 95, 102, 103, 112,
    115, 116, 195, 200, 201, 207
classify commodity (wine) salability grade, 20
classifying, 19, 20, 48–50
cloud, 211
CNN model, 17, 46–48, 198–200, 205, 207
CNNs. *See* convolutional neural networks
cognitive behavioral therapy, 210
cognitive computing, 1, 4, 9, 10, 123, 207,
    209–211, 213
collaboration, 10
Commodity Prices in Advance, 19, 33, 48, 49, 113
Commodity Saleable Grade Based on Their
    Attributes, 48–50
comparative, 13–15
competitive insight, 46
competitive intelligence, 4, 10, 210
compile the CNN, 201
compiling, 115
compliance, 211, 212
compute(), 15, 123, 125, 158, 159, 181, 200
confusion matrix, 23, 33, 51, 59, 60, 78, 79, 82,
    99, 101, 103

content analysis, 210, 211
contextually relevant, 9
contextual speech-to-text processing, 16, 117
continuous loopback feedback, 213
conversational AI, 15
convolution(-al layer), 200
convolutional neural networks (CNNs), 17,
    46–48, 195–201, 205–207
correlations, 4, 7, 14, 46, 115, 117
cross validation, 51, 92, 93
currency of the feedback, 213
customer, 4, 7, 13, 16, 19, 210
customizable, 9, 10
customizable AI, 10
custom models, 19

D

data and decisions storage, 211
data enrichment, 10
data governance, 3, 211
data integration, 3, 4
data lakes, 3, 4
data marts, 3
data patterns, 115
data preparation, 3, 19
data presentation, 3
data quality, 3, 10, 212
data science, 1, 4, 9
data scientist, 7, 9, 48, 49, 212
datasets, 14, 20, 23, 34, 35, 46, 50, 51, 59, 92,
    112, 113, 117, 118, 121, 122, 195, 200, 201,
    213
data sources, 3, 15
data standardization, 9
data virtualization, 3, 4
data visualization, 3, 7
data warehouse, 3
data wrangling, 19
date, 34, 36–45, 113, 117, 118
decision making, 1, 3, 4, 7–10, 13, 14, 17, 19, 33,
    48, 49, 123, 207, 210, 213
decision support, 3, 8, 10, 14, 123, 210
decision trees, 15, 20, 48, 50, 51, 70, 73, 92, 112,
    207
deep neural networks (DNNs), 7, 10, 15, 17, 48,
    113, 115, 117, 118, 120–124, 126, 158–160,
    182, 184, 195, 209
dense layer, 46, 117, 200

deployable, 15
depthwise location in the tree, 51
descriptive analytics, 10, 14–16, 20, 48, 50, 210
diagnostic analytics, 10, 210
dimension column, 35
dimension of rank 4, 200
dimensions, 3, 35, 53, 72, 81, 95, 102, 195, 200
DNNs. *See* deep neural networks
"down" sampling, 92
dropout (layer), 46, 200

E

emails, 212
embedded AI, 15, 16
embedding, 10
emotional intelligence, 10, 209
enabling BI, 1, 3
end user, 4, 7, 9, 17, 19, 48
enhancement, 4, 7, 14, 212
ensemble, 50, 51
enterprise BI, 7, 9, 10, 19, 49, 210
enterprise business benefits, 211
enterprise data, 19, 21, 34, 46
epochs, 47, 115, 119, 201, 204
error rate, 23, 51, 115
ethical, 209, 213
ETL/ELT. *See* Extract, Transform, Load/Extract, Load, Transform
ETS. *See* Exponential Triple Smoothing
evaluate the CNN, 201
evidence-based reasoning and hypothesis generation, 211
exceptions, 212
explainable, 212
exploration, 14, 15, 213
Exponential Triple Smoothing (ETS), 34, 35, 40
Extract, Transform, Load/Extract, Load, Transform (ETL/ELT), 3

F

F1SaleableCheap, 30, 33
F1SaleableCostly, 30, 33
F1 statistic, 50
F1 value, 20, 33
Facebook™ image tagging, 16, 117, 195
fact, 3, 13, 210
false negative (FN), 29, 30, 33

false positive (FP), 23, 29, 30, 33
fashion MNIST dataset of images, 195
feature bagging, 51
feature engineering, 16
feature extraction, 16, 46, 200
feature scaling, 51
feature selection, 16, 62
flexibility, 10, 14
FN. *See* false negative
forward-propagation phase, 113
FP. *See* false positive

G

generalize on new data, 121
generate new data, 14, 19
ggplot2(), 54, 73, 122, 125, 135, 169
gini, 72, 73, 78–83, 85, 92
governance, 3, 10, 209, 211–213
grade, 15, 19–26, 29, 48–50, 52–56, 58–61, 63, 70–75, 77–83, 93–102, 112
guided analytics, 15

H

harmonic mean, 29
hidden layers, 113, 115, 117, 123, 159, 200
higher and lower actuals, 182
"how it happened", 4, 7
how the product fares in the market, 16, 122
human intuition, 10

I

IBM®, 7, 211
image classification, 16, 201
image label, 46, 200
image recognition, 10, 16, 17, 19, 46, 48, 49, 117, 195, 198–200, 209
image tagging, 7, 16, 17, 46, 48, 117, 195, 200
imbalanced dataset, 50
important features, 50, 51
information gain, 83
input layer nodes, 113
instant liking, 126, 129, 159, 160, 163, 177, 180, 190
integrable, 210
intelligence, 1, 3, 4, 7, 9, 10, 13, 16, 19, 49, 209, 210, 212

intelligent decision making, 9, 13, 19, 49
intelligent healthcare solutions, 210
interactive, 3, 10, 14, 210
interactive dashboarding, 3
interpretable, 213
iterative and stateful, 210

K

Kaggle dataset, 122
Kappa measure, 50, 51
keras library, 113, 118, 195, 200
keras_model_sequential(), 117, 119, 203
key business drivers, 14, 15, 19
key performance indicators (KPIs), 1, 3, 7, 8, 14
key performance metrics, 20, 33
K-fold validation, 23, 116, 117
KPIs. *See* key performance indicators

L

layer to flatten input, 200
learning rate, 117
line-of-business, 212
logical dimensional model, 3
loss functions, 115
lower bound of the value of the interval, 35
lubridate, 117, 118

M

machine intelligence, 4, 10, 16
machine learning, 1, 4, 7, 10, 15, 17, 20, 33,
    48–50, 113, 117, 207–209
making decisions, 19
M(ean)S(quared)E(rror), 117
messaging, 212
metadata for AI/ML-based recommendations, 10
metrics, 1, 4, 7, 8, 14, 16, 20, 23, 29, 33, 48, 50,
    119, 204
Microsoft®, 7, 16, 117, 182, 183, 190
Microsoft® BI, 16, 117, 182, 183, 190
misclassifications, 29, 51
model build, 23, 50
model parameters, 51
MOLAP. *See* Multidimensional Online
    Analytical Processing
monetizing AI-driven models, 19

(month, day, year) of the predicted price, 35
Multidimensional Online Analytical Processing
    (MOLAP), 3

N

narrative, 14, 15
natural language generation and querying, 16, 117
natural language generation (NLG), 10, 15, 16,
    117
natural language processing (NLP), 10, 15, 209,
    211
natural language querying (NLQ), 10
neuralnet(), 122, 123, 125, 135, 144, 159, 169,
    180
neural nets, 51
next-gen, 9, 10, 211
NLG. *See* natural language generation
NLP. *See* natural language processing
NLQ. *See* natural language querying
nonlinearities, 115
number of filters, 200

O

observations, 23, 46, 53, 72, 81, 94, 95, 102
OLAP-based reporting and analysis, 7
OLAP-based solution, 3
one-hot encoding, 51, 200
on-premise, 9, 10, 211
on-the-fly reports, 212
on-the-go, 7, 9, 10, 15
on-the-go customer analytics, 7
OOB. *See* Out-of-Bag
operational BI, 3, 4, 7
optimizers, 113, 115, 117, 119, 204
Oracle®, 7, 16, 117, 182, 183, 190
Oracle® BI, 16, 117, 182, 183, 190
outcome optimization, 211
outliers, 10, 20
Out-of-Bag (OOB), 51
output layer, 46, 113, 115, 118, 123, 159, 201
overfitting, 46, 50, 51, 92, 103, 121, 200

P

parameter mtry, 50
percentage of accuracy, 20

performance curves, 49
personalized, 9, 10, 13, 16
pooling (layer), 46, 200
precision, 20, 29–31, 33, 212
PrecisionSaleableCheap, 30, 33
PrecisionSaleableCostly, 30, 33
predicted vs. actual, 201
predicting, 4, 15, 16, 19, 20, 23–25, 33, 48, 49,
    53, 57, 94, 113, 116–118, 122, 123, 159, 207
predicting precious metal prices, 33, 113, 118,
    207
predicting scale, 122
predictive analytics, 8, 10, 13–16, 33, 34, 48,
    113, 122, 123, 159, 160, 190–194, 210
predictive model-enabled charts, 10
predictor variables, 118, 159
predict the classes, 201
pre-process data, 50
prescriptive analytics, 10, 16, 17, 117, 122–124,
    182, 210, 213
price, 33–46, 113, 117–121
product, 7, 8, 13, 14, 16, 121–126, 128, 129,
    132, 135, 138, 141, 144, 147, 150, 153, 156,
    159, 160, 162, 163, 166, 169, 172, 175, 177,
    178, 181, 182, 184–194, 213
products having the highest scale, 122
Python®, 117, 200

Q

q14.Deodorant.overall.on.a.scale.from.1.to.10,
    123, 125, 126, 128, 129, 131, 134, 137, 140,
    143, 144, 146, 149, 152, 155, 158, 159, 161,
    163, 165, 168, 171, 174, 177, 180
quality, 3, 4, 10, 20, 50, 52, 54, 55, 58, 61, 70,
    71, 73, 74, 77, 83, 93, 95, 96, 98, 102, 103,
    127, 128, 130, 133, 136, 139, 142, 145, 147,
    151, 154, 156, 161, 162, 164, 167, 170, 173,
    175, 178, 183, 212
query context, 212

R

randomForest(), 51, 54
random forest, 23, 50–54, 56, 61–70, 92, 93, 95,
    97, 102–112
reason and decision automation, 10, 209
recall, 20, 29, 30, 32, 33

RecallSaleableCheap, 30, 33
RecallSaleableCostly, 30, 33
recognition, 10, 16, 17, 19, 46, 48, 49, 117, 195,
    198–200, 209–211
Recommender Systems, 15, 19, 46, 48, 49, 122
recommend the "optimal", 10, 123, 210
reduce the dimensionality, 200
redundancy, 211
regression, 50, 51, 115, 116
relational, 3
relevance, 4, 7, 13–16, 210
relu, 117, 119, 200, 203
remote use, 211
resampling, 56, 76, 79, 92, 95, 97, 102
response variable, 29, 34, 118, 120, 123, 159
result set context, 212
reusable components, 15
rf, 50, 51, 53, 54, 56, 57, 59–61, 71, 75, 94, 95,
    97–102
right result(s), 210
robotics, 1
rpart, 50, 70–73, 75, 76, 79

S

'SaleableCheap', 20, 21, 29, 30
'SaleableCostly', 20, 21, 29, 30
scalable, 9
schedulable, 15
score the model, 116, 118
Seasonal ARIMA, 34, 35, 37, 38, 44, 45
security, 209, 211, 213
self-driving cars, 1
self-service analytics, 1, 3, 4, 7, 13, 14
self-service data import, 15
semantic synthesis, 211
sentiment analysis, 16, 210, 211
separable classes, 51
separation of duties, 212
shape (dimension) of the input format, 200
sigmoid, 118
single decision trees, 50, 51
size of each filter, 200
smart data discovery, 9
SMOTE, 92
social engineering, 16
social intelligence, 16
softmax, 46, 118, 201, 203

splitting at each node, 50
SQL. *See* Structured Query Language
STAR schema, 3
Structured Query Language (SQL), 183

T

Tableau®, 7, 16, 117, 182, 183, 190
technical user, 9
Tensorflow® framework, 113, 195
test data, 33, 35, 43–46, 53, 54, 57–60, 71,
    72, 77–79, 81, 92, 94, 95, 98–100, 102,
    116–118, 122–126, 128, 129, 144, 147, 153,
    158, 159, 162, 163, 195, 200, 213
Theano, 117
the Before and After Forecast visualizations, 35
the predicted price, 35, 118
the upper bound of the prediction interval, 35
the value of the confidence prediction interval
    used for the ML forecast model, 35
three generations of BI, 1, 3, 8
tiers of nodes, 113
time series, 35
TN. *See* true negative
TP. *See* true positive
train the CNN, 201
train(), 50, 51, 53, 56, 71, 72, 75, 79, 94, 97,
    115–117, 119, 122–124, 126, 159, 160, 200,
    201, 203, 204
trainControl(), 51, 52, 56, 71, 75, 93, 97
training data, 20, 21, 23, 34, 36–42, 46, 50, 51,
    71, 76, 93, 97, 115, 200
transparent, 212
trControl(), 51, 53, 56, 71, 72, 75, 76, 79, 94, 97
true negative (TN), 29
true positive (TP), 29, 30, 33

trust, 209, 211–213
trustable AI, 212
type of values, 20, 34

U

unambiguously answerable, 13
unpruned, 51
"up" sampling, 92, 93, 103–110, 112
usage segmentation, 212
user feedback, 15, 210

V

validation, 4, 23, 27, 28, 31–33, 47, 115–117, 119,
    201, 212
validation data, 28, 31–33, 47, 115
variable importance plot, 51, 61, 62, 103
variable selection, 51
varImp plot, 92
viable product sources, 16, 122
visual, 7, 13–16, 210
visualize data distribution, 20
voice-based information, 210
voice-based visuals, 15

W

wearables, 16
weighted sum, 113
weights, 113
why of data analysis, 7
workflows, 15, 212

Y

ymd(), 117, 118

Printed in the United States
By Bookmasters